RAPE CULTURE 101
PROGRAMMING CHANGE

T0294493

Edited by Geraldine Cannon Becker and Angel T. Dionne

DEMETER

RAPE CULTURE 101
Programming Change

Edited by Geraldine Cannon Becker and Angel T. Dionne

Copyright © 2020 Demeter Press

Individual copyright to their work is retained by the authors. All rights reserved. No part of this book may be reproduced or transmitted in any form by any means without permission in writing from the publisher.

Demeter Press
2546 10th Line
Bradford, Ontario
Canada, L3Z 3L3
Tel: 289-383-0134
Email: info@demeterpress.org
Website: www.demeterpress.org

Demeter Press logo based on the sculpture "Demeter" by Maria-Luise Bodirsky www.keramik-atelier.bodirsky.de

Printed and Bound in Canada

Front cover artwork: *Hades and Persephone* by Jessica and Joanna Becker
Cover design and typesetting: Michelle Pirovich

Library and Archives Canada Cataloguing in Publication
Title: Rape culture 101 : programming change / edited by Geraldine Cannon Becker and Angel Dionne.
Other titles: Rape culture one oh one | Rape culture one hundred and one
Names: Cannon Becker, Geraldine, 1967- editor. | Dionne, Angel, 1989- editor.
Description: Includes bibliographical references.
Identifiers: Canadiana 2020025720X | ISBN 9781772582277 (softcover)
Subjects: LCSH: Rape culture. | LCSH: Rape—Social aspects.
| LCSH: Rape—Prevention.
Classification: LCC HV6558.R37 2020 | DDC 362.883—dc23

Acknowledgments and Dedications

All due thanks go to the publisher, Professor Andrea O'Reilly, first for acknowledging the importance of the topic after a brief query letter, and for extreme patience over the long haul of getting material submitted for readers to review, and finally for breaking the silence to share her own story on social media, inspiring me further in a difficult time.

We would like to thank WE LEARN (Women Expanding: Literacy Education Action Resource Networking), a community promoting women's literacy as a tool that fosters empowerment and equity for women for their support with the publication and for the inspiration of ongoing discussions around the important topic of rape culture.

Geraldine would like to acknowledge, in particular, her co-editors. Thanks to her former student, now friend and colleague, Jessica Boynton, for working with her on the first chapter and including excerpts of her own student response. Thanks also to Angel Dionne, co-editor of this volume, who is a former student, friend and colleague without whom this book would not have been possible.

Both Geraldine and Angel would like to thank the readers and reviewers of this book for their input and feedback, which we put to use to improve the book before publication.

We cannot fail to thank the contributors for allowing us to read and review their work in the first place, and for staying with us throughout the entire process, as this book has taken far longer than originally expected, due to various illnesses, deaths in families, setbacks due to election depression/court nomination anxiety, funding issues, the pandemic and job-related issues.

We would like to thank the artists, Jessica and Joanna Becker, of Bushi and Brush, for creating original work, called *Hades and Persephone*, to be used as the cover. In this work, Persephone reaches towards the distant caves, calling out for help as she is abducted, and is heard only by Hecate, who must tell Demeter what has happened. This image connects content we start hearing about at an early age through storytelling, to content we encounter for ourselves in society. How, like Demeter, do we fight for change?

Hades and Persephone is a stylized image inspired by various works depicting the abduction of Persephone, and it was also inspired by discussions of the romanticized Alfred Eisenstaedt photograph taken at Times Square at the end of WWII of the sailor George Mendonsa forcefully grabbing and kissing the nurse Greta Zimmer Friedman without her consent. Similarly, Demeter's daughter, Persephone, had no choice when she was grabbed in the garden as she joyfully picked her favorite spring flowers.

Special thanks go to each of our loved ones for putting up with us as we worked to get this book to publication. Finally, thanks to our universities for their continued support.

We certainly look forward to scheduling campus readings and book signings. This book is for you!

Contents

Introduction

Geraldine Cannon Becker and Angel T. Dionne

In a previously published newsletter column, which was the instigation for this book, Professor Geraldine Cannon Becker states the following: "Rape is a topic that is hard to think about, much less talk about for many people. Lots of people want to avoid it altogether, for one reason or another. Many people have been victims of rape, but we are all victims of what has been called a 'rape culture,' and this is a topic that deserves more attention towards education and prevention" ("Changing the Programming"). What is rape culture, exactly? Interestingly, rape culture has been defined in different ways by different people. We asked our contributors to define and clarify key terms, such as rape culture, as used in their work. However, generally speaking, Becker notes that "Rape culture is an idea that links rape and sexual violence to the culture of a society, and in which commonly-held beliefs, attitudes and practices normalise, excuse, tolerate, and even condone rape" ("Changing the Programming").

This edited collection examines rape culture in the context of the current programming—attitudes, education, and awareness. Authors explore changing the programming in terms of educational processes, practices, and experiences associated with rape culture across diverse cultural, historical, and geographic locations; they also explore the complexity of rape culture from a variety of contexts and perspectives. We include interdisciplinary academic submissions from educators and students as well as experiential accounts and perspectives from members of various community settings doing work that is aimed at making a positive difference.

Some of the original questions for engagement and topics for consideration are as follows: What do we teach our sons and daughters about rape culture and how do we teach them? Do we need to talk with children—both boys and girls—from an early age about stereotypes and focus on the strengths both boys and girls have? Do we need more stories and movies that feature strong and realistic female characters who do not need to be rescued by boys or men and who may even save the day for everyone, without sacrificing themselves in the process? What do these boys and girls currently see and hear on a daily basis through literature, media, social settings, surroundings, etc.? What do they experience? What about catcalling and street harassment? How do these factor into rape culture? What are some steps that could be taken towards appropriate education and prevention?

Educational awareness is something we looked into carefully. We were seeking specific ways to change or augment current cultural and academic education that could make a difference, and we thought that educators and learners may first want to start thinking about their own programming and ask themselves some of the following important questions. What are their thoughts on the topic of rape and how have their thoughts been formed over the years? What happens when victims speak out? Safe spaces need to be formed for people to be able to speak up and break the silence. We found that people wanted to tell their stories, in all kinds of ways, from writing more private journal entries and poetry, to writing memoirs, penning personal essays, and making audio recordings or using social media. Words on the page, stage, and screen speak volumes.

Indeed, the literature concerning rape culture is varied and plentiful. Although one may only think of the post-2000 era when first confronting the term "rape culture," the discussions surrounding rape culture are not merely a product of the 2000s. Through a brief survey of the literature touching upon this topic, it is evident that even older texts recognized the importance and urgency of addressing rape culture. Newer texts have investigated such topics as the interplay between social media, popular media, and rape culture. For example, in "Rape Culture and Feminist Politics of Social Media," Carrie Rentschler explores the use of social media as a vehicle for change in the context of feminist politics. Feminist bloggers, for example, have recently begun using social media to "respond to rape culture, and hold accountable those responsible for its practices when mainstream news media, police and school authorities do not" (Rentschler 67). This is a timely piece of research, as it comes at a time when police and school reactions to rape cases are coming under close scrutiny.

Other contemporary works also touch upon the perpetuation of rape culture in popular media, such as books, film, and music. Debra Ferreday's article "Game of Thrones, Rape Culture, and Feminist Fandom," for example, takes a look at fan narratives and how fandom can be used as a means of engaging in discourses concerning the "masculinity and futurity that contribute to rape culture" (Ferreday 21). Another article, "#AskThicke: 'Blurred Lines,' Rape Culture, and the Feminist Hashtag Takeover," by Tanya Horeck, tackles the music industry and the use of hashtags as a means of protest. Here, the analysis focuses upon hashtags as a means of "voiciferous discussion and debate about rape culture" (Horeck 1106).

Older texts of importance include *Transforming a Rape Culture* (Buchwald et al.), which focuses on strategies and programs serving the purpose of achieving a rape-free future. Many of these strategies and programs revolve around education. As a newer contribution to the literature surrounding rape culture and consent, the present collection, *Rape Culture 101: Programming Change*, is not the first of its kind. Other book-length essay collections concerning rape culture do exist, as do collections concentrating on the need for change, such as *Preventing Sexual Violence: Interdisciplinary Approaches to Overcoming a Rape Culture* (Henry and Powell), which also envisions a rape-free culture. Its essays thoroughly analyze societal attitudes towards sex and sexual violence, educational tactics to impart change, and the role of media in the perpetuation of rape culture.

There are some important similarities between this collection and the collections discussed in this review. Numerous essays in this collection discuss education, the media, as well as shifting perceptions in con-temporary society. What distinguishes this collection from others is the depth and breadth of the essays. The interdisciplinary backgrounds of the authors, as well as the interdisciplinarity inherent to each essay, are of particular interest, since they provide access in-depth discussions revolving around diverse topics (politics, media, law, culture, etc.). The collection does not focus on one sole aspect of rape culture, nor does it concentrate on one geographical location. In fact, three of the fifteen essays included in this collection discuss rape culture and media in India. The collection also contains a survey essay dedicated to depictions of rape in the ancient world as well as an essay probing the myth of "unrapeability"—that is, the mistaken notion that certain women are unrapeable). The diversity and depth of the essays found in this collection will appeal to a variety of readers, from professionals to laypersons. Those interested in education, media, cultural studies, literature, and politics will find something to pique their interest. The accessibility of the text is one of its main appeals.

Of course, the collection is not by any means the end-all and be-all of discussions surrounding rape culture and its impact on society. Certain topics, such as rape and the elderly as well as rape and the disabled, are missing. These are incredible important topics, which we hope to address in future publications. The elderly, disabled, and other marginalized groups are often neglected in discussions of rape and consent. We hope that future essay collections will be aimed at representing these at-risk populations.

The first chapter of this collection summarizes the original call and response essays that were the seed for this volume to grow, written by Geraldine Cannon Becker and Jessica Boynton, but this work had deep roots in the past. The next chapter, by Joseph E. Becker, briefly summarizes some ancient world literature with clear references to rape or abduction and focuses on how this work is still relevant to us today. The survey demonstrates the foundations of societal attitudes towards rape in representative cultures.

Next, in chapter three, Mary Bronstein addresses the role society, parents, and educators play in the creation and perpetuation of rape culture. She outlines the possible actions that can be undertaken to break down the beliefs and behaviours contributing to rape culture as well as explores the role of mothers in the perpetuation of the patriarchal values in which they themselves were raised. In chapter four, Emily Colpitts discusses recent efforts to educate men concerning the prevention of sexual assault and argues that the mere involvement of men in the prevention of sexual violence is not sufficient. The social constructions of gender norms that give rise to rape culture, gender-based violence, and gendered power relations must also be addressed.

In chapter five, Abigail L. Moser and Lynne M. Webb address the results of data collected from seven focus groups comprised of college women. The data showed that women in the samples voiced little agency in regards to sexual assault. Some college women held beliefs consistent with those perpetuated by rape culture, and the study suggests several changes to address these beliefs, including conversations with experts and incorporating rhetorical training programs. In chapter six, Katherine J. Denker and Faith R. Kellermeyer discuss the role memorable messages (which are verbal messages remembered for long periods of time) can play in the prevention of sexual assault through the analysis of qualitative interviews with students. Using constant-comparative analysis, the authors identified specific memorable messages that have the ability to both perpetuate and diminish rape myth acceptance, and they further developed them into thematic patterns.

Then, in chapter seven, Olga Marques and Jen Rinaldi focus on the articulation of cis-heteropenetrative sex acts as one of the key events of consequence masking sexual actors and relationships, which results in narrow definitions of consent. Marques and Rinaldi seek to rewrite the vocabularies of sex and sexual conduct by exploring different potentialities. Chapter eight, by Leigh Gaskin, discusses the historical contexts that have shaped political and social expectations for claims and prosecutions of sexual assault. By considering perceptions of who is a believable victim and who deserves justice for sexual crimes committed against them, Gaskin addresses the necessity of creating a cultural shift towards seeing sexual assault as unpredictable by overcoming the social and cultural taboos about sexuality and creating a nonpatriarchal means for its expression.

In chapter nine, Jodie Bowers and Carolyn M. Cunningham provide tools for identifying and addressing cyberbullying and cyberharassment, which are often normalized, and they offer an overview of bystander intervention and its importance in changing rape culture. In chapter ten, Erin R. Kaplan looks at incidents that serve as modes of affective production to help debunk and demystify the circular nature of American rape culture. This chapter hones in on how antirape-wear and rape-culture awareness can actually contribute to our already oversaturated, mediatized, and victim-blaming culture. Next, in chapter 11, Tracy Royce combines fat studies scholarship with personal narrative and journalistic accounts, and details the ways in which rape culture and fat oppression intersect. Additionally, the anti-fat practice of "hogging" is examined. The chapter concludes with recommendations for ways to meaningfully integrate material relevant to body size into academic and organizational antirape curriculum, thereby undermining rape culture and fat oppression alike.

Earlier chapters touched upon how American films have influenced rape culture. In chapter twelve, Kirthi Jayakumar looks at the Indian film industry at large, which includes films, music, and music videos from films. She makes the case for making sensitized cinema, as she argues that entertainment that may seem mindless to the intelligentsia can be, and oftentimes is, misinterpreted by those with little to no education or those who lack a more sensitized education. In chapter thirteen, Priyanka Nupur looks at the construction of a "moral woman," who is the harbinger of family and community honour under the cultural norms of India. Nupur explores how the manipulation of the idea of modesty of the victim is used to prove the innocence of the accused by demonstrating the victim's immorality of character, and she also discusses how the idea of a "loose woman" is normalized through the culture and how the idea also enters into the legal field. She further looks at various reforms in Indian laws regarding rape to see how far they conform to or depart from the idea of morality, which is defined by phallocentric standards. In chapter fourteen, Sona Kaur and Eileen L. Zurbriggen summarize several aspects of Indian culture and society that contribute to rape culture, and discuss Indian values concerning shame and honour, as both drive much of the socialization young girls receive around dating and sexuality. They also examine rape culture in Bollywood, India's leading film industry, and conclude by outlining some avenues for change to combat Indian rape culture, focusing on changing laws. Finally, in chapter fifteen, Carole Sheffield reminds us again of the importance of classroom strategies to tackle rape culture and argues that real, lasting change can only take place when society becomes uncomfortable with rape-supportive arguments.

Rape is indeed a difficult topic to discuss, but we must and in ways that do not continue to normalize it. We have to keep moving forward with the awareness of what has happened in the past. We have to break the old cycle and create a new one by being more comfortable in uncomfortable spaces. *Rape Culture 101: Programming Change* is our contribution to that process.

Works Cited

Becker, Geraldine Cannon. "Programming the Change." Email received by WE LEARN members, 7 Aug. 2014.

Buchwald, Emilie, et al. *Transforming a Rape Culture*. Milkweed Editions, 1995.

Ferreday, Debra. "Game of Thrones, Rape Culture and Feminist Fandom." *Australian Feminist Studies*, vol. 30, no. 83, 2015, pp. 21-36.

Henry, Nicola, and Anastasia Powell. *Preventing Sexual Violence: Interdisciplinary Approaches to Overcoming a Rape Culture*. Palgrave Macmillan, 2014.

Horeck, Tanya. "#AskThicke: 'Blurred Lines,' Rape Culture, and the Feminist Hashtag Takeover." *Feminist Media Studies*, vol. 14, no. 6, Feb. 2014, pp. 1105-7.

Rentschler, Carrie A. "Rape Culture and the Feminist Politics of Social Media." *Girlhood Studies*, vol. 7, no. 1, 2014, pp. 65-82.

Chapter One

Summary of the Call and Response to a Bigger Picture Issue: An Essay on Rape Culture–Programming Change

Geraldine Cannon Becker and Jessica Boynton

WE LEARN (Women Expanding: Literacy Education Action Resource Networking)—a community promoting women's literacy as a tool that fosters empowerment and equity for women—was seeking a topic for their general monthly newsletter, normally focusing on some "bigger picture" issue that would be up for further discussion by members. Geraldine Cannon Becker, on the WE LEARN board of directors, suggested that they focus on rape culture. WE LEARN asked her to present on this in the August 2014 newsletter column space, so Becker wrote a brief personal response to just a few sources that she had recently encountered in which rape and violence against women were a dominant theme, including fairy tales traditionally aimed mainly at young children.

Shortly after the newsletter was sent out, WE LEARN received some interesting responses. They also published some of these responses in the following months. One educator used the original column in her classroom and shared her student responses with WE LEARN. That is when Becker first reached out to Demeter Press with the query for a book expanding upon those initial ideas. This essay begins with selected content from the original column, which ended with a call for more reader input. We have included summarized classroom feedback, along with Jessica Boynton's student-writer response, which acknowledges the importance of inspirational, outspoken, and strong female role models in fairy tales and fantasy literature.

People write from their wounds, they say. So many poems, stories, and personal narratives over the years have followed all too similar and familiar patterns—from stories of untoward activities occurring while teens are babysitting, even in the homes of relatives or their own homes, to tales of sexual personal space violation in high school, when people may bump into other people on purpose just to touch a breast, for example. How many stories are there involving college and parties where alcohol or drugs may be involved? The young and the naive are often taken advantage of, in these kinds of cases, and they may end up questioning themselves later with regards to their own involvement. How could that unwanted event have been avoided? A person may ask themselves questions without clear answers. Friends and relatives cannot easily be avoided.

Many of us know of these kinds of stories, and far too many know them from personal experiences. Sometimes, people experience things they do not understand at the time, or things occur that they do not really identify as anything besides normal, even when the experiences are a far cry from normal. It may take years for a person to realize this and seek help through legal assistance and counselling, as may be needed. People who experience such violations may live a life of suffering in silence and try to forget the pain of the past, but they are often triggered when instances of sexual violence or incidents of rape are in the news. No one should be so harmfully silenced or fear shame or shunning when they do speak up.

In "Changing the Programming," the newsletter column Becker wrote for WE LEARN, she mentions how easy it is to find articles in which the victim stays silent in shame, thinking this is what is best to protect a career or children, as the perpetrator is often seen as an upstanding member of the community. This was the case when in 2014, as reported by the Associated Press, a Utah police officer who had drugged and recorded himself raping his wife ended up killing himself after he had killed her and their two children, along with his mother-in-law. The community was left in disbelief, trying to rationalize his actions.

Around the same time that this story was in the papers, Becker was teaching a summer course involving the close analysis of fairy tales. In "Changing the Programming," she talks about how she and her students had been examining a version of *Sleeping Beauty*, called "The Sun, Moon and Talia," by Giambattista Basile, in which an actual rape takes place. Becker says that Walt Disney's *Maleficent*, which premiered in theatres the summer of 2014, made her think of rape of a similar sort, date rape or sleep rape, when Maleficent is drugged and has her beautiful wings cut from her body while she sleeps. Angelina Jolie, who magnificently performed in the role of Maleficent, has indicated in various news reports that the rape analogy definitely was intentional (Hiblen). In this version of the old tale of *Sleeping Beauty*, viewers get more backstory on Maleficent and find out why she could make such a horrible curse on an innocent babe.

In most versions of *Sleeping Beauty*, there is no obvious rape, but Becker says she started thinking about that kiss without consent—often called "true love's kiss" and featured in many enchanting fantasy movies. It is a kiss given to a young maiden who is dead asleep (at least in most versions of *Sleeping Beauty* and *Snow White*). In "Changing the Programming," Becker reminds readers that there are other tales, of course, that feature young women who want a kiss and seem to be under tremendous pressure to get it even if they cannot speak (as happens in various versions of *The Little Mermaid*). With her students in the summer fairy tale course, she pondered the kinds of messages these tales and movies are sending. Her students wondered if kids were being programmed from an early age to dream of this kind of stolen kiss.

In the class, discussions of stolen kisses did not stay in the realm of the fantastic, as a reference was soon made to the famous and often romanticized Alfred Eisenstaedt *LIFE Magazine* V-J (Victory over Japan) Day photograph, which was taken August 14, 1945 at Times Square at the end of WWII. In the photograph, the sailor George Mendonsa forcefully grabs and kisses the nurse Greta Zimmer Friedman without her consent. They each have given their perspective of the unexpected event in various interviews, and the photograph has been the inspiration for statues and paintings by various artists. In fact, the cover illustration for this book, *Rape Culture 101: Programming Change*, is a stylized image called *Hades and Persephone*, which was created by two warrior artists, Jessica Becker and Joanna Becker, who teach people on the twofold path of both defense and creativity in their arts dojo, Bushi and Brush (*Bushiandbrush.com*). The image was inspired by various works depicting the rape and abduction of Persephone by Hades, but the pose itself is reminiscent of Eisenstaedt's Times Square photograph. In "Interview with Greta Zimmer Friedman," Patricia Redmond indicates that even though Mendonsa intended no malice in his actions, he gave her no choice but to endure his strong embrace. She rationalizes that he was only expressing great joy that the war was over, and sincerely believes that he was only showing his gratitude towards nurses. Yet, she felt like a bystander to his action and he did not take her feelings into consideration in that moment, which she also calls "an act of silence" (Redmond).

Similarly, Demeter's daughter, Persephone, had no choice when she was grabbed in the garden by Hades as she joyfully picked her favourite spring flowers. In the newsletter, "Changing the Programming," Geraldine Cannon Becker talks about the need for situational awareness and physical prowess:

> Women need to learn to feel as safe as most men seem to feel most of the time, and they need to get appropriate training for that from an early age.... However, it isn't just physical training that women need. They need to be ready to defend themselves against attack from people they know and love, too. This can be even harder to prepare for, because often the abuse will come from someone a woman knows and thinks she can trust.

In karate or self-defense classes, students run through various scenarios and act out some possible ways to avoid or counter attacks. Becker notes also that "We have to develop situational awareness, and give ourselves permission to defend ourselves in all cases, to the extent that is necessary. Being prepared can help a person be more at ease."

Students in Becker's fairy tale course discussed ways they might have been programmed to think in specific ways from an early age, in part through the words and images they had been exposed to repeatedly. Jessica Boynton, a student in the course, responded to the "Changing the Programming" newsletter, writing the following:

> There is no question about the influence that literature has on people and their cultures, traditions, values, and beliefs. At times, this influence can be a good thing. It can help people to

better understand not only their own role(s) in society, but also the roles that other people have.... Literature can change how people see themselves, each other, and the world; it can also address social, political, and humanitarian issues facing our world today. However, the influence literature has over people and society can also be detrimental.

She gives examples of works explored in the course, such as *Snow White* and *Beauty and the Beast*, noting that recently people had seen and learned about them "through the animated Disney movie versions." She continues: "The amount of influence the tales and movies have over men, women, society, and the media is a problem. It is a problem because they not only give people unrealistic expectations of life and love, but they also subject both men and women to stereotypical roles, which are supposedly equivalent to what is expected of them by society." In her complete response, which WE LEARN should have archived and may eventually feature on its website for teachers of this subject, Boynton discusses home and work stereotypes as well as love interests in those two movies in some detail before acknowledging that literature was changing. She notes that there have been strong female characters that break the bounds of traditional expectations in recent popular films and literature, such as the *Hunger Games* trilogy by Suzanne Collins.

In fact, the following excerpt of Boynton's student response essay addresses this change nicely and summarizes significant female warrior role models:

> The protagonist, Katniss Everdeen, volunteers to save her sister by taking her place to compete in the hunger games, a televised fight to the death between the twelve districts. Each district sends two competitors, one boy and one girl, to the Capitol which led by President Snow, controls the districts (Collins 17, 22-23). Katniss's counterpart, Peeta Mellark, initially saves her before the games began. After her father dies, Katniss's mother becomes depressed and does not care for her children. Knowing that she and her young sister are about to starve to death, Katniss becomes desperate and scours trash bins behind businesses for food and eventually finds herself behind the bakery. Peeta, a baker's son, sees her and tosses two partially burnt loaves of bread, which save her and her sister (Collins 26-32). Katniss

later remembers that her father taught her to hunt and begins to return to the meadow to hunt and provide food for her family. She is determined that what happened before will not happen again, and she uses what her father taught her for survival. When Katniss competes in the hunger games, she is once again on her own but is a contender. She hunts and traps animals for food and returns the favour by finding Peeta and nursing him back to health after he is injured (Collins 164). Katniss is brave, courageous, strong, and self-reliant. She has strong male figures in her life (including her father, Peeta, Gale, and her mentor, Haymitch Abernathy), but she does not wait for someone to save her. She is a great role model and symbol for any person who is afraid. She is strong but also relatable. Throughout the trilogy, her fear and terror from the games and her fear that her actions from the previous games will be taken out on her loved ones are evident. Katniss is a flawed character but also a strong character that young women can look up to and admire.

Disney has also made films that centre around a strong female character, most notably *Brave* (2012) and *Mulan* (1998). However, I will only focus on *Mulan* here, because Merida does not have a "true love" interest. *Mulan* is about a girl who goes to fight in a war in the place of her father, Fa Zhou, who is aging and ill. She pretends that she is a man but is later found out to be a woman after she is injured. Mulan was initially ridiculed for not knowing her place in society and for not acting ladylike by both her family and a matchmaker, but by the end of the movie, even the emperor of China is grateful to her because her actions saved China. *Mulan* is another excellent example of what children should admire and idolize. Again, Mulan is not perfect (she is gutsy and impulsive), but she is another strong female character. By the end of the movie, Mulan and Li Shang have developed feelings for each other, but they did not magically fall in love and get married instantly. Their romance gradually built up over time, which made the movie both more believable and more realistic.

Hopefully, more characters like Mulan, Katniss, and even Merida can come along and break the traditional stereotypes and expectations that people, society, and the media have to help "change the programming." Hopefully, these characters can help reinforce the fact that women can be strong and independent, and loving and courageous. I know these characters helped me to learn and understand that women can be heroes too, even if they do not fit the traditional or ideal view of a hero.

Later that year, in the fall of 2014, in a classroom at Berry College, Dr. Susan Conradsen discussed Geraldine Cannon Becker's WE LEARN newsletter, "Changing the Programming," with students in her women's and gender studies course. In personal correspondence dated February 26, 2015, Becker got a summary of those student reactions. Conradsen writes:

> When the class discussed this article, one of the things that I found that was very cool as a professor was that it generated a lot of sharing of experiences and lots of discussion. It touches on a range of different things, making good points, and asked questions that could facilitate discussion.... These are some of the other things that came up:

> [There is] difficulty in getting people to take rape seriously: spoke about rape memes, rape jokes. When [people] speak out about rape, as a victim or supportive of a victim, they are punished and ... it is much easier to conform and not speak out.

> Men don't realize sometimes what they are doing is rape. We need to stop demonizing rapists and abusers as pure evil, since it prevents men from seeing [such behaviour] in themselves and in their friends because they don't see the person they know as evil, and if all rapists are evil...

> They really like the rape analogy in *Maleficent*. (Some of them had not thought or read about that.)

> [There was a lot] of sharing about their experiences in school of having to wear certain length skirts etc. so [they] wouldn't distract boys. But the boys didn't have to do anything. And that here at college with no dress code, somehow the boys are still able to concentrate! (This section led to lots of personal examples, including one student sharing how a boy pulled her skirt down,

and she punched him in the eye, and she got in trouble, but he didn't.)

[There was discussion about how] some areas are a hub of toxic masculinity—law enforcement, military, etc.

They liked talking about Disney and asked ... what new stories should we tell our children to combat [rape culture]. [They talked about] how the male leads saved the world ... but for the females love is primary and [their] only identity.

[They wished] there was more discussion about rape culture and talked about more ways to challenge it.

Overall, it led to great discussion, and I will assign it again. Personally, I like how it touches on a number of things, so there is both breadth and depth; it makes points that get folks thinking, which then can be expanded on.

All of the responses to Becker's WE LEARN newsletter on rape culture and "Changing the Programming" got the wheels turning and the ball rolling for a query letter to Demeter Press as well as for a call for submissions to this collection on ways to challenge rape culture through education and in our daily lives. Becker talked with colleagues and former students, including her co-editor for the current volume, Angel Dionne, her co-author for this chapter, Jessica Boynton, as well as the WE LEARN board of directors. All of them were in agreement that this important topic deserved more attention than it had been getting at the time, in 2014. Since then, of course, lots of drastic changes have taken place in the world concerning rape culture.

The most devastating setback to writing on this topic while working on this book had to be the depression so many of us felt after the election of Donald Trump as president of the United States, as he had openly bragged about his mistreatment of women. Then, the #MeToo movement drew more needed attention to rape culture and its influences, starting in the film and news industries. This gave many people hope. More stories were shared. More silenced voices were being heard. Bill Cosby and Harvey Weinstein were even charged and sentenced. However, then Trump's Supreme Court pick, Brett Kavanagh, was accused by Christine Blasey Ford of attempted rape, and the way this played out in the system in America was reminiscent of what had happened with Anita Hill in 1991. Women are still fighting to be heard and people are struggling for basic rights.

Now, as this book finally goes to press, we are in the midst of a pandemic due to the outbreak of the COVID-19 virus, and lots of victims of violence may be held in lockdown with their abusers. The battle may seem never ending on many fronts. With lives on the line, the call to take action with awareness is important. We do not have to be silent bystanders to life. We can speak up and help break the silence. We all can. And we can all be ready to listen when people are talking and to become more informed while taking necessary action, legal or otherwise, towards the prevention of violence. Readers, you may ask yourselves about your own programming when it comes to rape culture. What are your thoughts and how have they changed over the years? We can participate in ongoing conversations and begin to make important changes one step at a time.

Works Cited

Associated Press. "Texts Reveal Cop Who Killed Family Had Raped Wife." *New York Post*, 8 July, 2014, nypost.com/2014/07/08/texts-reveal-officer-who-killed-family-had-raped-wife/. Accessed 17 May 2020.

Basile, Giambattista. "The Sun, Moon and Talia." *Uncoy.com*, 17 May 2006, uncoy.com/2006/05/sleeping_beauty_1.html. Accessed 18 May 2020.

Becker, Geraldine Cannon. "Changing the Programming." Email received by WE LEARN members, 7 Aug. 2014.

Boynton, Jessica. "Response to Geraldine Cannon Becker's 'Changing the Programming.'" *WE LEARN Newsletter*, email received by WE LEARN members, 7 Sept. 2014.

Collins, Suzanne. *The Hunger Games*. Scholastic Press, 2008.

Conradsen, Susan. "Class Reactions." Email to the author, 26 Feb. 2015.

Hiblen, Carolyn. "'We were very conscious that it was a metaphor for rape': Angelina Jolie reveals the powerful meaning behind harrowing Maleficent wing-tearing scene." *Daily Mail*, 11 June 2014, www.

dailymail.co.uk/tvshowbiz/article-2655642/Angelina-Jolie-reveals -harrowing-Maleficent-wing-tearing-scene-metaphor-rape.html. Accessed 18 May 2020.

Maleficent. Directed by Robert Stromberg, Walt Disney Films, 2014.

Mulan. Directed by Tony Bancroft and Barry Cook, Walt Disney Films, 1998.

Redmond, Patricia. "Interview with Greta Zimmer Friedman." *Veterans History Project*, Library of Congress, American Folklife Center. 23 Aug. 2005, memory.loc.gov/diglib/vhp/story/loc.natlib. afc2001001.42863/transcript?ID=sr0001. Accessed 18 May 2020.

Chapter Two

Depictions of Rape in the Ancient World: A Brief Survey

Joseph E. Becker

R ape in ancient world literatures is presented in various forms, including abduction, coercion, violent assault, and other violations of bodily autonomy. Among the most ancient depictions of rape occurs in the Sumerian epic *Gilgamesh*, wherein the titular hero of the work is shown violating the cultural norms associated with his priest-king status in his city-state of Uruk (square brackets denote reconstructed text): "Yet he is the shepherd of the Uruk-the-Sheepfold, / Gilgamesh, [the guide of the] teeming [people.]/Though he is their shepherd and their [protector,]/powerful, pre-eminent, expert [and mighty,]/Gilgamesh lets no girl go free to her bride[groom]" (I.87-91). The people of Uruk cry to their god, Anu, begging for aid against the apparently unappeasable sexual appetite that Gilgamesh exhibits, which clearly contravenes Sumerian cultural norms. Anu consults with the goddess Aruru, who creates the wild man Enkidu, who will be a "match for the storm of his heart" (I.97). In short, although any recompense for the victims of Gilgamesh's actions is left unwritten, the gods find that the best way to deal with the ardor of Gilgamesh is by distracting him via the agency of Enkidu—thereby channelling his energy away from the people.

Indeed, even though the various ancient cultures had rules and stipulations regarding sexual conduct, these varied widely, as those depicted in Hebrew scripture illustrate. Two exemplary texts focus on the violation of hospitality and the quest of vengeance when a rape occurs. In the first, Genesis 34, Dinah, the daughter of Jacob's first wife, Leah, is assaulted by one Shechem, who "seized her and lay with her by force" (2). He then apparently "loved the girl, and spoke tenderly to her" (3) before requesting that she be acquired as his wife. Jacob's sons plot revenge once they learn of Shechem's violation of Dinah (who is silenced throughout the tale—keeping the physical and psychological aftermath of her rape unrecorded). Jacob's sons trick Shechem and his fellow male tribal members into getting circumcised as a prerequisite for marrying Dinah (13-24). The brothers attack Shechem and his compatriots while they are recovering; they slay them all, remove Dinah from Shechem's house, and plunder the land (25-9). Jacob is upset by their actions, although his sons ask, "should our sister be treated like a whore?" (32).

Another tale found in 2 Samuel 13 concerns the rape of Tamar by her half-brother, Amnon, who conceives an unnatural desire for her. When she proves reluctant to acquiesce, despite her protestations, "he would not listen to her; and being stronger than she, he forced her and lay with her" (14). In a situation with some parallels to Genesis 34, we have another male with a lack of self-control who overpowers a female victim and rapes her. In this story, both the rapist's and the victim's reactions are depicted. Amnon develops "a very great loathing for her" (15), and Tamar castigates him for deciding to cast her out, yet she states that "sending me away is greater [wrong] than the other that you did to me" (16), since Mosaic law, as promulgated in Deuteronomy, required marriage in such situations. Tamar adopts mourning attire and "went away, crying aloud as she went" (19). Eventually, her full brother, Absalom, plots revenge on his sister's behalf, and some two years later holds a feast where Amnon and all of King David's sons are slain—an event that triggers a period of civil discord (22-29).

The Hebrew scriptures depict rape in various ways, though often as a violation of hospitality (i.e., the rape of Dinah) or as a violation of familial bonds (i.e., the rape of Tamar); the victim may be punished for failing to sufficiently defend herself in the eyes of the patriarchal society, and social/kinship bonds are disrupted by rape and the revenge often enacted afterwards by the male relatives of the victim. Despite various prohibitions and prescriptions regarding sexual behaviour, divinely sanctioned rape in time of warfare is condoned in Numbers 31.

For the Greco-Roman world, some of the most famous myths

underpinning their cultural paradigms depicted rape. For example, a number of nymphs and (primarily) female demigods are assaulted by Zeus, including Leah, Io, Europa, and Demeter, among others. Many of them are unfairly punished by Hera for their failure to avoid Zeus's advances. Other gods also pursued and assaulted a range of victims, usually female: Hermes chases the nymph, Syrinx, who is transformed into reeds by her sister to avoid violation by the messenger god (who fashions the pan flute from the reeds, nonetheless). Apollo becomes enamored of Daphne, whom he attempts to assault, but she cries out to her father, the river god Peneus, who transforms her into the laurel tree from the leaves of which Apollo fashions a wreath. In both cases, Hermes and Apollo do not sexually consummate their desires, but they still manage to take something from the nymphs and utilize it without their permission.

Perhaps the most famous rape portrayed in Greco-Roman literature is that of Persephone by Hades. Demeter, the Greek goddess of agriculture and sister of Zeus, was raped by him and gave birth to Persephone. As depicted in *The Homeric Hymn to Demeter*, the young girl (Persephone) is lured by a beautiful flower she sees in a meadow. As she grasps the flower, the earth opens up, and Hades emerges in his chariot, who abducts the young woman "and bare[s] her away lamenting" (Evelyn-White, ll. 19-32). While Zeus hears her cries, "he [is] sitting aloof, apart from the gods, in his temple where many pray, and receiving sweet offerings from mortal men" (ll. 19-32) and does not stop his brother's abduction of Persephone. Demeter is devastated by her daughter's abduction, and rather than seeing Persephone's reaction to her assault, readers of the myth perhaps see it by proxy in Demeter's anguish: "Bitter pain seized her heart, and she rent the covering upon her divine hair with her dear hands: her dark cloak she cast down from both her shoulders and sped, like a wild-bird, over the firm land and yielding sea, seeking her child" (Evelyn-White, ll. 40-53).

Eventually, Hecate and Helios, the only witnesses of the rape, reveal to Demeter that Hades has abducted Persephone with the acquiescence of Zeus. After learning the truth, she becomes even more outraged: "Thereafter she was so angered with the dark-clouded Son of Cronos that she avoided the gathering of the gods and high Olympus, and went to the towns and rich fields of men, disfiguring her form a long while" (Evelyn-White). She withdraws her blessing from the earth, which plunges the world into a winter-like period of famine. As the famine makes the people more desperate, their cries are finally heard by Zeus, who intervenes and strikes a bargain with Hades: Persephone is allowed to return for part of the year, and Demeter restores fertility to the lands. During the other portion of the year, the land is dormant, as Demeter mourns for Persephone, who had unwittingly partook of a pomegranate in the Underworld, thereby tying her to that realm—she must return to Hades in the Underworld during the winter season.

In this myth, a mother doggedly seeks her daughter and finds some modicum of justice. The story also presents a powerful depiction of the consequences of rape on a mother. Although the myth does not reveal much from Persephone's perspective, the pain and anguish Demeter experiences on account of her daughter's abduction and rape are some of the most detailed in ancient literature.

In India, the *Ramayana* contains a depiction of feminine behaviour that has both inspired and exasperated readers. Rama is an avatar of Vishnu, who incarnates as the mortal son of a human king to defeat Ravana, a demon living on the island of Lanka, who can only be defeated by a mortal. Over the course of the epic, Rama wins the hand and heart of Sita, a princess found in a furrow of a field by a childless king who adopts her as his own. In the course of the epic, Sita is abducted by Ravana and taken to Lanka. Rama, with this assistance of his brother Lakshmi and the monkey-god Hanuman, mounts a rescue mission and eventually defeats Ravana.

After the demon's demise, Rama and Sita are reunited. However, because of doubts about her chastity held by his followers, Rama asks that Sita undergo an ordeal in order to confirm her purity, which she successfully undertakes by striding, unburnt and unharmed, through intense flames. Nonetheless, after the end of their exile and Rama's restoration to the throne, rumors continue to abound questioning Sita's behaviour with Ravana, and as the populace grows more restive over the matter, Rama agrees to exile her to a forest, where she lives for a time and gives birth to twin sons before returning to her mother, the Earth. Some scholars believe Sita's purity ordeal was added by later and more patriarchal authors and does not reflect the overall tone of the ancient epic. Regardless, Sita's character has had a deep influence on Indian perceptions of femininity. Archana Pathak Bhatt notes the following: "Sita gives everything up to follow her husband into exile. Despite her deep seated loyalty and commitment, Sita is continuously tested, questioned and doubted. Even when she passes the most rigorous of tests for fidelity ... doubt remains and ultimately she is punished with banishment" (155). With Sita as a model, many Indian women have traditionally been trained to be docile, self-effacing, and devoted to their husbands, regardless of their behaviour. In modern India, women who are raped are still customarily seen as damaged, impure, or at fault, and women who fail to meet societal standards suffer ostracism, despite laws to the contrary that have been too infrequently enforced.

Rape is a difficult and painful subject to examine, and the attitudes displayed in ancient literatures are sometimes difficult for modern readers to comprehend. Nonetheless, rape cultures are often rooted in the many ancient works that reference or depict sexual assault, and by reading them, we may better assess and address the current cultural attitudes that these works have inspired.

Works Cited

Bhatt, Archana Pathak. "The Sita Syndrome: Examining the Communicative Aspects of Domestic Violence from a South Asian Perspective." *Journal of International Women's Studies*, vol. 9, no. 3, 2008, pp. 155-73.

The Bible. The New Oxford Annotated Version, 3rd ed., Oxford University Press, 2001.

Evelyn-White, Hugh G., translator. *Homeric Hymns.* 1914. Project Gutenberg, 2008. Retrieved November 7, 2018. http://www.gutenberg.org/files/348/348-h/348-h.htm#chap37 George, Andrew, translator. *The Epic of Gilgamesh.* Penguin, 1999.

Chapter Three

All Rapists Go to Preschool:
A Call to the Radical Reformation of the Normalization and Aggrandizement of Violence, Domination, Misogyny, and Entitlement in American Boyhood

Mary Bronstein

Introduction

> "We've begun to raise daughters more like sons ... but few have the
> courage to raise our sons more like our daughters."
>
> —Gloria Steinem

To acknowledge the existence of rape culture as a pervasively infectious cornerstone of American society, one must also acknowledge this reality: rape culture is not something that has been done to society from the outside by a legacy of misogynist deviants; it is something created, perpetuated, enacted, and propagated from within. It is not an abstracted mode of oppression or an invisible entity hiding in dark corners of society. It is society; it is an essential component of the well-oiled patriarchal system that we live in. In fact, the term "rape culture" is somewhat misleading in itself, as Western culture and rape culture are one and the same. To think that they can be seen or discussed as separate systems is false. Psychologist Alfred Adler discussed rape culture decades before the term existed when he stated that hegemonic masculinity could be seen as "the arch evil of our culture, the excessive pre-eminence of manliness" (qtd. in Connell 16). Thus, in discussions of rape culture, it is important to discuss men and boy and not some men and some boys. Of course, not all boys will be reared towards becoming rapists, and not all men rape or even condone rape. However, when living in a society in which one in every five American women experiences rape in their lifetimes (Harding 5), concentrating on the individual men and boys who do not participate in rape belies the fact that it is the institution of patriarchy that must be problematized, not the individuals who commit specific crimes.

Jackson Katz points out the importance of the semantic distinction between the claim that boys learn to see girls as the "other" and that boys are taught this: "To say that boys *learn* to mistreat girls shifts attention away from the role that adult men play in *teaching* boys to mistreat girls. When you shift the topic of conversation back to how men *teach* boys to be violent it puts the onus for change back on adults" (232). I would go further: men are not the only or even the most important teachers of young boys. This role belongs to women, both in the home and in educational programs. To accept that rape culture starts with boys below elementary school age is to question everything that is considered normal and natural about American boyhood. It is also to consider the role of both men and women in the problematic process of rearing a male infant into a man. Perhaps, most importantly, it is to understand that it is largely the work of women to radicalize the way they raise and educate male children. This is not a condemnation of the role of mothers and female caregivers in the existence of rampant rape culture; instead, it is a hopeful that what has been created can also be counteracted and dismantled through strong vision and new choices.

This chapter understands rape culture as the man-made creation of a society that normalizes the dominance, humiliation, sexualization, dehumanization, commodification, monetization, abuse, and objectification of women by men so that rape is allowed, ignored, condoned, normalized, and even encouraged. Rape is always a gendered crime: it is a system of terrorism by which all women are kept in a state of fear because of their sex and gender. Gender must be understood as a structure of rules invented and perpetuated in order to oppress people on the basis of sex much the same way caste systems work in other parts of the world. With these conceptual definitions in place, it can be possible to dismantle modes of oppression and terror masquerading as natural and normal. Identifying the relationship between rape culture and gender highlights how man-made oppressive systems can also be destroyed. Action in the form of educational programs and campaigns aimed towards adolescent and adult men to reprogram them into people who do not rape or participate in rape culture have been implemented sporadically and to varying degrees and results. In any case, programs that target young men are inadequate at best and illogical at worst, at least on their own. To chip away at something as large, normalized, and all-consuming as rape culture, simply reeducating boys at the brink of male adulthood is not the answer. Boys and men are not members of a cult and cannot be deprogramed through classes or group therapy to the necessary standard. In *The War Play Dilemma*, Diane Levin and Nancy Carlson Paige state the following: "Children's immediate environment plays a crucial role in influencing the content of early political learning. Political attitudes change the most up to about the age of thirteen and are less subject to change thereafter" (32). Ending rape culture demands educating boys long before puberty begins and before sexual urges, fantasies, practices, and attitudes start to solidify.

Sexual violence against women is also not just a women's issue. When less than 1 per cent of rapists are women (Katz 5) and the rest are men, regardless of the victim's gender, it must be understood that rape is very much a men's issue. Rape affects women in egregious ways, but it stems from the acts and practices of men. Researchers, academics and anyone interested in creating solutions to the problem of rape must accept that by looking backwards in the lives of men is where the process starts. We must look at male infants. We must look at little boys. We must do what the perpetuators of rape culture do: we must get them young.

The Scope

This chapter is concerned with the radical deconstruction and reorganization of the development of masculinities in boys, from infancy through five years old, with the goal of creating a generation of men who function completely outside of behaviours and beliefs that contribute to rape culture. The ways in which boys are encouraged to play (and the toys marketed towards boys) and are socialized through the modality of play are the main focus of this discussion. This chapter will only discuss toys and play that they encourage; the Internet and video gaming will not be included here. The presence of the Internet, personal electronics, and video games in the lives of young boys is pervasive enough that it deserves an in depth discussion of its own and is beyond the scope of this chapter. Indeed, work and research have been done in this area, and the connections between Internet pornography, violent/ misogynist video games, and rape culture have been explored and widely accepted. But there are no significant theoretical works that deal specifically with the types of toys, play, and socialization that are deemed normal and healthy (and, in fact, are even encouraged) in the lives of young boys and their connection to rape culture. Such a gap in research is surprising because of the influence toys, play, and peers have for boys five years old and younger, but this blind spot is certainly not shocking. Adult men and women, including parents and teachers, do not want to accept that small children are involved in rape culture. They certainly do not want to see their little boys as potential rapists, purchasers of sex workers, consumers of violent pornography, abusers of women, or any type of contributor to a world in which rape culture is the norm. In order to create a different kind of man, concerned members of Western society need to give our boys different tools with which to understand the world.

The Miseducation of Women: The Myth of the Normal Boy

> "Older men hate boys because they still have the stink of women on them. War purifies them, washes off the female stink."
> —Andrea Dworkin 51.

In their groundbreaking work about the emotional lives of boys, Dan Kindon and Michael Thompson tell us "it is the responsibility of people who raise boys to train them specifically to be good, empathic partners to girls and women" (216). It may be assumed that since men are responsible for the invention and perpetuation of a toxic masculinity contributing to rape culture, they must, too, be the ones to take on the cause of reimagining how boys are raised to understand their future as men in relation to women. Fathers and other male role models play an influential part in the shaping of the young boy into a man. The father is usually the first, if not only, male figure to demonstrate adult male gender performativity in the life of a small boy. But it is also true that the vast majority of male children have a woman as their primary caregiver and, subsequently, as their substitute caregivers and early childhood teachers. The role of women in the young boy's life must be understood as the relationships that do the most to shape his understanding of the world and his place in it. This does not mean that women are responsible for the creation of rape culture and its participants; rather, it is paramount to understand that mothers, female caregivers, and female educators have often become a pawn in the self-perpetuation of the patriarchy within which they too were raised. The dismissal of the level of influence women have in the formation of the male psychology is a product of misogyny in itself. Women are vitally important in this regard, perhaps exclusively important.

In addition to the myriad contributions to master narratives that make rape culture possible (which have been covered extensively by second-wave feminist scholars, including Simone de Beauvoir and Betty Friedan), Sigmund Freud also contributed to the development of rape culture through his theorizations concerning male sexuality. In the early 1900s, Freud introduced to Western culture a nonresearched, theoretical imagining of male psychosexual development known as the Oedipal complex. The theory hinges on the idea that in order for a boy to develop into a high functioning, heterosexual, and hegemonic man (indeed, the only type of man Freud, as a reflection of the staunchly patriarchal culture at the time, considered psychologically healthy), he must sever emotional ties with his sexually possessive and oppressive mother in favour of his inherently intimidating father. If this does not happen in early childhood, if the boy succumbs to the feminizing mother instead of the masculine father, the boy will grow into a feminized, gender non-conforming, and sexually perverse man. A healthy boy is strong, penis proud, vulva fearing, and stoic. Of course, this is an overly simplified summation of an in-depth work written by Freud but purposefully so, as it has been the crux of the information trickled down to popular culture over nearly one hundred years and accepted as completely factual and logical. William Pollack, the author of *Real Boys*, acknowledges that it has not just been Freud's theory that has created this narrative about what healthy male development entails: "Our view of boys is so influenced and distorted by our myths about them. Over the years a thousand models of boyhood have accumulated and become melded into an all-purpose stereotype" (xxii). He goes further to say, "these models, (many of which date from the 19th century) simply have no relevance to today's world" (xxiv).

The practical negative effects of patriarchal theories of male development can be observed from the time a male infant is born. Mothers have received the message that separation from her is the most important developmental task a male child must complete if he is to become a man. In fact, Pollack goes so far as to state that the cultural imperative of gender differentiation "lies under the push toward separation" (28). If society believes that male children need less of their mother for fewer years than female children, then it also tacitly acknowledges that from birth, there is a fundamental emotional, social, and relational difference between girls and boys—boys do not need as much love or emotional intimacy from their mothers as girls do. Dan Kindlon and Michael Thompson remind us that "all boys are born with the potential for a full range of emotional experience" (10), yet as a culture, we engage in a process of shaming the vulnerability, emotions, or the mother love that young boys display. Pollack calls this process "The Boy Code," which is a set of rules that are "inculcated into boys' by our society—from the very beginning of a boy's life." He further argues that "In effect we hold up a mirror to our boys that reflects back a distorted and outmoded image of the ideal boy" (xxv). An essential aspect of this formula to creating manly boys is the denial of the first security and love that infants find in the world. By encouraging separation from the mother and discouraging identification with her, society begins a process of identity building that hinges on opposition. A male child comes to understand that he is a boy because he is not a girl. He is his father not because he identifies positively with him but because he is not his mother. He needs to follow the rules of boyness, lest he discover that he is feminized, since feminine means being weak, passive, and (perhaps the most terrifying in this context) different from other boys and men.

Mothers and other women are the primary caretakers of the majority of male infants and little boys. Thus, it is logical to expect that a perfectly healthy child of either sex would come to seek identity cues in women. By internalizing both subtle and overt cultural cues that they should not identify with the very people who care for them the most, boys are left in a confusing position in relation to their conception of both self and other. The realization by the male child that he is not female—and therefore (according to society) somehow drastically and importantly different than the woman who provides love, comfort, and security for him—is a pivotal and traumatic psychological event. Indeed, the very young infant has no self at all and views the world and people around it as an extension of its own existence. As psychologist D. W. Winnicott so eloquently states, "there is no such thing as an infant" (585). Understanding this fact reveals that the male child spends a portion of his earliest life with no concept of himself as separate in any way from his mother specifically and, therefore, from the female in general. In her essay, "How Rape is Encouraged in American Boys and How to Stop it," Myriam Miedzian says that as boys slowly realize "they will not be able to grow breasts, have a baby, or nurse it, their efforts to develop a male identity often includes deprecating and rejecting everything female" (167). Miedzian defines this type of negative reactionary gender development as "hypermasculinity" (an extreme concern of boys with proving their masculinity) and "protest masculinity" (a masculine identity formed out of rejecting the feminine) (168). The boy is so angered and disappointed that he is not female and he is different from his mother and may be rejected by her because of it that he pushes away from her femininity and embraces the construct of the male gender wholeheartedly. This starts a lifetime of affiliating manliness with that which is not female.

Discovering that not being female is an imperative ingredient to being male must be painful and frightening to a young boy who understands the world through the lens of his mother and other women. When it becomes important that a boy is different from girls and women, anything female becomes scary; the female body itself becomes something to revile and control all at once. In her essay "The Dread of Woman," Karen Horney states the following: "The fear of the mother is deep seated and repressed. Boys feelings of inadequacy lead them to withdraw emotional energy from the mother and focus it on themselves and their genitals" (428). Since his penis is a tangible thing that he has and his mother does not, the penis becomes both frightening and dangerous as well as something to project worthiness and power onto. But during this process, femaleness still holds tremendous power. To restore order to his world, the work of the boy becomes turning this idea around so that femaleness is the state of wrongness, that anything female is dangerous to his very being and that part of living as a male person requires the constant opposition to and subordination of the female. As boys turn into men, it is not coincidental that this opposition and subordination are often done with the penis, both in abstract and literal ways.

Discussing the childrearing process in the context of societal problems always runs the risk of being misinterpreted as yet another cornerstone of patriarchal culture: mother-blaming. Let it be understood in the clearest terms: mothers are no more to blame for raising boys according to the rigid gender imperatives of society than the child himself. The important detail to understand is that this is a deeply ingrained process. After all, women are raised in patriarchy too and have been given the same untruths about boys that boys receive. Michael Kimmel tells us that part of the problem of the push towards nonfemale identification through early separation from the mother is that it begins a "hardening process" that involves "a narrowing of emotional express-iveness" (40) for the young boy, which continues throughout childhood. Mothers react differently to the emotions and expressions of male infants from birth: they tend not to take time to understand the reasons or desires behind emotions of sadness or frustration as they may in female infants; instead, they maintain a constant state of distraction, dismissal or denial of those emotions (Kimmel 42). The effects of this (along with the adherence to such rules taught by parents as "boys don't cry") lead to boys not only becoming divorced from the meaning of their own feelings but also feeling ashamed of having them in the first place. Kimmel emphasizes that "how we respond to our baby boys and young sons—the manner in which we cuddle, kiss and reassure, teach, comfort and love—not only determines a young boy's capacity for a healthy emotional start in life but deeply effects a boy's characteristic style of behaviour" (57). Kindlon and Thompson call this "emotional illiteracy"—boys "act with careless disregard for the feelings of others at home, at school or on the playground" (5). Adults are comfortable with little boys who are emotionally illiterate because they project a sense of invulnerability and strength, which is how society dictates men should be.

Tools of Domination and Emotional Avoidance: The Toys We Give To Boys

> "Man's discovery that his genitalia could serve as a weapon to generate fear must rank as one of the most important discoveries in prehistoric times, along with the use of fire and the first crude stone axe."
>
> —Brownmiller 14

In his book *The Macho Paradox*, Katz states that boys "learn to be abusive in the same way they learn to be a men" and that "they do not just learn to be violent, they learn that violence is manly" (229). An important way that culture teaches young boys about violence and its place in the work of boyhood is through the toys that are custom designed for them. Reviewing and detailing specific toys on the current or historical market is beyond the scope of this chapter and is not the best way to understand the effects of toys on the developing boy. The pervasively limited categories of play materials that boys are encouraged to use have been consistent to varying degrees since the invention of mass marketed toys; they also are a contributing factor towards problematic gender development in boys. Perhaps the only difference between the toys of the last three decades and those previously produced is that modern toys are even more specific in their prescribed uses for violent play. A look at the bestselling and top-rated toys marketed for boys and sold through *Amazon.com*, supports this argument. Some examples include Nerf N-Strike Tristrike Blaster, with the tagline "Boys can build their own blaster for each mission with the NERF Modulus Tri-Strike Blaster from Hasbro! The Tri-Strike Blaster features three different ways to blast that can all be used separately, or combined, for custom configurations. Bring an entire arsenal to the battlefield with the versatility and power of the Tri-Strike Blaster! Start building with the Elite Dart Blaster and attachable ten-dart clip combo. Precision-fire Elite darts or fire ten in a row using rapid-sliding-bolt-action!" (Hasbro). *Amazon.com* also carries a multitude of Pokémon products, which centre around the stalking, capturing, and training of tiny creatures for the purposes of having them fight each other for entertainment. There is also the Lego Star Wars Imperial Assault Hover tank, with the following tagline:

With a rotating and elevating turret gun with dual spring-loaded shooters, elevating side guns, opening two-minifigure cockpit, storage container and "hover-look" transparent wheels, the Imperial Assault Hovertank is the ultimate urban patrol vehicle. [It] features heavy-armor detailing, transparent wheels, rotating and elevating turret gun with dual spring-loaded shooters, storage container and opening two-minifigure cockpit and elevating side guns. (Lego)

The online store also sells a complete swat team kit, which includes a bulletproof vest, dagger, and billy club, described as "THE CUTEST LITTLE POLICEMAN IS HERE TO ARREST YOU!—Now your toddler can spend endless hours of fun playing cops and robbers with these SWAT toys and pretend to be a real police officer with our durable and sturdy police outfit accessories set!" The page for this toy even includes a photograph of a young girl chasing after a young boy dressed in full swat team gear (Dress Up America).

The messages contained in these toys are striking. If children's toys as tools are understood as tools through which children work out their place in, and their understanding of, the world, these toys are problematic at best and harmful at worst. They are emissaries of masculinity meant to encourage boys to believe in certain myths about themselves.

The role of violence in play, as well as its position and place in early childhood environments, is an ongoing debate. One of the most frequently used validations for the idea of the natural occurring imperative of boys' violent and aggressive play is the work of Bruno Bettelheim. In favor of the noninterference with violent tools and themes in play, the psychologist states the following: "As playing with blocks does not indicate that a child will become an architect, so playing with toy guns tells nothing about what a child will do and be later in life" (47). In fact, the overarching theme of Bettelheim's work about children involves the idea that children must be able to enact their fantasies, no matter how scary or misunderstood by adults, so that the real world is less scary to them. Bettelheim's arguments appear sound when taken in the conceptual abstract, or even in practical terms for previous generations, but they are not applicable when used as an argument in favour of the modern play materials boys are encouraged to use. Whereas in the first half of the twentieth century, children reinterpreted the uses of found objects or nonviolent materials for violent fantasy play or used simple props to enact those fantasies, modern children are handed toys that have very limited and specific purposes. Nancy Carlsson-Paige and Diane Levin agree: "In the past children determined the content of their war play. They made guns out of whatever materials they could find and they invented pretend enemies using their imaginations. They used their play in the service of their development" (16). Modern toys are not a blank slate on which a boy can project his fear-based fantasies; instead, they are actual products of the fully realized fantasies of adults. They are prepackaged narratives given to children so that they may enact adult male fantasies of violence, domination, and superiority. They are products of, and therefore tools for, the patriarchal ideal of masculine development. Carlsson-Paige and Levin believe these toys "can inhibit the kind of creative play necessary for a child's growth" (44). The majority of toys marketed to young boys do not inspire open-ended play; they prescribe action-oriented and prepackaged symbols of masculinity.

Since the toys that are marketed and given to boys are products of the minds of adult men, it makes sense that these toys are overly concerned with themes of power and violence. These men project the anxiety they feel over the validity of their own fully formed masculinity onto the boys they produce toys for. The toys become another way for men to communicate to boys about gendered expectations. Toys become a tool with which boys can practice the rules of male gender and begin to bond with other boys through performative masculinity: "The most common way that boys proved their masculinity and established themselves as being one of the boys was by expressing interest in boys toys and activities" (Chu 64). Judy Chu observes that this ultimately results in boys focusing on guns and gunplay and opposing dolls and doll play: "The main allure of guns and gun play seemed to be that they provided (and proved to be) a quick, effective and distinctively masculine way for the boys to engage and bond with each other" (66). These toys also encourage the divide between boys and girls from the youngest age. Through bonding on violence and female opposition, boys come to see their bonds and play as centrally focused on an aversion to femininity—reifying a worldview that has already been developing.

The main theme of boys' toys is power. Superheroes and other action heroes explicitly embody such power. When discussing where boys learn to equate manliness with violence, Katz explains that "they learn it on Saturday morning cartoons and trips to the toy store, where action heroes with rippled muscles convey the powerful lesson that might makes right" (229). According to Carlsson-Paige and Levin, giving boys instruments for imitating and enacting violence and domination is inherently developmentally dangerous: it makes the child "focus on the action and excitement of the fighting, [but] they do not think about the pain and suffering that might result" (20). Whereas girls are marketed with toys that have themes such as nurturance, emotions, imagination, and creativity (although, of course, some of these categories and their corresponding toys suffer from their own brand of gender stereotyping), boys are given toys that demand a narrative of good versus bad and us versus them. Regardless of whether the boy is taking the role of the good guy or the bad guy, violence is the way that he demonstrates power and details the narrative of play when using superhero toys or action figures. Vivian Gussey Paley notes in her observations that even though they are labeled "good," superheroes are still destructive: "They save people while knocking down buildings; they jail bad and good people indiscriminately and set off explosives everywhere. Like monsters, they are uncompromisingly aggressive" (26). From infanthood onwards, boys are encouraged to play with superheroes and identify with them. As a culture, we need our boys growing up believing they are strong, powerful, admired and righteous, yet we are then surprised when these same boys are confused about the boundaries between their bodies and the bodies of girls and woman.

This confused identity surrounding good guys and bad guys comes to light when looking at toy guns, swords, and other imitation weapons or accessories of violence. In the world of boys' toys, weapons are used and fetishized by both heroes and villains alike. The only difference seems to be who uses these weapons most effectively against the other. We know that in all children's narratives, the hero always wins. However, many boys are more excited by identification with the villain. Paley notices the following: "Luke Skywalker is much admired, but Darth Vader's name is uttered with awe. The bad guys always promise more power—or more freedom—than the good guy" (25). For boys who have been stripped of their ability to express a full range of emotions and are frustrated by the push to separate from their mothers in favour of bonding with other boys, it makes sense that bad guys would hold a special interest for them. These figures represent the ultimate masculinity: they dominate, intimidate, and conquer everyone. Their downfall ends up being that they want too much power. When the good guy takes them down and regains power, the bad guy gets up and tries again. He never goes away. This situation is a metaphor for how boys understand masculinity itself, since the only way to diminish the threat and its danger is to use violence to control and contain it. Violence is posited as inevitable. The only question in these games becomes whether to use violence for good or for evil. The notion that there is even such a thing as good violence further limits the ways in which boys believe they can be effective, accepted, and valued in the world. Violence, action, and conquest become normalized, whereas as talking and expressing feelings become part of the reviled feminine.

Instead of providing boys with the opportunity to become fully emotionally literate, our culture provides boys with weapons and toys that promote violent play; boys then internalize a sense of violence and understand it as a normal way to express emotions or resolve a conflict. Combined with an already developing sense of fear and opposition to the feminine and a desire to feel powerful in the wake of this problematic (but somehow imperative) division of himself from girls and women, these tools normalize the rage and aggression that boys feel at their inability to be seen or heard as emotional beings. Boys are encouraged to be loud, disruptive, aggressive, physical, and violent; they are commanded to avoid anything feminine. Boys learn to become violent through playing with violent toys and enacting narratives with characters that are nothing more than human weapons. By embracing violence, a boy can have a sense of power that eases the confusing nature of performing masculinity. Harnessing and enacting this type of power is also understood to be the basis for rape itself. Susan Brownmiller states that since the beginning of time, "forcible entry into her body, despite her physical protestations and struggle, became the vehicle of his victorious conquest over her being, the ultimate test of his superior strength, the triumph of his manhood. Man's discovery that his genitalia could serve as a weapon to generate fear must rank as one of the most important discoveries of prehistoric times, along with the use of fire and the first crude stone axe" (14). It would be too simple to state that toys teach boys to use their penises as weapons. However, by providing violent toys to boys, society encourages their understanding that an appendage on the male body has the potential to look, feel, and act like a weapon.

When parents and other adults provide these kinds of hypergendered toys to boys, they are encouraging the boys' separation from girls. The best way to ensure maltreatment of a group is to position them as the "other." When girls are defined as the "other," they become nonhuman, mysterious, repulsive, and even terrifying. Not only is bonding or empathizing with girls positioned as the ultimate way to be seen as not a-boy, but also the very presence of girls becomes frustrating. Instead of retreating from girls and absolutely avoiding them, boys go out of their way to commit acts of aggression against girls as early as preschool. In my experience as an early childhood specialist, I have found that when a group of girls are engaged in play that one or more boys will seek to disrupt them in an aggressive manner. Preschool boys begin to play with the physical dominance they can have over female peers by knocking over their block towers, chasing them, excessively touching them or taking up their physical space. Preschool girls often complain and are confused about this behaviour from boys. They do not have an innate interest in disrupting or infiltrating the self-segregated space of boys. But they do mourn the male friends they had before they stopped playing with girls. As Paley states, "the girls remember when boys were more at ease" (xiv). Whereas girls come to internalize this shift in boys' behaviour as shame and blame for their femaleness, boys continue to position them as enemies. Carlsson-Paige and Levin argue that "all play has political content" (34), and through such an understanding, it is easy to see how early childhood play can lead to situations where sexual assault is possible.

Change the Expectations, Change the Outcome: How Encouraging Different Kinds of Play in Boys Can Change a Rape Culture

> "Boys will be boys—to my mind the four most depressing words in education policy today."
>
> —Kimmel 72

In his book about adolescent masculinity, Michael Kimmel calls the world that adolescent males live in "Guyland." He explains that there are three main dynamics that Guyland relies on: "a culture of entitlement, a culture of silence and a culture of protection" (59). According to Kimmel, entitlement is a learned feeling that says if a boy follows the rules of being a boy, he will get to be a man, which means having power, and any attempts to prevent him from acquiring such power are met with violence (61). The culture of silence Kimmel refers to is the phenomenon of boys and men learning to be silent in the face of violence committed by other men and boys. Being a silent witness to violent acts or talk demonstrates a loyalty to maleness, which is imperative to maintaining male friendships and validity as a masculine being (62). Finally, the culture of protection speaks to the learned rule that boys and men must protect one another at all costs (63). The culture of silence and protection includes the idea that even when boys and men choose not to participate in acts of violence—even if they leave the scene, turn away, or simply remain silent—they are complicit in whatever act has been committed because their inability to speak or act against it reinforces these codes (67). Kimmel agrees that in order to change the rate of sexual violence perpetuated on women, these dynamics need to be prevented from forming in early childhood. Waiting until they are solidified before attempting to dismantle them is missing the point. It is not good enough for a boy or man to abstain from committing acts of violence against women; they must be able to speak and act in direct opposition to these acts so that they are not accepted as normal among men. Teaching boys not to rape is a waste of time and is as beside the point as teaching girls not to get raped. Boys must be taught to actively oppose sexual violence: "Since these types of violence are so closely linked to men's beliefs about what it means to be a man, it is also important to provide boys with alternative ideas about manhood to counter-balance all of the hypermasculine posturing and misogyny they encounter" (Katz 229).

To stop boys from normalizing rape and power, they need to be given different tools with which to develop a sense of themselves in the world. Mothers need to be educated about the emotional needs of their male infants and encouraged to disregard previously held views about how and when young boys should emotionally separate from their mothers. Boys should be encouraged to be physically and emotionally cuddled and supported until the point of a natural child-led separation process, which should occur at the same time or later than the same process in a little girl. Boys need to be taught emotional literacy as thoroughly as possible if any change in rape culture is ever going to occur, which means instilling a deep sense of validation to all vulnerable feelings the boy has. Young boys should be allowed to cry freely and should be taught how to articulate feelings of anger, frustration, anxiety and jealousy with words, expressive arts, and play. Boys should be touched and held affectionately as much as possible. All of these statements seem so simple and obvious, but they are not done in most homes where boys are raised. The only way for the Boy Code and Guyland to die out is for fewer and fewer boys to be indoctrinated within their messaging. For parents, as Katz maintains, "the responsibility is not just to shield their sons from harm; it is to raise sons who will not mistreat women and girls—or remain silent when their peers do" (234). In order for parents to teach their sons not to mistreat women and girls, they must first teach them that they have the capacity to be a fully emotional, caring, and loving human being.

A more complicated piece of this puzzle is how to prevent boys from being pushed away from the feminine in order for them to develop their masculine identities. The most effective means for stopping the development of toxic masculinity is to target the toys boys play with. To work towards eventually chipping away at rape culture, the violent toys that are marketed and sold to boys need to be boycotted and removed from their playrooms. In order to restore a sense of emotional literacy and relational skills needed to develop into a kind, empathetic, and compassionate person with creative problem-solving skills, boys need to be supplied with play tools that work towards these cognitive and emotional ends. Such open-ended toys as dollhouses, baby dolls, generic people figures, animal figures, and building toys need to be supplied. Giving a boy a doll or a dollhouse is currently incredibly stigmatized by the masses; most boys know this by preschool age. If these toys are introduced at a young age, they will become normalized in the child's home environment. At home, parents and caregivers can play with these materials to encourage rich imaginative play in which any number of stories can be enacted. Without toys tied to media characters, boys will be given the chance to explore their own feelings, fantasies, fears, and anxieties instead of covering these up with prescribed narratives laden with adult masculinities. No toys or figures that involve guns, weapons, or hypermasculinized characteristics should be provided to boys. The idea is to expose the boy to more options for their male identity than soldiers, superheroes, firefighters, or police officers. As the boy gets older, the sophistication of the toys should grow with him, but they should not be replaced with traditionally masculine toys. By encouraging imaginative play and discouraging aggressive or action-oriented play, the boy will continue to see himself as a person with a full range of feelings as well as ways to express them. By not forcing early separation and steeping him with tools of violent masculinity, the mother becomes a point of identification for the boy instead of a point of contention and frustration. It is, therefore, imperative that the mother engages with the boy in this type of play as much as possible.

All boys should be given dolls from a young age and encouraged to play with them. Dolls are such a rich play tool because they symbolize people who are there to be cared for and loved. To play effectively with a doll, children must be willing to fully engage with their imagination in order to project life onto the doll. The doll becomes a screen on which to project the child's emotions, fears, fantasies, and ideas. Boys should be provided with both girl and boy dolls, baby dolls, as well as toddler-aged dolls. Bonding with a doll requires a boy to be vulnerable, loving, and gentle. Dolls with removable clothing and anatomically correct features are especially useful, as these dolls can provide opportunities for exploration of body parts and discussions about boundaries and bodily agency.

The early childhood classroom is a place where the earliest sex and gender segregation takes place. In America, early childhood education refers to any schooling attended by a child through the end of kindergarten, most commonly at the ages of two, three, four and five years old. It is vitally important that these classrooms become a place where integration and equalization between boys and girls is prioritized. The differences between boys and girls should be acknowledged, but they should also be celebrated and presented as positive and interesting. A central focus of the early childhood program must be social and emotional education and development. All three years of early childhood programming should include daily discussions, activities, or organized learning about emotions, relationships and kindness. Children of both sexes benefit from these social and emotional curriculum areas, but the benefits to boys can be immeasurable. The opportunity to practice verbalizing emotions and desires as well as to freely express emotions, thoughts, and fantasies (both in literal and abstract terms) should be woven into the work of each school day. If boys and girls see each other as having the same propensity for experiencing and displaying a full range of emotions, they will learn to see themselves as more alike than different. They will be better able to develop a sense of empathy that is required in developing compassion, understanding, and nonviolent conflict resolution.

The toys used in early childhood classrooms should be entirely free of commercial characters or symbols. There should be no war toys or toys that include violent themes in any early childhood classroom, and there should be a full range of toys that encompass both traditionally gendered and gender neutral materials. Ideally the gendered materials would be in close proximately to each other in order to deemphasize a sense of separation between those who play with the materials. A large domestic play area is paramount and should be one of the major content areas of the classroom. Pretend kitchens, dolls, doll furniture, pretend food, pretend baby care items, strollers and grocery carts are all excellent props for domestic play. Boys and girls should be encouraged to play with these materials, and designated times should be set aside where it is the main organized activity. Teacher-led games about playing house or family should be included in the curriculum on at least a weekly basis. This focus on domestic play does several things; for one, it encourages girls and boys to interact through play around themes of family, baby care, and household living. Doing this for many years helps boys internalize the idea of themselves as caring and cooperative individuals. Playing about caring for babies helps boys develop a sense of themselves as loving and nurturing, and allows for the working out of emotional feelings about their own relationship with their mothers. Through this type of play, boys will also internalize the idea that there is nothing inherently threatening about playing cooperatively with girls and their toys. Indeed, by encouraging boys and girls to play in this way, the themes and materials of this domestic play with lose their stigma for boys. Myriam Miedzian makes the following interesting argument related to this discussion: "In order to significantly decrease violence, including rape, we must begin to protect our boys from violent entertainment and to teach them, from the youngest age, to view themselves as future, nurturing, nonviolent, responsible fathers" (162). By making this a theme of early childhood play, professionals can attempt to break the pattern of expecting that boys' play must be destructive, rough, and violent. Just as boys yearn for emotional connect-edness and expression, they are also hungry for opportunities to nurture and be seen as capable of loving others.

Some critics may feel that I am encouraging the censorship of children's play, which I reject. Rather than censoring naturally occurring predispositions towards certain types of play materials, I am calling for a drastic rethinking about why violent toys and violent play are seen as natural for boys. All children experiment with violence and domination through play and social interactions. But as a society we children the rules of being a productive member of society by teaching them that hitting, biting, screaming, grabbing, and bullying are not appropriate ways to behave in the world because treating other people with respect and kindness is the cornerstone of a civilized society. It would be difficult to find an adult who believes that children should be allowed to freely exhibit these aggressive ways of dealing with conflict or difficult feelings. The message for boys becomes confusing when they are being taught these rules of behaviour but are also being given toys and shown media that teach them that aggression, violence, and destruction are a natural part of who they are as boys and who they should be as boys. To change rape culture, society must change its assessment of what a boy naturally is. Katz states "there is general agreement among researchers in the domestic and sexual violence fields that boys' and men's violence against girls and women is not the expression of innate, biological impulses, but it is the result of some combo of personal experience and social conditioning" (228). Providing boys with tools that narrowly define how they play and how they think they should play is more severely censoring of the natural inclinations and purposes of play in childhood than any attempt to redirect, reframe, and widen expectations surrounding boys' play. Shaming boys into gravitating towards toys that only serve the purpose of strengthening their sense of themselves as a dangerous force in the world is censorship in a pure form. Telling boys that they are not capable of anything besides violence, destruction, domination and social aggression is what should be criticized.

The societal mandate toward keeping the features of destruction, violence, anger, aggression, nonfemininity, and domination in boyhood is so thorough that the phrase "boys will be boys" has become a ubiquitous explanation for any disruptive or violent behavior in a young boy. This rationalization begins in toddlerhood and continues through adulthood to account for many aspects of male behaviour, including and especially sexually based crimes. Pollack says this type of excuse for the negative behaviour of boys propagates the myth that "boys are prisoners of biology, that their behaviour is premeditated and an inherent part of their nature" (52). There have been major movements against the stereotyping of young girls and action taken to encourage the acceptance that girls should be offered many options through play and experience to teach them that they are not just pretty, passive, and future housewives but are capable of choosing their own life path. Why has this work not been done for boys? Where is the anger about the narrow ways in which boys are defined? Kimmel criticizes the "boys will be boys" philosophy because it implies "such abject resignation: boys are such wild, predatory, aggressive animals that there is simply no point in trying to control them" (72). Eradicating the "boys will be boys" mentality means teaching boys that they are not entitled to be disruptive to whatever they choose. They are not entitled to be destructive without consequence or remorse. And they do not have a right to touch or harm another person's body. This eradication of perceived male rights that begins in early childhood is the crux of the work needed to stop rape culture at its very roots.

Conclusion

"Emotional neglect lays the groundwork for the emotional numbing that helps boys feel better about being cut off. Eruptions of rage in boys are most often deemed normal, explained by the age-old justification for adolescent patriarchal misbehaviour, 'Boys will be boys.' Patriarchy both creates the rage in boys and then contains it for later use, making it a resource to exploit later on as boys become men. As a national product, this rage can be garnered to further imperialism, hatred and oppression of women and men globally"
—hooks 51

The work of reframing boyhood in an effort to prevent the continuation of a society that does not actively oppose and prevent the rape of women and girls is daunting but vital. I have established that training boys to accept violence as an integral part of their masculine identity is an essential part of perpetuating rape culture. The process of treating boys as future men and training them from birth in this regard is positive. The work must involve deep reflection and thinking on the part of parents and early childhood professionals about what the next generation of men should embody in order to dismantle the rules of masculinity that inform rape culture. Ideally, this utopian generation of men would see women as complete equals and full human beings, would be caring, nurturing, and loving, would not be afraid or ashamed of their emotions, would fully and actively embrace fatherhood, and would be horrified by the rape, sexual harassment, and sexual assault of women and girls. This new generation of men would be as invested in ending rape culture as women are. Once this image of men is fully formed in our minds, we can begin to work backwards. How should we treat little boys if we want them to turn out this way? What toys should we give them to practice at being this type of adult? How should we talk to them about violence, guns, and aggression? Once we acknowledge that all male infants have the possibility to grow up to either confront or condone rape culture and that it is not biologically predetermined, it becomes an obligation of all adults to actively choose which path to encourage. It becomes the responsibility of all adults to prevent toys promoting harmful notions of masculinity from ending up in the hands of little boys, lest they grow up to be an unquestioning participant in rape culture. As Kate Harding asks, "Will your son stand up to him? Will your son know what that guy is doing is wrong? Will your son use his phone to call 911 if he witnesses a rape or to take a video of it?" (40).

Works Cited

Bettelheim, Bruno. "The Importance of Play." *The Atlantic*, vol. 259, no. 3, 1987, pp. 35-46.

Brownmiller, Susan. *Against Our Will: Men, Women and Rape.* Open Road Media, 2013.

Carlsson-Paige, Nancy, and Diane E. Levin. *The War Play Dilemma: Balancing Needs and Values in the Early Childhood Classroom*, 1987.

Chu, Judy Y. *When Boys Become Boys: Development, Relationships, and Masculinity.* New York University Press, 2014.

Connell, Raewyn. *Masculinities.* 2nd ed. University of California Press, 2005.

Beauvoir, Simone de. *The Second Sex*. Random House, 2014.

Dress Up America. "Ultimate All in One Police Officer Costume for Kids." *Amazon*, www.amazon.com/Ultimate-All-One-Police-Officer/dp/B075MP3W76/ref=sr_1_1?dchild=1&keywords=swat+team&qid=1588374932&s=toys-and-games&sr=1-1. Accessed 7 May 2019.

Dworkin, Andrea. *Pornography: Men Possessing Women*. Plume, 1989.

Friedan, Betty. *The Feminine Mystique*. WW Norton & Company, 2010.

Harding, Kate. *Asking for It: The Alarming Rise of Rape Culture—And What We Can Do about It*. Da Capo Press, 2015.

Hasbro. "NERF Modulus Tri-Strike Blaster Toy." *Amazon*, www.amazon.com/Nerf-Modulus-Tri-Strike-Blaster-Toy/dp/B01BP6GPX8. Accessed 7 May 2020.

hooks, bell. *The Will to Change: Men, Masculinity, and Love*. Square Press, 2004.

Horney, Kate. "The Dread of Women." *The Psychoanalytic Review (1913-1957)*, vol. 25, 1938, pp. 428-440.

Katz, Jackson. *Macho Paradox: Why Some Men Hurt Women and How All Men Can Help*. Sourcebooks, Inc., 2006.

Kimmel, Michael S. *Guyland: The Perilous World Where Boys Become Men*. Harper, 2008.

Kindlon, Dan, and Michael Thompson. *Raising Cain: Protecting the Emotional Life of Boys*. Ballantine Books, 2009.

Lego. "LEGO Star Wars Imperial Assault Hovertank 75152 Star Wars Toy." *Amazon*, www.amazon.com/LEGO-Imperial-Assault-Hovertank-75152/dp/B01CVGV93C/ref=sr_1_1?dchild=1&keywords=lego+star+wars+imperial+assault+hovertank&qid=1588374378&s=toys-and-games&sr=1-1&swrs=AF5B754DFF2FAA8BDA238ACC35626D8C. Accessed 7 May 2020.

Miedzian, Myriam. "How Rape Is Encouraged in American Boys and What We Can Do to Stop It." *Transforming a Rape Culture*, 2004, pp. 153-63.

Paley, Vivian Gussin. *Boys and Girls: Superheroes in the Doll Corner*. University of Chicago Press, 2014.

"Pokemon Search Results." *Amazon*, www.amazon.com/s?k=pokemon&i=toys-and-games&ref=nb_sb_noss_1. Accessed 7 May 2019.

Pollack, William. *Real Boys: Rescuing Our Dons from the Myths of Boyhood.* Macmillan, 1999.

Steinem, Gloria. "Leaps of Consciousness." Women and Power Conference. Omega Institute, Sept. 2004, New York, Keynote Speech, awpc.cattcenter.iastate.edu/2017/03/21/leaps-of-consciousness-sept-2004/. Accessed 7 May 2020.

Winnicott, Donald W. "The Theory of the Parent-Infant Relationship." *The International Journal of Psycho-Analysis,* vol. 41, 1960, pp. 585-95.

Chapter Four

Men, Masculinities, and Responses to Rape

Emily Colpitts

Introduction

Efforts to engage men in preventing rape have become increasingly prevalent around the world over the past decade (Jewkes et al. 1580). These efforts are important for several reasons, including the fact that men are responsible for perpetrating the majority of acts of gender-based violence, including rape (Pease 6). Furthermore, although most men are not violent, male complicity in the structures and systems that underpin rape, such as rape culture and patriarchal gender relations, is widespread. As such, efforts to engage men in preventing rape represent an important shift away from victim blaming by placing the onus of prevention on those primarily responsible for perpetration. Arguably, addressing the underlying structures and systems that contribute to rape necessitates men's involvement, given that they continue to hold power within these structures and systems and may, therefore, act as gatekeepers to change (Connell, "Change among the Gatekeepers" 1802). Moreover, men are increasingly showing an interest in preventing sexual violence, and, as such, these antiviolence efforts present an opportunity for them to become involved (Connell, "The Role of Men" 7). However, merely involving men is insufficient; preventing rape requires addressing social constructions of masculinity and the ways in which these constructions are intertwined with rape culture.

To better understand why addressing social constructions of masculinity is an essential component of rape prevention, this chapter begins with an overview of the complex relationships between men, masculinities, power, and violence. Having established the importance of addressing social constructions of masculinity, this chapter then explores the literature on engaging men in rape prevention efforts, along with the challenges and tensions inherent in this work. Finally, this chapter briefly considers men's rights activism as a response to feminist efforts to address inequitable gendered power relations and gender-based violence, including rape.

Why Engaging Men and Addressing Social Constructions of Masculinity Matters

Raewyn Connell's concept of hegemonic masculinity presents a useful starting point to understand how social constructions of masculinity interact with power and violence. According to Connell, hegemonic masculinity can be defined as "the configuration of gender practice which embodies the currently accepted answer to the problem of the legitimacy of patriarchy, which guarantees (or is taken to guarantee) the dominant position of men and the subordination of women" (*Masculinities* 77). In this sense, hegemonic masculinity serves to define and police what it means to be a so-called real man in a given society, whereas alternative masculinities are obscured (Morrell, "Of Boys" 608). Hegemonic masculinity frames masculinity as socially constructed rather than innate or natural, and it highlights the social processes through which this configuration of masculinity is reproduced as normative (Jewkes et al. 1582).

Although the majority of men's lived and embodied experiences of masculinity do not conform to hegemonic masculine norms, they often remain complicit, given the power and privilege conferred by patriarchy (Connell, *Masculinities* 79). Furthermore, men may be oblivious to their own complicity; privilege tends to remain invisible to those who experience it, and, in this sense, "not having to think about gender is one of the patriarchal dividends of gender inequality" (Kimmel, "Forward" xii). It is important to note that men do not access the power conferred by patriarchy equally. The intersections of masculinity, race, class, sexuality, (dis)ability, etc. shape how men experience, embody, and express their masculinity and the extent to which they experience patriarchal privilege (Morrell, *Changing Men* 10). Kimberlé Crenshaw notes, for example, that racism and patriarchy are inextricably linked, as racism prevents racialized men from experiencing power and privilege in the same way as white men (1258). Similarly, Michael Kimmel argues that "the fear of humiliation, of losing in the competitive ranking among men, of being dominated by other men ...reinforce[s] traditional notions of masculinity as a false sense of safety" ("Men, Masculinity"146). As these examples demonstrate, while men do not access the power conferred by patriarchy equally, they often remain complicit with patriarchal gender relations and with hegemonic masculinity to avoid being labelled weak or feminine (Kimmel, "Men, Masculinity" 146).

Social constructions of masculinity are intimately connected to the perpetration of rape and to the reproduction of rape culture. The ideals represented by hegemonic masculinity contribute to rape culture in that "culture produces rapists when it encourages the socialization of men to subscribe to values of control and dominance, callousness and competitiveness and anger and aggression, and when it discourages the expression by men of vulnerability, sharing and cooperation" (Herman 49). As Kimmel explains, men's anxiety about living up to hegemonic masculine norms fosters a culture in which "men often will use their sexual conquests as a form of currency to gain status among other men" ("Men, Masculinity" 147). Isak Niehaus notes that rape is more prevalent in contexts where male entitlement and control of women are central features, yet he suggests that rape perpetration is not necessarily limited to men who closely approximate hegemonic masculine norms (65). Like Kimmel, Niehaus argues that the pressure to conform to the normative definition of what it means to be a man contributes to the perpetration of rape as a means of asserting one's masculinity (69). The intersections of social constructions of race and masculinity are also intimately connected to rape, since racism shapes popular notions of which men perpetrate violence (Haritaworn 65). As Angela Davis explains, for example, the myth of the Black rapist is "distinctly a political invention" that was and continues to be used to justify the incarceration and lynching of Black men (184).

As such, efforts to address rape culture and prevent rape must seek not only to engage men but also to address social constructions of masculinity. In other words, addressing rape culture and preventing rape means challenging hegemonic masculinity and promoting nonviolent, gender-equitable alternative constructions of masculinity. It is imperative that this work is grounded in a feminist analysis of gendered power relations that seeks to dismantle patriarchy and male privilege (Walsh 135). As Harsha Walia argues, "no one would disagree that there is a critical role for men in ending violence against women, but that role should be to dismantle patriarchy, not simply to redefine and authenticate the social constructions of manhood." Unfortunately, as the following section demonstrates, existing efforts to engage men tend to fall short of meeting these criteria.

Efforts to Engage Men in Preventing Rape: Challenges, Compromises, and Concerns

Engaging men and addressing social constructions of masculinity are essential in preventing rape and addressing rape culture. Overall, perhaps because of their relative newness or their tendency to focus on prevention, antirape efforts targeted towards men tend to be met with enthusiasm and the men involved in these efforts have been branded as heroes by some (Messner et al. 150). However, the literature on men's antiviolence efforts highlights a number of key challenges and worrisome trends. In general, efforts to engage men tend to focus on addressing individual men's violent behaviour rather than challenging the broader structures and systems that contribute to their use of violence (Jewkes et al. 1583). Indeed, the majority of antiviolence campaign posters targeted towards men in North America tend to focus on interpersonal violence against women almost exclusively, with a few notable exceptions that address interpersonal violence within male homosexual relationships. Although the majority of victims/survivors of gender-based violence, including rape, are women, this narrow focus renders invisible violence against queer, trans, and nonbinary populations (Goldscheid 313-14) and also collapses the complexities that shape vulnerability to and experiences of violence. Furthermore, the focus on interpersonal violence obscures the broader violent systems and structures that contribute to men's violence, including patriarchy, hegemonic masculinity, and rape culture.

The emphasis on interpersonal violence and changing individual men's violent behaviour is consistent with a broader trend of depoliticizing antiviolence efforts. Michael Messner et al. illustrate this trend: "During the first decade of the millennium, several other well-established anti-rape and anti-domestic violence organizations changed their names, and in most cases, 'rebranding' included removing 'women' from the organizational name and replacing negative terms such as 'rape' with positive language that pointed to peaceful futures" (96). There are a number of factors that contribute to this trend, including increasing state involvement in antiviolence organizations (Bumiller 2) and the fact that many of these organizations have begun offering services to queer, trans, and nonbinary victims/survivors of violence as well as to male victims/survivors (Messner et al. 102). Furthermore, this trend of depoliticization may relate to the desire to secure funding—that is, it may serve to make antiviolence organizations more appealing to "funding agencies that might balk at overt expressions of feminism" (Messner et al. 102). The depoliticization of efforts to address rape and other forms of gender-based violence has the potential to reinforce the narrow emphasis on changing individual men's violent behaviour rather than addressing the violent systems and structures that contribute to this violence, which may ultimately limit their effectiveness.

There are numerous examples of the ways in which existing efforts to engage men in preventing rape fail to challenge hegemonic masculinity and address inequitable gendered power relations. For example, the discourse of so-called real men is prevalent in antiviolence efforts targeted towards men, as evidenced by the Real Men Don't Rape campaign. The so-called real men represented in these antiviolence efforts often reproduce the norms established by hegemonic masculinity by employing such characteristics as strength, power, and bravery to distinguish real men from men who perpetrate rape (Masters 39). By labelling such traits as masculine, these antiviolence efforts reproduce gender difference, which contributes to the perpetration of rape and the perpetuation of rape culture (Boswell and Spade 134). In this sense, through the discourse of real men, "male privilege is re-defined, but not negated, in a way that leaves masculinity unchallenged and still dominant" (McCarroll).

The Real Men Don't Rape campaign title is also problematic because it reproduces the notion that there is a singular way to be a man. Although the campaign's version of a real man is one who does not rape, this discourse has the potential to exacerbate the anxiety generated by the discrepancy between men's lived and embodied experiences of masculinity and the normative definition of what constitutes real men, which, as discussed above, may contribute to rape. This argument is illustrated by the White Ribbon Campaign's (WRC) New Code of Manhood initiative. As Beth Lyons explains, "the stuff in WRC's *New Code* is good, but it's still a code, and codes are prescriptive—even when expanded—and can be punitive to those who violate them." As such, instead of reproducing the notion that there is a singular normative definition of masculinity to which men must ascribe, it may be more productive to explore the diversity of masculinities that exist and to encourage men to develop a range of nonviolent alternatives.

Deploying the discourse of real men also has the effect of creating a clear distinction between men who rape and men who do not, effectively othering men who rape (Masters 38). In this sense, the discourse of real men is strategically deployed to appeal to men by allowing them to feel like part of the solution rather than part of the problem. In so doing, this framing seeks to address the feelings of blame and alienation that men may associate with antiviolence efforts that are perceived to engage with men as potential perpetrators (Masters 39). However, by othering men who perpetrate rape and by framing the majority of men as part of the solution, this discourse renders invisible the ways in which men are often complicit with the broader systems and structures that contribute to rape (Masters 43).

The tensions inherent in framing men as part of the solution are evident in certain approaches to bystander interventions, which are popular in the military and on postsecondary campuses (Messner et al. 121). Although approaches to bystander interventions vary, Messner et al. argue that they may "harnes[s] men's sense of responsibility to the male group, [whereby] intervening in a potential sexual assault preserves the integrity of the team, the frat or the military unit by preventing men in the group from getting into trouble" (121-22). Put differently, in the context of the military or fraternities, bystander interventions have the potential to strengthen the patriarchal cultures engrained in these institutions rather than challenge them: "In positioning the male group and the individual men in the group as inherently good, and only in need of mustering some (traditionally masculine) strength and courage, a key feminist insight is potentially lost: that sexual objectification, conquest and domination of women—scoring—is a central organizing principle of many such male groups, not an individual aberration" (Messner et al. 123). As such, bystander interventions serve as an important example of the risks of depoliticization and of the necessity of grounding men's antiviolence efforts in a feminist analysis of gendered power relations.

The prevalence of the discourse of men as protectors in antiviolence campaigns, such as the My Strength Is Not for Hurting campaign, presents similar challenges. Although this discourse may appeal to well-meaning men by providing a positive image of men involved in antirape efforts, it reproduces paternalistic ideology (Scheel et al. 265) and performs "a sort of masculinity triage" (McCarroll), wherein "by flattering men's strength and asking them to use it to protect women, we once again place men in the driver's seat" (McCarroll). This discourse also frames men as part of the solution while rendering invisible the ways in which they may be complicit with broader structures and systems that contribute to men's violence (Scheel et al. 265-66) and reproduces the notion that strength is an inherently masculine attribute.

A further complication emerges in relation to how men involved in antirape efforts exercise the privilege and power conferred by patriarchy to organize and lead these efforts. Some have argued that because men hold power, they will be trusted and listened to more than women will, particularly by other men, and are more capable of attracting male involvement, which serves to justify their roles as leaders in efforts to engage men in antirape activism (Walsh 139). However, this solution distances men's violence from patriarchy and contributes to the depoliticization of antiviolence efforts (Walsh 139). Messner et al. highlight the problematic nature of the rise of the so-called male rock stars of the antiviolence movement, who tend to be paid more for speaking engagements than women in the sector (145-46) and tend to receive an unmerited level of praise for their efforts, whereas the long history of women's antiviolence efforts is rendered invisible or diminished (138-39). J. A. McCarroll explains it as such:

> There is certainly something to be said about using the language of the patriarchy to subvert the patriarchy, or of using privilege to end privilege, but it's not clear that's what being done. Rather, it looks as if men are given a privileged place in the feminist movement, one where they are praised for simply not being terrible and their much-vaunted power remains intact.

Other challenges related to male leadership in the antiviolence sector include agenda-setting power, accountability to women's organizations and others working in the sector, the risk of men speaking over or for women as well as queer and trans populations, and the possibility that efforts to engage men may divert scarce attention and resources away from services for victims/survivors of violence (Walsh 139).

As discussed above, because men do not access the power conferred by patriarchy equally (Morrell, *Changing Men* 10; Crenshaw 1258), it is important to analyze efforts to engage men in preventing rape from an intersectional perspective. How do these efforts construct race? Are racialized men disproportionately represented as perpetrators and white women as victims? By centring gender, do these campaigns commit or perpetuate other forms of violence, such as racism, cisnormativity, ableism, and/or heteronormativity? For example, Walia argues that although the Consent Is Sexy campaign is effective to the extent that it is catchy and challenges the misogynist notion that coercion is sexy, it fails to recognize that constructions of what is sexy are inherently connected to race, class, (dis)ability, gender, and body size, etc. As Walia notes, "given the disproportionate magnitude of sexual violence against those who are deemed inherently 'undesirable' and hence 'rape-able'—Indigenous women, migrant women, Black women, trans women, poor women, sex workers, women with disabilities—it is potentially dis-astrous to sexualize consent and link it to desirability." She concludes that challenging rape culture and developing a culture of consent requires centring the diverse experiences of racialized and poor women to avoid reproducing the violent structures of racism, capitalism, and colonialism. As this example demonstrates, if violence is only concept-ualized through a gendered lens rather than from an intersectional perspective, there is a risk that the complexities that shape vulnerability to and experiences of violence will be obscured.

The intersections of gender and sexuality provide another useful illustration of the importance of approaching efforts to engage men in preventing rape from an intersectional perspective. As discussed above, with the exception of a few notable examples, the majority of antirape campaigns targeted towards men specifically pertain to violence in the context of heterosexual relationships, thereby reproducing hetero-normativity. Similarly, transphobic "man up" discourses (Walia) and the invisibility of violence against queer, trans, and nonbinary populations highlight the ways in which antirape campaigns targeted towards men reproduce a binary understanding of gender and cisnormativity. Tristan Bridges argues that the WRC's Walk a Mile in Her Shoes events, in which men raise money for women's shelters and services by walking a mile in high heels, reinforce patriarchal and heteronormative masculine norms by reproducing gender and sexual difference (25). Bridges reports that men who are perceived to walk in high heels with relative ease are taunted and subject to homophobic slurs (17). Moreover, the wearing of high heels has the effect of framing men's participation in the walk as a gender transgression, thereby feminizing antiviolence activism (20). According to Bridges, feminizing men's antiviolence activism is problematic for a number of reasons:

> First, it confirms our worst fear about acknowledging men doing feminism: that they will only adopt feminist agendas in certain situations or that their performances of feminist politics will be inauthentic in some way. Second, it contextually situates gender inequality as women's problem by presuming that concern over these issues is "feminine," casting women alone in search of solutions. Third, when gender and sexuality are not understood as socially constructed and differences are assumed to be natural … individuals fail to see the ways in which inequality and ideologies of difference are deeply connected. (20-21)

In this way, the feminization of antiviolence activism reproduces gender difference and preserves patriarchal power and privilege. This example also powerfully demonstrates the importance of approaching efforts to engage men in antirape activism from an intersectional perspective to avoid perpetuating other forms of violence, including heteronormativity and cisnormativity.

As many of the examples highlighted above demonstrate, there is often a tradeoff or compromise involved in efforts to engage men in preventing rape. On the one hand, appealing to men as part of the solution may be a more effective means of soliciting men's involvement, yet on the other hand, this framing renders invisible the structures and systems that contribute to men's violence—including hegemonic masculinity, rape culture, and inequitable gendered power relations— and the ways in which non-violent men may be complicit in these systems. The WRC's New Code of Manhood initiative also illustrates the compromises often involved in efforts to engage men. The posters for the initiative, which were displayed around Toronto in November 2012, featured statements such as "put her in her place," "tears are weak," "feelings are for chicks," "stop acting gay," "grow some balls," and "say it with fists" (Lyons). Lyons argues that while these statements are meant to be provocative and are effective at drawing attention to the initiative, they are potentially triggering to people who have experienced violence or marginalization based on their gender or sexuality. She juxtaposes this potential for discomfort with the measures that the initiative takes to make men feel comfortable. Although the campaign encourages men to demonstrate affection with other men, it frames this as "shar[ing] a #manhug," which, by virtue of being differentiated as a "manhug," ensures that the gesture is not viewed as feminine and preserves hegemonic masculine norms. As Lyons concludes, "I'm not sure it's fair for the lion's-share of the emotional risk-taking to be thrust upon on those who are already marginalized by gender-based oppression, all for the sake of promotion, while the emotional risk for the men WRC's targeting is minimized for the sake of increasing engagement." Thus, in evaluating efforts to engage men in rape prevention, it is important to recognize these compromises and to ask whether there are ways of appealing to men while still addressing the structures and systems that contribute to rape.

Antifeminist Men and Men's Rights Activism

Thus far, this discussion has focused on men's positive responses to feminist antirape activism, but it is important to recognize that this is not the only way that men have responded to these efforts. Specifically, it is necessary to address antifeminist men and men's rights activism as well as the ways in which they contribute to the structures and systems that foster rape and gender-based violence more broadly. As Kimmel explains, the emergence of men's rights activism can be traced to the men's liberation movement, which developed alongside the women's liberation movement in the 1970s and promoted the idea that tradition-al gender roles are harmful for both women and men (*Angry White Men* 104). Tensions emerged within the men's liberation movement between men who pursued a therapeutic model of self-discovery and men who became involved in activism to address inequitable gender relations and violence against women (Messner et al. 43). Contemporary men's rights activism evolved from the therapeutic branch of men's liberationists (Kimmel, *Angry White Men* 104).

According to Messner et al., some feminists felt that the "therapeutic focus on men's pain was not only self-indulgent but, worse, kept men from diving into crucially important work, using their positions as men to stop rape" (52). This notion relates to a broader concern that as men "appropriat[e] the personal, there has been a tendency to forget the political and ignore the vested interest many men have in resisting change" (Cornwall and Lindisfarne 34). Kimmel suggests that one of the reasons why feminist analyses of patriarchal power relations do not resonate with many men is that men do not feel powerful, especially men who are marginalized. (*Angry White Men* 185). However, as Kimmel points out, "as men experience it, masculinity may not be the experience of power. But it is the experience of *entitlement* to power" (*Angry White Men* 185). This sense of entitlement to power over women fosters antifeminist backlash and fuels contemporary men's rights activism, as feminist gains are perceived to threaten men's ability to access this power.

Although men's rights activism emerged from a critique of traditional gender roles, that critique has morphed over time into claims of gender discrimination against men and "a celebration of all things masculine and a near infatuation with the traditional masculine role itself" (Kimmel, *Angry White Men* 107). Men's rights activism tends to deploy the discourse that there is a crisis of masculinity generated by feminist gains and to posit the suppression of feminism and the revalorization of hegemonic masculinity as the solution to this supposed crisis (Blais and Dupuis-Déri 22). Men's rights activists' antifeminist discourses affect not only feminists but also profeminist men, including those involved in efforts to prevent rape, by labeling them as "traitors to their sex, self-haters, haters of their maleness, in sum, not 'real' but 'castrated' men, and probably gay" (Blais and Dupuis-Déri 27). In this sense, contemporary men's rights activism reproduces the traditional gender roles that the earlier men's liberationist movement sought to challenge.

By defending and reproducing hegemonic masculinity and male entitlement, men's rights activism contributes to the structures and systems that fuel men's violence. For example, the Canadian Association for Equality (CAFE), a men's rights group, launched a billboard campaign in Toronto in 2015 that claimed that spousal violence against men is as prevalent as spousal violence against women and decried the lack of support services for male victims/survivors of spousal violence ("Domestic Violence"). The CAFE campaign suggested that policies regarding support for services for women who experience violence are biased on the basis of gender and are, thus, discriminatory against men. CAFE president Justin Trottier defended the campaign by arguing that "policies should be built on facts rather than bound by ideologies" ("Domestic Violence"). However, although the Statistics Canada survey cited by the CAFE campaign found that men and women reported experiencing spousal violence with similar prevalence, it also found that women are more than twice as likely to be injured by spousal violence, more than six times as likely to receive medical attention, and three times as likely to experience more serious forms of violence, including sexual assault and being choked or threatened with a weapon (Statistics Canada 10). CAFE conveniently ignored these facts in promoting their antifeminist agenda. Citing spousal violence prevalence statistics in isolation fails not only to differentiate between the severity and forms of violence reported but also to account for whether violence was used in self-defence. As such, CAFE's campaign misrepresents the reality of spousal violence in Canada and undermines the notion that spousal violence is gender based and disproportionately affects women.

As the CAFE example demonstrates, men's right activism contributes to the structures and systems that fuel men's violence. This dynamic is also visible with respect to men's rights activism and antifeminist backlash around the issue of rape, particularly as it relates to false reporting (Gotell and Dutton 74). Men's rights activists have, for example, filed injunctions against antirape campaigns on the basis that they allegedly promote a negative image of men (Blais and Dupuis-Déri 33). In 2013, Men's Rights Edmonton launched a Don't Be That Girl counter-campaign in response to the Don't Be That Guy antirape campaign. The Don't Be That Girl campaign featured posters with statements such as "just because you regret a one night stand doesn't mean it wasn't consensual." Men's Rights Edmonton defended their actions by claiming that the Don't Be That Guy campaign amounts to hate speech, since "it specifically targets a gender and all members of that gender as perpetrators of rape" ("Don't Be That Girl"). Not only does this counter-campaign have the potential to discourage victims/survivors from reporting rape, but it also denies the ways in which nonviolent men are complicit in the structures and systems that contribute to rape as well as the necessity of addressing social constructions of masculinity in order to prevent rape. Similarly, the notion that feminists encourage false reporting was central to the threats made against feminists at the University of Toronto in September 2015 (Hopper). The threats, which were posted online, included the following: "next week when a feminist at the University of Toronto tries to ruin your life with false sex rape allegations, rent a gun from a gang and start firing bullets into these feminists at your nearest Women's Studies classroom" (Hopper). As these examples demonstrate, feminist organizing against rape is a site of antifeminist backlash and men's rights activism.

Furthermore, men's rights activists and antifeminist men often use the threat of rape, among other forms of violence, against feminists. For example, Yasmine Mehdi, a student journalist at the University of Ottawa who exposed the Science Students Association's pub-crawl known as the Vet's Tour, faced threats of rape and violence (Schnurr). Following her report on the pub-crawl, wherein participants allegedly earned points for acts such as performing oral sex on the judges and eating a doughnut off a judge's penis ("University of Ottawa"), Mehdi received racist, sexist, and Islamophobic threats on her social media accounts, including "I will be laughing when your father murders you in an honor killing. You terrorist breeder" and "don't spoil it for everyone else, you filthy f***ing sand******. I hope your imam rapes you" (Schnurr). As this example demonstrates, antifeminist men and men's rights activists not only challenge feminist antirape organizing but also use the threat of rape against feminists.

Ultimately, the prevalence of masculine entitlement in men's rights discourses and in antifeminist backlash, including antifeminist violence, further reinforces the necessity of transforming gendered power relations and addressing social constructions of masculinity. The urgency of this task is underlined by the fact that men's rights discourses and male sexual entitlement inspired Elliot Rodger to commit the Isla Vista attack in 2014, which, in turn, inspired Alek Minassian to commit the 2018 van attack in Toronto ("Facebook Post"). Contemporary men's rights activism also contributes to rape culture and men's violence by denying the persistence of patriarchy and by reinforcing hegemonic masculinity rather than challenging it. In this sense, men's rights activism undermines efforts to engage men in preventing rape.

Conclusion

Efforts to engage men are an important part of preventing rape and addressing rape culture, not only because men perpetrate the majority of rape and are complicit in structures and systems that contribute to its perpetration but also because men are increasingly recognizing the importance of becoming involved in feminist antirape efforts. In order to effectively prevent rape and challenge rape culture, antirape efforts must go beyond merely including men to challenge the systems and structures that contribute to rape. Specifically, efforts to engage men in preventing rape must address hegemonic masculine norms and promote nonviolent, gender equitable alternative constructions of masculinity.

A review of the literature demonstrates that existing efforts to engage men in preventing rape present several challenges and concerns. There are numerous examples of how antirape campaigns targeted towards men reinforce hegemonic masculinity and gender difference. Furthermore, some men's antirape campaigns are not grounded in a feminist analysis of gendered power relations, as the prevalence of the discourse of men as protectors shows. The examples cited in this chapter also demonstrate the need to approach men's antirape efforts from an intersectional perspective to account for the complexities of men's lived and embodied experiences of masculinity, as well as the factors that shape vulnerability to and experiences violence, and to avoid perpetuating other harms, such as heteronormativity, cisnormativity, and racism. In recognizing the shortcomings of existing efforts to engage men, it is important to acknowledge that they often represent a compromise between, for example, encouraging men's involvement by framing them as part of the solution and addressing the structures and systems that contribute to men's violence by recognizing male complicity as part of the problem. In this sense, additional research is needed to determine whether the potential benefits outweigh the limitations.

Finally, this chapter briefly explored the emergence of contemporary men's rights activism and its relationship to rape. Although it has its roots in a movement that sought to challenge traditional gender roles, men's rights activism serves to reproduce hegemonic masculinity and contributes to antifeminist backlash. Men's rights activists seek to discredit feminist antirape efforts and deploy the threat of rape against feminist activists. As such, the example of men's rights activism reinforces the importance of addressing social constructions of masculinity to prevent rape.

Works Cited

Blais, Melissa, and Francis Dupuis-Déri. "Masculinism and the Antif-eminist Countermovement." *Social Movement Studies*, vol. 108, no.1, 2012, pp. 21-39.

Boswell, A. Ayres, and Joan Z. Spade. "Fraternities and Collegiate Rape Culture: Why Are Some Fraternities More Dangerous Places for Women?" *Gender & Society*, vol. 10, no. 2, 1996, pp. 133-47.

Bridges, Tristan. "Men Just Weren't Made to Do This: Performances of Drag at 'Walk a Mile in Her Shoes' Marches." *Gender and Society*, vol. 24, no. 1, 2010, pp. 5-30.

Bumiller, Kristin. *In an Abusive State: How Neoliberalism Appropriated the Feminist Movement against Sexual Violence.* Duke University Press, 2008.

Statistics Canada. *Family Violence in Canada: A Statistical Profile.* Catalogue no. 85-224-X. Minister of Industry, 2011, Connell, Raewyn. *Masculinities.* University of California Press, 1995.

Connell, Raewyn. "The Role of Men and Boys in Achieving Gender Equality." *United Nations Expert Group Meeting on The Role of Men and Boys in Achieving Gender Equality*, 7 Oct. 2003. Brasilia, Brazil. United Nations Division for the Advancement of Women, pp. 1-39.

Connell, Raewyn. "Change among the Gatekeepers: Men, Masculinities, and Gender Equality in the Global Arena." *Signs: Journal of Women in Culture and Society*, vol. 30, no.3, 2005, pp. 1801-25.

Cornwall, Andrea, and Nancy Lindisfarne. *Dislocating Masculinities: Comparative Ethnographies.* Routledge, 1994.

Crenshaw, Kimberlé. "Mapping the Margins: Intersectionality, Identity Politics and Violence against Women of Color." *Stanford Law Review*, vol. 43, no. 6, 1991, pp. 1241-99.

Davis, Angela. *Women, Race and Class.* Random House, 1981. "Domestic Violence against Men Target of Controversial Campaign." *CBC News*, 10 Mar. 2015, www.cbc.ca/news/canada/toronto/domestic-violence-against-men-target-of-controversial-campaign -1.2989105. Accessed 27 Apr. 2020.

"'Don't Be That Girl' Campaign: Men's Rights Edmonton Say They're Not Advocating Rape." *The Huffington Post Alberta*, 12 Jul. 2013, www.huffingtonpost.ca/2013/07/12/dont-be-that-girl-mens-rights-edmonton_n_3587808.html. Accessed 27 Apr. 2020.

"Facebook Post Linked to Toronto Van Attack Points to Insular, Misogynistic World of 'Incels.'"*CBC News*, 25 Apr. 2018, www.cbc.ca/news/canada/toronto/what-is-an-incel-toronto-van-attack-explainer-alek-minassian-1.4633893. Accessed 27 Apr. 2020.

Goldscheid, Julie. "Gender Neutrality and the 'Violence against Women' Frame." *University of Miami Race and Social Justice Law Review*, vol. 5, 2015, pp. 307-324.

Gotell, Lise, and Emily Dutton. "Sexual Violence in the 'Manosphere': Antifeminist Men's Rights Discourses on Rape." *International Journal for Crime, Justice and Social Democracy*, vol. 5, no. 2, 2016, pp. 65-80.

Haritaworn, Jin. "Beyond 'Hate': Queer Metonymies of Crime, Pathology and Anti/Violence." *Jindal Global Law Review*, vol. 14, no. 2, 2013, pp. 44-78.

Herman, Dianne, F. "The Rape Culture". *Women: A Feminist Perspective*, edited by Jo Freeman, Mayfield, 1984, pp. 45-53.

Hopper, Tristin. "Online Posts About Killing Feminists Prompt University of Toronto to Increase Campus Security." *National Post*, 10 Sept. 2015, news.nationalpost.com/ toronto/online-posts-about-killing-feminists-prompt-university-of-toronto-to-increase-campus-security. Accessed 27 Apr. 2020.

Jewkes, Rachel, et al. "From Work With Men and Boys to Changes of Social Norms and Reduction of Inequities in Gender Relations: A Conceptual Shift in Prevention of Violence Against Women and Girls." *Lancet*, no. 385, 2015, pp. 1580-89.

Kimmel, Michael. Forward. *Masculinities Matter! Men, Gender and Development*, edited by Frances Cleaver, Zed, 2002, pp. xi-xiv.

Kimmel, Michael. "Men, Masculinity, and the Rape Culture." *Transforming Rape Culture*, edited by Emilie Buchwald, Pamela R. Fletcher, and Martha Roth, Milkweed, 2005, pp. 139-158.

Kimmel, Michael. *Angry White Men: American Masculinity at the End of an Era*. Nation Books, 2013.

Lyons, Beth. "On White Ribbon's Be-A-Man.ca Launch." *Shameless*, 11 Dec. 2012, shamelessmag.com/blog/entry/on-white-ribbons-be-a-manca-launch. Accessed 27 Apr. 2020.

Masters, N.Tatiana. "'My Strength is Not for Hurting': Men's Anti-Rape Websites and Their Construction of Masculinity and Male Sexuality." *Sexualities*, vol. 13, no. 33, 2010, pp. 33-46.

McCarroll, J. A. "The Language of Dude Feminism." *Sherights*, 24 Apr. 2014, sherights.com/2014/04/24/the-language-of-dude-feminism/. Accessed 27 Apr. 2020.

Messner, Michael, et al. *Some Men: Feminist Allies in the Movement to End Violence against Women.* Oxford University Press, 2015.

Morrell, Robert. "Of Boys and Men: Masculinity and Gender in Southern African Studies." *Journal of Southern African Studies* vol. 24, no. 4, 1998, pp. 605-30.

Morrell, Robert. *Changing Men in Southern Africa.* University of Natal Press, 2001.

Niehaus, Isak. "Masculine Domination in Sexual Violence: Interpreting Accounts of Three Cases of Rape in the South African Lowveld." *Men Behaving Differently: South African Men Since 1994*, edited by Graeme Reid and Liz Walker, Double Storey Books/ Juta, 2005, pp. 65-87.

Pease, Bob. *Issue Paper 17: Engaging Men in Men's Violence Prevention: Exploring the Tensions, Dilemmas and Possibilities.* Australian Domestic and Family Violence Clearing House, 2008.

Scheel, Elizabeth D., et al. "Making Rape Education Meaningful for Men: The Case for Eliminating the Emphasis on Men as Perpetrators, Protectors or Victims." *Sociological Practice: A Journal of Clinical and Applied Sociology* vol. 3, no. 4, 2001, pp. 257-78.

Schnurr, Joanne. "U of O Newspaper Editor Receives Backlash after Exposé on Pub Crawl." *CTV Ottawa News*, 19 Oct. 2016, ottawa. ctvnews. ca/u-of-o-newspaper -editor-receives-backlash-after-expos% C3%A9-on-pub-crawl-1.3122435. Accessed 27 Apr. 2020.

"University of Ottawa Won't Commit to Investigating Sexualized Pub Crawl." *CBC News*, 20 Oct. 2016, www.cbc.ca/news/canada/ ottawa/university-ottawa-pub-crawl-vet-s-tour-1.3813408. Accessed 27 Apr. 2020.

Walia, Harsha. "The bell hooks Phone Line Bothers Me." *Rabble*, 18 June 2014, rabble.ca/columnists/2014/06/bell-hooks-phone-line-bothers-me. Accessed 27 Apr. 2020.

Walsh, Shannon. "Addressing Sexual Violence and Rape Culture: Issues and Interventions Targeting Men and Boys." *Agenda*, vol. 105, no. 29.3, pp. 134-41.

Chapter Five

U.S. College Women's Reports of Rape, Resistance, and Prevention: A Case Study of One Campus

Abigail L. Moser and Lynne M. Webb

T he Center for Disease Control describes sexual assault as a significant problem in the United States (U.S.). College women are
particularly vulnerable to attack (Littleton), as evidenced by a
recent meta-analysis concluding that approximately 20 per cent of
college women will be raped at least once during their educational years
(McCauley and Casler). Multiple popular press writers blame campus
rape culture (e.g., Kingkade; MacDonald) for the widespread sexual
violence, which has prompted a national conversation about "the
prevalence of and strategies for addressing sexual assault on college
campuses" (McCauley and Casler).

In 2016, the American College Health Association recognized "sexual and relationship violence as a serious public health issue affecting
college and university campuses" (ACHA). How can this issue be best
addressed? To date, universities rely primarily on free, on-campus, rape-
prevention training. Spurred on by earlier reports detailing the extent
of sexual violence on college campuses (Fisher, Cullen, and Turner), the
U.S. government imposed the requirement that universities receiving
federal funds must provide rape-prevention training for their students
(Security on Campus). These prevention programs have had mixed
success in changing attitudes and behaviours on U.S. campuses (Banyard; Gidycz et al.).

Some rape-prevention training programs are far more successful than others. Programs exist that lower college men's likelihood of becoming perpetrators of sexual assault (Stewart). Although the male-oriented programs are not as widely implemented as sexual assault victim advocates would prefer, they demonstrate promise for changing men's behaviour on a large scale (Foubert; Miller et al.). These programs were created and modified with the input of male participants to become increasingly effective (Foubert and Marriott). Female participants, however, have not been afforded this same level of involvement in development and implementation of programs for college women. Sexual assault intervention programs for women typically address beliefs about sexual assault, rape myths, and double standards for men and women; trainers present this material to change rape-supportive attitudes, lower levels of women's future victimization, and decrease the likelihood of men's future perpetration of rape.

College women's lack of participation in program creation can be attributed to multiple causes. For example, trainers may fear that focusing on changing women's behaviour to stop sexual assault could contribute to victim blaming. However, if the success of men's programs increased following the inclusion of college men's input, then it may be possible to develop more effective training programs by asking college women how to improve the programs designed to keep them safe. A first step in this direction would be to present the ideas typically covered in sexual assault prevention programs to female focus groups and ask college women for their thoughts about these common curriculum components. We took this first step and report our findings in this chapter.

Review of the Literature

Virtually every U.S. college campus offers free sexual assault prevention training programs designed for women. Such programs focus on teaching women risk-reduction strategies, such as avoiding isolated areas of campus at night (Bedera and Nordmeyer). These programs have employed multiple training techniques, including videos, workshops, and skits (Rothman and Silverman) as well as more in-depth techniques involving peer education (Foubert and Marriott 1996) and the bystander intervention approach (Katz and Moore 2013). These programs often contain multiple cognitive elements, but most typically discuss three specific topics: rape myths, traditional gender roles, and the sexual double standards for men and women. Each of these elements is discussed in detail below.

Rape Myths

Rape myths are beliefs that transfer the etiology of the crime from the perpetrator to the victim (Ward). Susan Brownmiller has identified four such myths: All women want to be raped; no woman can be raped against her will; the woman was asking for it; and if a woman is going to be raped, she may as well enjoy it (246). Martha Burt has also discussed four somewhat different rape myths: Nothing happened; no harm was done; she wanted it or liked it; and she asked for it or deserved it. These myths "suggest that women, not men, are to blame for sexual assault" (Ward 25). Collen Ward also has recognized additional prevalent myths: "Rape is impossible; women want to be overpowered and ravished; women provoke rape and get what they deserve; rape is a crime of sexual passion; women often make false accusations of rape" (37). Discussion and debunking of these myths are common features of sexual assault prevention programs (e.g., Breitenbecher and Scarce; Currier and Carlson) but have had mixed success (e.g., Hayes, Abbott, and Cook). Nonetheless, these myths can be viewed as undergirding rape culture and, thus, worthy of continued attention in sexual assault prevention training.

Rape myths may facilitate rape, but they also influence the way a rape victim may be treated following an attack, which is a contributing factor to rape culture. When women are blamed for their own rape, they can experience the need or desire to defend themselves in the court system and in the community. Often, the "victim may even come to accept the judgment of others that she asked to be raped, that she was somehow guilty of precipitating the assault" (Laws and Schwartz 205). Judy Mann has found that these myths are so deeply ingrained in our culture that they are held by sixth to ninth graders. A large percentage of these young students believed that a man has the right to kiss or to have sex with a woman against her will if he has spent money on her or if she dressed in a seductive way.

Ability to Prevent Sexual Assault: Agency

Related to rape myths, but worthy of review as a distinct area of research, is the notion of perceived victims' agency to prevent rape. Can (and do) women perceive that they have the ability to prevent their rape or, alternatively, is it simply a matter of luck and circumstances typically beyond the victim's control whether or not she is raped? Kate Harris provides evidence that women may experience the term "rape" itself as denying them agency. Similarly, Stacy Young and Katheryn Maguire have noted that counsellors at a local rape crisis centre avoided the term "rape" and instead used the term "sexual assault" with their clients. Sexual assault prevention training programs for women typically focus on rape prevention techniques (e.g., never walk alone at night on campus) as action items. Such a focus may set the stage for women to view their agency in addressing an actual rape incident as limited if they fail to prevent such a situation from developing. If women view men as appropriately aggressive in sexual matters, then they may view rape as inevitable in a serious, romantic relationship.

Traditional Gender Roles

Belief in rape myths and blaming rape victims strongly correlate with an adherence to, and the belief in, traditional gender roles (Johnson, Kuck, and Schander). These traditional gender roles include the belief that men should be assertive, tough, and willing to resolve disputes through violence (Bourgois); furthermore, they need to control women by using violence if women step beyond their traditional roles (Haywood and Swank). Rape resistance training for women is hindered by these gender norms, which create associations between femininity and the characteristics of vulnerability and weakness (Guthrie). Additionally, men who subscribe to these traditional gender roles are more likely than other men to be sexually coercive and to commit rape and/or sexual assault (Berkowitz).

Double Standards

Different or double standards of sexual permissiveness exist for women and men (Crawford and Popp). Double standards employ gendered expectations: Men are permitted, and perhaps expected, to be sexually active (even promiscuous), whereas women are expected to display a lack of interest in sexual activities. Many studies discuss sexual double standards for women and the relationship of double standards to rape myths because, according to traditional gender roles, the responsibility for allowing or not allowing sex falls to women (versus men). Therefore, women become responsible for outcomes in sexual encounters, including rape. In contrast, men are not expected to control their sexual desires or actions (Haywood and Swank). Many men learn that sexual conquests are expected of them and that violence can be useful in such conquests. Because traditional gender roles in heterosexual relationships assign responsibility for sexual purity to women, male sexual violence can be viewed as necessary to overcome women's resistance and, thus, achieve consummation.

The extent to which an individual believes in rape myths may be connected to how strongly he or she participates in rape-supportive cultures. However, multiple studies (Foubert) document that education can dispel these beliefs. A collegiate education often asks students to think critically about themselves and their cultural assumptions. Thus, the completion of college courses could influence students' beliefs about women and rape (Forbes and Adams-Curtis; White and Robinson-Kurpius). For example, general education classes help reduce students' acceptance of rape myths; classes focusing specifically on sexism lead to larger reductions in those beliefs (Hinck and Thomas). Furthermore, scholars have linked multiple components of university life, including rape prevention training (Klaw et al.), to perpetuating or dismantling rape culture (Boswell and Spade; Burnett et al.; Folchert). As a reasonable next study in this line of research, we undertook an investigation of college women's beliefs in ideas that support rape culture to inform designers of sexual assault prevention programs about appropriate content for such programs.

The specific purpose of the study was twofold: (a) to examine one sample of college women's understandings of sexual assault, including beliefs about sexual assault, rape myths, and double standards for men and women—all typical content in sexual assault prevention programs—and (b) to discover if college women voiced agency with regard rape prevention. To these ends, we posed the following research questions:

- Research Question 1 (RQ1): Do college women voice consciousness of rape myths?

- Research Question 2 (RQ2): Do college women voice acceptance of rape myths?

- Research Question 3 (RQ3): Do college women voice a belief in traditional gender roles and double standards for men and women?

- Research Question 4 (RQ4): What agency, if any, do college women voice with regard to rape prevention?

Methods and Procedures

We collected data from focus groups. Researchers have used focus groups extensively to examine sexual issues (e.g., Burnett et al.) and to assess health education messages (e.g., Lederman and Stewart). Focus groups are especially useful for discovering information that provides the basis for future education and training (Salmon and Murray-Johnson).

Following a meta-analysis of sixty-nine studies examining sexual assault education programs, Linda Anderson and Susan Whiston concluded that program efficacy varied with the gender of the audience. A recent parallel meta-analysis of twenty-eight studies with follow-up assessments also recommends continued separation of male from female students for sexual assault prevention training (Newlands and O'Donohue). Thus, we thought it seemed reasonable to conduct studies of potential female program participants separately. Consistent with the purpose of the study, we elected to recruit only female college student to participate in our study.

Consistent with Patricia Fabiano and Linda Lederman's suggestion of employing same-sex discussants and facilitators to foster an atmosphere of open and honest communication, a female facilitated our all-female focus groups. Following Kim Golombisky's work, we structured our focus groups to create a gendered communication context that encouraged our female participants to disclose honestly their interpretations of their lived realities. By privileging women's voices in all-female focus groups, we attempted to transform each focus group into a "private world" (Golombisky 174)—a world in which participants felt sufficiently comfortable to describe their experiences in detail as well as to "share gossip and secrets" (183) about unwanted sexual advances.

Using focus groups as a research technique has multiple advantages. The communication and discussion integral to the effectiveness of focus group research can reveal how people "think and why they think that way" (Kitzinger 311). Furthermore, Lederman noted that focus groups offer group synergy, which may produce more data and more accurate data than one-on-one interviews ("Assessing"). Because of the level of interaction created through the use of focus groups, participants may expound extensively, describe their views in detail (Kitzinger), and identify beliefs that have not been clearly identified previously. Interview protocol questions were phrased neutrally to facilitate group discussion.

Recruitment

For two consecutive semesters, student participants were recruited at the "flagship," public university in Arkansas, the U.S. state with the highest incidence of rape in the southeastern region of the United States (i.e., 42.3 per 100,000). According to FBI statistics, only four states in the country experienced higher incidences of rape in 2012 (Sutter).

We recruited student participants from communication courses. We reasoned that students trained to be successful communicators might be more articulate in challenging conversations and capable of in-depth discussion. We requested that communication professors allow recruitment from their courses and, if possible, offer extra credit for student participation. Some professors offered extra credit and some did not, but all professors encouraged their students to participate in the study. Although men could not participate in the focus groups, they could earn extra credit by recommending females aged eighteen to twenty-two years of age who participated. Most participants who participated received extra credit for their participation (87.50 per cent). Potential participants were provided instructions on how to access online signup sheets for focus group time slots (*signupgenius.com*).

Sample

The sample consisted of forty female participants across seven focus groups. Focus groups ranged in size from four to seven participants (M =5.71; SD=1.11). Participants ranged in age from eighteen to twenty-two years (M=19.64; SD=1.14) and reported the following classifications: 37.5 per cent freshmen (n=15); 32.5 per cent sophomores (n=13); 12.5 per cent juniors (n=5); and 17.5 per cent seniors (n=7). The majority of participants were heterosexual (97.5 per cent); one participant self-reported as bisexual. The majority of the participants self-identified as Caucasian (n=35). However, other participants self-reported as mixed ethnicity (n=3) and Hispanic (n=2). All but one of the participants reported being a U.S citizen. Half (50 per cent) of the participants reported living in dormitories (n=20); 25 per cent reported living in an apartment (n=10); 15 per cent reported sharing a home (n=6); 5 per cent reported living in sorority houses (n=2); and the remaining 5 per cent reporting living at home with their families (n=2). The majority of participants were single, never married (77.5 per cent, n=31); 17.5 per cent were in committed relationships but did not live with their partners (n=7); 2.5 per cent were not married but lived with their part-ner (n=1); and 2.5 per cent were married and living with their spouse (n=1). Given that sexual assault training programs on the campus were voluntary, as is typical across the U.S., only one quarter (25 per cent, n=10) of the participants reported that they had attended such a program.

Interview Protocol

A semistructured interview protocol guided the focus group conver-sations. We designed the interview questions to facilitate discussion that addressed the research questions. We specifically queried women's beliefs in rape myths, traditional gender roles, and double standards for men and women. When necessary, the facilitator asked probing questions to elicit additional information to understand participants' beliefs. The authors designed the protocol and refined it across seven pilot tests. We made slight changes to the wording of the protocol following each pilot test until the discussion proceeded smoothly with few follow-up questions required. Data collection began and pilot testing ceased when the revised protocol prompted an hour of on-going conversation in the seventh pilot group.

Data Collection

A twenty-eight-year-old, Caucasian, heterosexual, female served as facilitator for the focus group sessions. Focus groups were conducted in an on-campus research laboratory; recordings were made with a digital handheld voice recorder that provided excellent quality audio. The recordings were transcribed and analyzed via thematic coding.

Each focus group session began with the completion of the demographics questionnaire, confidentiality forms, and extra credit sheets. Then, the facilitator reminded the participants of the discussion topic and provided assurances of confidentiality in an environment free of judgment. Each discussion began with a prompt (a reference to idea that all school children in the U.S. are taught to not talk with strangers because strangers can represent danger connected to the idea that college women may fear strangers as potential rapists); if that prompt did not elicit sufficient conversation, then the facilitator offered another prompt (a personal story about her mother). Next, the facilitator proceeded through the interview protocol asking broad questions to prompt discussion.

Each group session lasted approximately one hour. As discussion came to a close, participants were asked for any final thoughts on the topic or further contributions they wanted to have noted. They were reminded of the facilitator's email address as well as the contact information for the psychological services on campus if they wanted to talk further about the topics raised in the discussion groups. Participants were encouraged to email questions or comments to the facilitator and then were thanked for their time and contributions.

Analysis

The recordings were transcribed, including notations designating group interactions (e.g., group laughter) and line numbers for easy reference. Transcripts were labelled according to date, and participants were assigned fictitious aliases according to their group (e.g., Group B; Barbara, Brittney, Bridgette). The transcriptions, totalling 135 double-spaced pages containing 3,032 lines of data, were analyzed for emergent themes.

Thematic content analysis is the "scoring of messages for content, style, or both for the purpose of assessing the characteristics or experiences of persons, groups, or historical periods" (Smith 1). Following Richard Boyatzis's work, themes were identified as they emerged from the data rather than imposing preselected categories on the data. Our thematic analysis identified participants' "recurring similar assertions" (Reinard 182) relevant to the research questions. We employed William Foster Owen's criteria for themes: repetition (relatively the same language to describe a phenomenon), recurrence (differing language but similar meanings for a phenomenon), and forcefulness (ideas strongly stressed verbally or nonverbally).

The facilitator conducted the thematic analysis as an expert analyst; she had extensive knowledge of the scholarly literature surrounding the research topic, and she conducted the seven pilot focus groups as well as the seven research focus groups. Similar to any analytic inductive technique based in grounded theory, the facilitator functioned as a textual critic interpreting language: "Thus, reliability [was] not established by intercoder agreement. Instead, integrity of the analysis [was] established through a constant comparison process" (Krusiewicz and Wood 791). Insights from later responses influenced themes and, when appropriate, prompted the reinterpretations of previously reviewed responses and/or recorded themes (Charmaz).

Following each focus group, the facilitator examined the transcribed text to discover themes relevant to the research questions. Next, she completed a reading to find any counter evidence to previously identified themes and to pinpoint instances of group interactions that may have relevance to the emergent themes. She completed a final reading of the transcript to ensure all relevant data were identified. As the coder examined the transcript of each additional focus group using the constant comparison process, no new theme emerged after analysis of the transcript from the seventh focus group. Thus, the emergent thematic categories were deemed saturated, as per grounded theory protocol (Glaser and Strauss), and data collection ceased. The coder reviewed all the transcripts one final time to ensure coding of all incidences of the identified themes and to discover any counter evidence for the identified themes. When no new findings emerged following this reading, the analysis was deemed complete.

Results and Discussion

The purpose of the present study was twofold: (a) to discover one sample of college women's understandings of sexual assault, including beliefs about sexual assault, rape myths, and double standards for men and women—all typical content in sexual assault prevention programs—and (b) to discover if college women voiced agency in rape prevention.

This study was novel in that it asked college women to discuss the common components of campus sexual assault prevention training programs. Focusing on women's voiced concerns and beliefs allowed for unexpected themes to emerge. The analysis revealed multiple themes relevant to the research questions.

RQ1: Do college women voice consciousness of rape myths?

Every participant reported knowing about the falsehood of common rape myths. They said college instructors, parents, and church members informed them about the truth concerning rape myths. They were able to say who had told them about the myths or to describe what logic had led them to acknowledging them as myths. They reported not believing rape myths and instead believing the following:

- Rapes and assaults were most likely to be perpetrated by someone the victim knows.

- Women are not raped because of their clothing. After all, children do not dress provocatively and are sometimes raped. Therefore, it is clear that women are not raped because of their clothing.

RQ2: Do college women voice acceptance of rape myths?

Participants did discuss the rape myths they believed in, although they did not call them "myths." Such beliefs emerged in discussion of other topics and included the following:

Theme	Illustrative Quotation
Victim fabrication: Participants did not believe women who claim they were raped if they believe the victim to be "that kind of girl" or a liar.	Jan: "You can lie about it. I feel a lot of girls say they're raped too, and they're really not." Leah: "Let's be honest. There's all girls [here]. Like everyone knows someone who was like, 'Yeah, I think that someone raped me last night.'"
Women can behave in ways that provocatively invite sexual assault.	Melanie: "Why did you make out with him and lead him on? You knew he was going to want to go further." Macy: "A lot of people say they put themselves in that situation, so it is what it is." Jade: "There are girls that proclaim to be very innocent but act like a wild child and dress like a hooker off the streets. Just wait! One day that will come back to you."
Many attackers are strangers who do not know their victims. Participants believed the urban legend of a man hiding under cars and cutting women's Achilles tendons.	Helen: "Where I was growing up, there was a big case going on 'cause there was this guy that would hide under cars; and, when women would walk up to get in their cars, he would cut their Achilles tendon." Nadia: "... slit their Achilles tendon, because then they can't get away. So now I'm just really paranoid that I'm just going to be walking [and be attacked]."

Participants claimed to have been well versed in the truth behind rape myths but nonetheless still believed in some of those ideas. They believed that some women lied about rape, that sometimes women "asked for it" by engaging in facilitative behaviours, and that strangers were common perpetrators of assault. People who think they do not believe in rape myths, but in fact accept some of the myths, unknowingly perpetuate rape culture. "Cultural acceptance of rape myths and communities that tolerate sexual aggression create environments in which many individuals are disempowered" (ACHA).

A belief in these specific rape myths could potentially be counteracted through specific education concerning sexual assault. Based on our findings, sexual assault prevention programs should continue to focus on debunking rape myths, especially the myths that women ask for it that women lie about rape and that rapists are often strangers.

RQ3: Do college women voice a belief in traditional gender roles and sexual double standards for men and women?

Consistent with previous studies (e.g., Haywood and Swank), our participants noted the heterosexual double standards that exist for men and women as well as the traditional gender roles in heterosexual romantic relationships. They voiced their frustration with these roles and standards and questioned why they existed. Ironically, not one participant mentioned rape culture or its perpetuation. Two relevant themes emerged.

Theme	Illustrative Quotation
Current social norms require women to control and limit their sexual encounters, whereas men are free to have sex with whomever they want and whenever they want.	Naomi: "My Dad always says boys are the gas, and girls are the brakes." Melanie: "[When men are sexually aggressive,] they're just 'being a guy.'"
In heterosexual relationships, generally, men are the leaders.	Melanie: "I think normally the guy is the one to initiate sex. You don't see a girl all coming onto a guy all the time. You expect the guy to come onto the girl. It's her decision whether she lets him or not."

The college women who participated in our focus groups openly discussed their frustration with the double standards they reported experiencing in heterosexual relationships. Because double standards contribute to victim blaming and beliefs in rape myths, it is rational and important to teach men and women to confront these double standards. Sexual assault programs can help to move beyond discussing double standards to encouraging women to confront traditional gender roles and sexual double standards when they encounter them. Communication skills such as assertiveness and making effective arguments could reasonably become part of such training. In this way, programs could teach women to become agents of positive change via effective communication skills.

RQ4: What agency do college women voice in rape prevention?

We also investigated whether college women could or would voice their beliefs, understandings, and perceived vulnerabilities (i.e. their agency regarding rape). We discovered that they welcomed a venue for such discussions. The majority of our participants reported that they had never been asked their opinion on sexual assault issues that influence where they go and how they act on a daily basis. Participants reported a complete absence of venues to voice their fear of sexual assault and how that fear influenced them. The majority reported a desire to address questions about sexual assault to experts with information on the subject.

In each focus group, participants identified the limitations they place on their own behaviours in an attempt to minimize their vulnerability to rape. Four themes concerning rape prevention strategies emerged.

Theme	Illustrative Quotation
Never be alone.	Lana: "You use the buddy system, go in pairs. I would never go anywhere at night, even on campus. I would be afraid to walk somewhere by myself, so I always ask a friend to go with me."
	Odele: "Last year, after I took that one-hour [rape prevention] class too, they said the best method of prevention is not ever being alone. Don't ever be alone."

Theme	Illustrative Quotation
Be careful in public places.	Melanie: "I make sure I don't park next to any unmarked vans, especially if I'm driving by myself, [and] to park with the passenger's side door facing the van. I could get out of the car and get pulled right into the van." Kat: "If you're ever at a party) [and] you set your drink down, [walk away], and [then] come back to it, you throw it away [because it could contain a date-rape drug]."
Don't carry a Taser or mace because it can be used against you.	Kendra: "I'm not real strong. Somebody could just turn my hand, and use it [the Taser] on me."
You can intervene on your friend's behalf, but then you become vulnerable yourself.	Laura: "And my friend will be like, 'No, this isn't my dorm,' and he'll just say, 'Just come back with me anyways.' And I say, 'No, she's staying in this car. You can leave.' I've had to say that before to guys, 'No. You don't know this girl. She's not going with you!'" Nadia: "She came in crying because he was doing [sexual] stuff to her—not rape but other things that she didn't want to happen. And so later that night when they were dropping us back off, I said something to him. I didn't realize it [that he could come after me and rape me as an act of revenge] at the time, but I did later. I was scared almost that he would come back and do something to me."

Furthermore, in each focus group, participants clearly stated that they regularly found themselves in situations where they could do nothing to prevent a sexual assault if a perpetrator elected to attack them. In sum, they were never safe—a conclusion consistent with colleges' and universities' website tips on campus safety (Bedera and Nordmeyer). Our participants acknowledged taking steps to avoid placing themselves in situations that increased their vulnerability (e.g., walking alone in a dark place late at night)—the typical action item of campus sexual assault training programs. However, they viewed these measures as simply diminishing their chances of rape. Ultimately, however, they saw themselves as powerless to stop a determined rapist and that in an actual rape situation, they were helpless. They viewed attempting to have an assailant punished as futile and more damaging to the victim than the assailant. Four relevant themes emerged.

Theme	Illustrative Quotation
Sexual assaults are inevitable.	Jasmine: "If somebody is determined—and I'm a little girl—they're going to overpower me no matter what." Ohara: "I think there is always going to be a rape/sexual assault problem because there's always going to be that one guy that's just a creeper."
Society encourages women to keep quiet about rape and sex in general.	Kat: "Sex is something personal. You talk to your friends about it and stuff, but you aren't going to announce it to the whole campus. It's more personal than anything else. It's not something you're going to want everyone to know, like in the newspaper." Kaylee: "It's awkward to talk about." Kelsey: "It's the personal stories [of rape] that really open your eyes. [But] not everyone wants to talk about it."

Theme	Illustrative Quotation
Rape is embarrassing for women. Thus, reporting rape causes more negative outcomes for the female victim than if she deals with it alone.	Kat: "I think when it comes to reporting it [rape] ... you are super attached to your dignity. It's degrading. You don't want to share that with everyone. You don't want to be like, 'I got raped and everyone should know.'" Ophelia: "Most women don't report because they don't want to relive it or face their attacker or go through the emotional stress again. They believe that they can't find them [the assailant], so what's the point of reporting?"
A woman has to have all of the facts before reporting an attack to the police because her accusation could damage the man's reputation.	Kaley: "You have to have all the facts. I understand that you need the facts, that you can't just accuse somebody." Megan: "Or you've grown up with that person and so maybe they think 'Oh, that's not how they really are' or deep down, that's not their true self so maybe they think ... they wouldn't want to tarnish their reputation."

Consistent with previous reports (Harris; Young and Maguire), our participants voiced the belief that there was nothing they could do to prevent rape. They described scenes from their daily lives and explained how they would not be able to protect themselves if a man attempted to sexually assault them. For example, one participant said, "I get very nervous if I'm alone in any situation because I don't know if I could protect myself or defend myself if anything were to ever happen."

Such feelings of helplessness are particularly concerning among college students, as "students cannot learn in an atmosphere in which they do not feel safe" (ACHA). This sense of vulnerability is particularly disturbing when combined with student lifestyles at a twenty-first-century research institution. Women believe they openly risk rape if they go running in the evening or if they work alone late at the library or the laboratory. They believe they should not enroll in any class that ends after dark at any point in the four-month semester, thus limiting enrollment options and potentially crippling timely graduations if required classes are only offered in the late afternoon or evening, as is often the case on urban campuses. They cannot attend project or study group meetings after dark. It is difficult to imagine a talented student in any major completing their degree with such limitations.

Perhaps of even greater concern, these women have extremely limited opportunities for leadership experience outside of sorority life, especially if they are unable to attend the evening meetings of clubs, associations, and student government activities. Yes, they could attend with a friend, but if the woman has no friend also interested in the activity, she will have to cross that event off her list of options. Finally, it is concerning to think that these women will not benefit from the vast majority of the cultural events on the campus, as many concerts, plays, and dance recitals are presented only at night. Art gallery openings occur in the evenings, as do campus debates as well as the speaking engagements of most visiting lecturers and public officials. All students pay expensive activity fees to underwrite the cost of these events, but it appears that female students are underwriting the cost of male students' attendance at these events—as, because of their timing, these events are largely open to only male students unless the female student has a friend who will accompany her to the event. The situation seems eerily reminiscent of the 1800s, when no respectable women would appear in public unaccompanied. Now, this also has become true for women on college campuses after dark.

Our participants reported believing that if they were raped, society would rather they keep quiet about the assault than embarrass themselves or tarnish the reputation of the attacker by reporting the assault. Consistent with previous research (Burnett et al.), the college women who participated in this study had been taught that rape is a humiliation for women that should not be discussed.

As recommended by the White House Task Force to Protect Students from Sexual Assault (DeGue), encouraging college women to have open conversations about rape-supportive culture could be beneficial in addressing this set of perceptions and beliefs. Furthermore, campus sexual assault prevention programs would do well to train women in self-defence to decrease their feeling of vulnerability (see Hollander for evidence of the efficacy of such programs) and to provide women with rhetorical strategies to confront supporters of rape culture, who suggest that women should keep quiet about sexual assaults.

Limitations and Suggestions for Future Research

This study is not without its limitations. All participants were from one university campus, and the majority of participants were heterosexual and Caucasian. Limited diversity might have reduced variation in participant responses. Future studies could replicate this research using more diverse focus groups to determine whether the emergent themes relate only to heterosexual, Caucasian college women or if they extend across ethnic boundaries and sexual preferences.

This study focused solely on eighteen- to twenty-two-year-old college women. Examinations of nontraditional age college women's beliefs about sexual assault could expand the scope of this line of research in fruitful directions. Furthermore, future research could examine female students in high school and middle school, as many of the participants in this study reported exposure to the effects of sexual assault from a very young age and began forming their beliefs at that time.

Because of the sensitive nature of the subject, participants' self-reported data might have been skewed by a social desirability bias. Participants might have altered their responses to fit what they believed the researcher and the other focus group participants, the participants' peers, wanted them to say. People may not want to be honest about a sensitive subject like sexual assault or may experience an inability to be honest even when desiring to do so (Lederman and Stewart). Although this is a risk with any self-report research, it may be mitigated in future research by using multiple forms of data acquisition (e.g., questionnaires and surveys).

Conclusions and Recommendations

Despite the limitations listed above, this study contributes to our understanding of the necessary components of effective campus sexual assault prevention training programs. We asked a sample of college women their thoughts on commonly used curricular components of such programs. Their feedback (i.e., our results) document the need for more in-depth and fact-based rape education for women as well as more assault prevention interventions, and more focus on addressing gender inequality.

The college women in this sample voiced beliefs in some rape myths and some traditional sex roles. They also expressed their unhappiness with the sexual double standards for men and women. Our findings document the need for sexual assault prevention training programs to continue to include such topics in their curricular materials—and to explain their interconnections in more depth. The more we understand about the etiology of rape (McPhail), the more important it becomes to identify contributing factors and their connections to call out this phenomenon as a behaviour that is unnecessary and preventable. Early reports on the success of such integrated programs that discuss rape culture are promising (Jozkowski).

Furthermore, the participants voiced concerns regarding their lack of sexual education, a lack of venues in which to engage in meaningful dialogue regarding sexual assault, and their lack of agency in rape situations. Perhaps campus sexual assault prevention training programs could be meaningfully reframed as conversation and dialogue sessions that provide empowerment as well as education. Thus, our results document the desirability of both retaining the traditional curricular components of campus rape prevention training programs for women and moving beyond the traditional curricular elements to add two new elements to such programs: self-defence training to provide a sense of agency in rape situations as well as communication training to rhetorically confront gender inequities and rape culture.

Works Cited

American College Health Association (ACHA). "ACHA Guidelines: Addressing Sexual and Relationship Violence on College and University Campuses." ACHA, 2016, www.acha.org/documents/About/ACHA_AnnualReport_2015-2016.pdf. Accessed 28 Apr. 2020.

Anderson, Linda A., and Susan C. Whiston. "Sexual Assault Education Programs: A Meta-analytic Examination of their Effectiveness." Psychology of Women Quarterly, vol. 29, no. 4, 2005, pp. 374-88.

Banyard, Victoria L. "Improving College Campus-Based Prevention of Violence against Women: A Strategic Plan for Research Built on

Multipronged Practices and Policies." *Trauma Violence & Abuse*, vol. 15, no. 4, 2014, pp. 339-51.

Bedera, Nicole, and Kristjane Nordmeyer. "'Never Go Out Alone': An Analysis of College Rape Prevention Tips." *Sexuality & Culture*, vol. 19, no. 3, 2015, pp. 533-42.

Berkowitz, Alan D. *Men and Rape: Theory, Research, and Prevention Programs in Higher Education*. Jossey Bass, 1994.

Boswell, A. A., and Joan Z. Spade. "Fraternities and Collegiate Rape Culture: Why Are Some Fraternities More Dangerous Places for Women?" *Gender and Society*, vol. 10, no. 2, 1996, pp. 133-47.

Bourgois, Philippe I. *In Search of Respect: Selling Crack in El Barrio*. Cambridge University Press, 1995.

Boyatzis, Richard E. *Transforming Qualitative Information: Thematic Analysis and Code Development*. Sage, 1998.

Breitenbecher, Kimberly H., and Michael Scarce. "A Longitudinal Evaluation of the Effectiveness of a Sexual Assault Education Program." *Journal of Interpersonal Violence*, vol. 14, no. 5, 1999, pp. 459-78.

Brownmiller, Susan. *Against Our Will: Men, Women and Rape*. Simon & Schuster, 1975.

Burnett, Ann, et al. "Communicating/Muting Date Rape: A Co-Cultural Theoretical Analysis of Communication Factors Related to Rape Culture on a College Campus." *Journal of Applied Communication Research*, vol. 37, no. 4, 2009, pp. 465-85.

Burt, Martha R. "Rape Myths and Acquaintance Rape." *Acquaintance Rape: The Hidden Crime*, edited by Andrea Parrott and Laurie Bechhofer, John Wiley, 1991, pp. 26-40.

Charmaz, Kathy. "The Grounded Theory Method: An Explication and Interpretation." *Contemporary Field Research*, edited by Robert M. Emerson, Little, Brown, 1983, pp. 109-26.

Crawford, Mary and Danielle Popp. "Sexual Double Standards: A Review and Methodological Critique of Two Decades of Research." *Journal of Sex Research*, vol. 40, no. 1, 2003, pp. 13-26.

Currier, Danielle M., and Jessica H. Carlson. "Creating Attitudinal Change through Teaching: How a Course on 'Women and Violence' Changes Students' Attitudes about Violence Against Women." *Journal of Interpersonal Violence*, vol. 24, no. 10, 2009, pp. 1735-54.

DeGue, Sarah. "Preventing Sexual Violence on College Campuses: Lessons from Research and Practice. A Report Prepared for the White House Task Force to Protect Students from Sexual Assault. Part One: Evidence-based Strategies for the Primary Prevention of Sexual Violence Perpetration," *National Center for Campus Public Safety*, 2014, www.nccpsafety.org/assets/files/library/Preventing_Sexual_Violence _on_College_Campuses.pdf. Accessed 28 Apr. 2020.

Fabiano, Patricia M., and Linda C. Lederman. *Top Ten Misperceptions of Focus Group Research. Working Paper #3: The Report on Social Norms.* PaperClip Communications, 2002.

Fisher, Bonnie S., Francis T. Cullen, and Michael G. Turner. "The Sexual Victimization of College Women. Research Report," U.S. Department of Justice, 2000, www.ncjrs.gov/pdffilesl/nij/182369.pdf. Accessed 28 Apr. 2020.

Folchert, Kristine J. E. *The Role of Institutional Discourses in the Perpetuation and Propagation of Rape Culture on an American Campus.* 2002. University of British Columbia, MA thesis, circle.ubc.ca/bit stream/handle/2429/1449/ubc_2008_fall_englefolchert_kristine.pdf?sequence=1. Accessed Apr. 28 2020.

Foubert, John D. "The Longitudinal Effects of a Rape-Prevention Program on Fraternity Men's Attitudes, Behavioral Intent, and Behavior." *Journal of American College Health*, vol. 48, no. 4, 2000, pp. 158-63.

Foubert, John D., and Kenneth A. Marriott. "Overcoming Men's Defensiveness toward Sexual Assault Programs: Learning to Help Survivors." *Journal of College Student* Development, vol. 37, no. 4, 1996, pp. 470-72.

Forbes, Gordon B., and Leah E. Adams-Curtis. "Experiences with Sexual Coercion in College Males and Females: Role of Family Conflict, Sexist Attitudes, Acceptance of Rape Myths, Self-Esteem, and the Big-Five Personality Factors." *Journal of Interpersonal Violence*, vol. 16, no. 9, 2001, pp. 865-89.

Gidycz, Christine A., et al. "Concurrent Administration of Sexual Assault Prevention and Risk Reduction Programming: Outcomes for Women." *Violence against Women*, vol. 21, no. 6, 2015, pp. 780-800.

Glaser, Barney G., and Anselm L. Strauss. *The Discovery of Grounded Theory: Strategies for Qualitative Research.* Aldine. 1967.

Golombisky, Kim. "Gendering the Interview: Feminist Reflections on Gender as Performance in Research." *Women's Studies in Communication,* vol. 29, no. 2, 2006, pp. 165-92.

Guthrie, Sharon R. "Liberating the Amazon: Feminism and the Martial Arts." *Women and Therapy,* vol. 16, no. 2-3,1995, pp. 107-19.

Harris, Kate L. "The Next Problem with No Name: The Politics and Pragmatics of the Word Rape." *Women's Studies in Communication,* vol. 34.1, 2011, pp. 42-63.

Hayes, Rebecca M., Rebecca L. Abbott, and Savannah Cook. "It's Her Fault: Student Acceptance of Rape Myths on Two College Campuses." *Violence against Women,* vol. 22, no. 13, 2016, pp. 1540-555.

Haywood, Holly, and Eric Swank. "Rape Myths among Appalachian College Students." *Violence and Victims,* vol. 23, no. 3, 2008, pp. 373-89.

Hinck, Shelly S., and Richard W. Thomas. "Rape Myth Acceptance in College Students: How Far Have We Come?" *Sex Roles* vol. 40, no. 9-10, 1999, pp. 815-32.

Hollander, Jocelyn A. "Does Self-Defense Training Prevent Sexual Violence against Women?" *Violence against Women,* vol. 20, no. 3, 2014, pp. 252-69.

Hollander, Jocelyn A. "The Importance of Self-defense Training for Sexual Violence Prevention." *Feminism & Psychology,* vol. 26, no. 2, 2016, pp. 207-26.

Johnson, Barbara E., Douglas L. Kuck, and Patricia R. Schander. "Rape Myth Acceptance and Sociodemographic Characteristics: A Multidimensional Analysis." *Sex Roles,* vol. 36, no. 11, 1997, pp. 693-707.

Jozkowski, Kristen N. "Beyond the Dyad: An Assessment of Sexual Assault Prevention Education Focused on Social Determinants of Sexual Assault among College Students." *Violence against Women,* vol. 21, no. 7, 2015, pp. 848-74.

Katz, Jennifer, and Jessica Moore. "Bystander Education Training for Campus Sexual Assault Prevention: An Initial Meta-Analysis." *Violence and Victims,* vol. 28, no. 6, 2013, pp. 1054-67.

Kitzinger, Jenny. "Introducing Focus Groups." *BMJ: British Medical Journal*, no. 311, 1995, pp. 299-302.

Kingkade, Tyler. "College Administrators Pushed to Tackle Rape Culture." *Huffington Post*, 22 Sept. 2014, www.huffingtonpost.com/news/college-rape-culture/. Accessed Apr. 28 2020.

Klaw, Elena L., et al. "Challenging Rape Culture: Awareness, Emotion, and Action through Campus Acquaintance Rape Education." *Women & Therapy*, vol. 28, no. 2, 2005, pp. 47-63.

Krusiewicz, Erin S., and Julia T. Wood. "'He was our Child from the Moment We Walked in that Room': Entrance Stories of Adoptive Parents." *Journal of Social and Personal Relationships*, vol. 18, no. 6, 2001, pp. 785-803.

Laws, Judith L., and Pepper Schwartz. *Sexual Scripts*. University Press of America, Inc., 1981.

Lederman, Linda C. "Assessing Educational Effectiveness: The Focus Group Interview as a Technique for Data-Collection." *Communication Education*, vol. 3, no. 2, 1990, pp. 117-27.

Lederman, Linda C., and Lea P. Stewart. "Using Focus Groups to Formulate Effective Language for Health Communication Messages: A Media Campaign to Raise Awareness of Domestic Violence on a College Campus." *Qualitative Research Reports in Communication*, vol. 4, no. 4, 2003, pp. 16-22.

Littleton, Heather. "Interpersonal Violence on College Campuses: Understanding Risk Factors and Working to Find Solutions." Trauma, Violence, & Abuse, vol. 15, no. 4, 2014, pp. 297-303.

MacDonald, Heather. "The Culture of 'Campus Tape.'" *National Review*, 11 Oct. 2014, www.nationalreview.com/article/390084/culture-campus-rape-culture-heather-mac-donald. Accessed 28 Apr. 2020.

Mann, Judy. "Twisted Attitudes Taint Youth." *Washington Post*, 6 May 1988, D3, 24.

McCauley, Heather L., and Adam W. Casler. "College Sexual Assault: A Call for Trauma-Informed Prevention." *Journal of Adolescent Health*, vol. 56, no. 6, 2015, pp. 584-85.

McPhail, Beverly A. "Feminist Framework Plus: Knitting Feminist Theories of Rape Etiology into a Comprehensive Model." *Trauma, Violence, & Abuse*, vol. 17, no. 3, 2016, pp. 314-29.

Miller, Elizabeth., et al. "'Coaching Boys into Men': A Cluster-Randomized Controlled Trial of a Dating Violence Prevention Program." *Journal of Adolescent Health*, vol. 51, no. 5, 2012, pp. 431-38.

Newlands, Rory, and William O'Donohue. "A Critical Review of Sexual Violence Prevention on College Campuses." *Acta Psychopathol*, vol. 2, no. 2, 2016, pp. 1-14.

Owen, William Foster. "Interpretive Themes in Relational Communication." *Quarterly Journal of Speech*, vol. 70, no. 3, 1984, pp. 274-87.

Reinard, John. *Introduction to Communication Research*. McGraw-Hill, 1998.

Rothman, Emily, and Jay Silverman. "The Effect of a College Sexual Assault Prevention Program on First-Year Students' Victimization Rates." *Journal of American College Health*, vol. 55, no. 5, 2007, pp. 283-90.

Salmon, Charles T., and Lisa Murray-Johnson. "Communication Campaign Effectiveness." *Public Communication Campaigns*, 3rd ed., edited by Ronald E. Rice and Charles K. Atkin. Sage, 2000, pp. 168-180.

Security on Campus, Inc. "Jeanne Clery Disclosure of Campus Security Policy and Campus Crime Statistics Act Text," *Security on Campus*, 2002, securityoncampus.org/schools/cleryact/text.html. Accessed Apr. 28 2020.

Smith, Charles P. *Motivation and Personality: Handbook of Thematic Content Analysis*. Cambridge University Press, 1992.

Stewart, Andrew L. "The Men's Project: A Sexual Assault Prevention Program Targeting College Men." *Psychology of Men & Masculinity*, vol. 15, no. 4, 2014, pp. 481-85.

Sutter, John D. "List: States Where Rape Is Most Common." *CNN Opinion*, 3 Feb. 2014, www.cnn.com/2014/02/03/opinion/sutter-alaska-rape-list/. Accessed 28 Apr. 2020.

U. S. Center for Disease Control, Injury Prevention & Control, Division of Violence Prevention. "Sexual Violence," *CDC*, 2015, www.cdc.gov/ViolencePrevention/sexualviolence/index.html. Accessed 28 Apr. 2020.

Ward, Colleen A. *Attitudes toward Rape: Feminist and Social Psychological Perspectives*. Sage Publications, 1995.

White, Bradley H., and Sharon E. Robinson-Kurpius. "Attitudes toward Rape Victims Effects of Gender and Professional Status." *Journal of Interpersonal Violence*, vol. 14, no. 9, 1999, pp. 989-95.

Young, Stacy L., and Katheryn C. Maguire. "Talking about Sexual Violence." *Women & Language*, vol. 26, no. 2, 2003, pp. 40-52.

Chapter Six

Memorable Messages in Campus Sexual Assault Prevention

Katherine J. Denker and Faith R. Kellermeyer

M emorable messages are "verbal messages which may be remembered for extremely long periods of time and which people perceive as a major influence on the course of their lives" (Knapp, Stohl, and Reardon 27). Memorable messages have been studied for their influence on variety of health behaviours (Reno and McNamee 1; Smith et al. 293) as well as their impact on organizational socialization (Dallimore 214; Ellis and Smith 97). However, no previous study has explored the role of memorable messages in sexual assault prevention training, let alone with first-year students on college campuses. Beginning in 2014, all federally funded universities in the United States (U.S.) were required to provide their students with sexual assault prevention training, and it is important to ensure that these training programs impart messages that stick with students (Schroeder 1197). This study examined a midsized, Midwestern university's online training program for new students, which was designed to deliver messages about sexual assault prevention, bystander intervention, safe drug and alcohol practices, and indicators of healthy and unhealthy relationships.

In this study, we conducted qualitative interviews with students. Because attempts to quantify the subject have led to such widely different conclusions (Krakauer xiii-xv), utilizing a qualitative approach provided a complementary and more nuanced context from which to understand the experiences of students. Additionally, as the online training that new students were required to take automatically provided some quantitative data, a qualitative research design helped fill in gaps left by the quantitative survey research. Through our use of constant-comparative analysis, specific memorable messages were identified and developed into thematic patterns.

Campus Prevention Programs

Central to any discussion about issues of sexual assault and campus safety are the norms and expectations of rape culture. A rape culture is an "environment that supports beliefs conducive to rape and increases risk factors related to sexual violence" (Burnett et al. 466). The frequency with which sexual assault happens in the U.S. indicates that it has a culture that condones rape and perpetuates rape myths (Earle 417). Stereotypes and myths that support rape culture create a climate that is hostile to victims (Burt 229).

Since college campuses are high-risk environments for sexual assault, there is a demand for innovations in prevention tools and training (Banyard et al. 65-67). Early prevention programs perpetuated the idea that women are most likely to be victimized by strangers, resulting in such prevention efforts as blue emergency lights and security phones (Schwartz and DeKeseredy 141). These approaches were problematic not only because they ignored the reality of acquaintance rape but also because they placed the onus for rape prevention on victims. Additionally, rather than increasing safety on campus, teaching women to avoid being alone served to reduce the value of their college experience, preventing them from participating in extracurricular activities or from attending night classes (Schwartz and DeKeseredy 139-41).

In recent years, there has been greater variability in the extent to which colleges and universities in the U.S. have sought to prevent sexual assault (Karjane, Fisher, and Cullen 3-8). One tactic enacted by universities has been to create print and online campaigns focused on sexual assault prevention (Masters 34). There is a rising trend for such campaigns to target men, which was largely inspired by a well-known visual campaign called My Strength Is Not for Hurting in the early 2000s (Murphy 113). Visual campaigns can raise awareness and potentially bring rape myths to attention, but they are less effective in changing attitudes (Rodriguez et al. 230), as they rely entirely on the viewer to adopt prescribed attitudes without providing any further support or guidance.

The majority of sexual assault intervention models utilized by college campuses consist of didactic lectures and passive forms of learning, such as online training modules or guest speakers (Rodriguez et al. 230-31). Although this type of intervention model is typically efficient in terms of cost and time for universities, didactic teaching negates education and knowledge acquisition as a process of inquiry (Friere 53).

More interactive efforts to prevent sexual assault on college campuses include bystander intervention training, acquaintance rape workshops, and interactive performances (Earle 418; Karjane, Fisher, and Cullen 7-8, Rodriguez et al. 231). Bystander intervention occurs when individuals speak up and act if they witness a situation they perceive could lead to a sexual assault (Hust et al.106). This intervention moves the focus of prevention efforts to peers and community members, placing emphasis on changing community interactions (McMahon and Banyard 3). Programs that utilize a community approach to teach bystanders appropriate ways to intervene have reported a high level of success with multiple groups on college campuses, and they are especially beneficial for reaching higher risk populations, such as members of fraternities and sororities and athletes (Bannon, Brosi, and Foubert 73).

Unfortunately, prevention programs in general have not significantly reduced the number of sexual assaults or influenced reporting behaviour on college campuses (Bannon, Brosi, and Foubert 75). Although bystanders have the ability to help victims by both directly intervening and by advocating for behaviours that do not support sexual violence, personal factors can decrease the likelihood of a bystander to intervene (Hust et al. 108). For example, individuals with higher acceptance of rape myths are less likely to recognize the ubiquity of sexual assault and more likely to blame victims (Hust et al. 115). The lack of sexual assault reduction may be a result of the type of program implemented or the lack of continuous support from university officials (Bannon, Brosi, and Foubert 73).

Identity Formation

Communication theory of identity (CTI) draws a layered perspective of identity, integrating community, communication, social relationships, and self-concepts into identity formation and management (Hecht and Choi 138). To better understand how students learn campus norms (including their attitudes towards sexual assault prevention), CTI provides insight into the identity formation that takes place when individuals become socialized to a new organization. Compared to other identity theories, CTI focuses more on mutual influences between identity and communication; it asserts that identity is stored within the communication between relational partners and group members (Hecht, Jackson, and Ribeau 214).

CTI identifies four frames of identity—personal, enacted, relational, and communal (Jung and Hecht 266)—that interact with and are influenced by one another (Hecht and Choi 140). The personal layer of identity is an individual's self-concept or self-image, which includes a person's self-cognitions, feelings about the self, and spiritual sense of being (Hecht and Choi 140; Jung and Hecht 266). The enacted layer of identity is constructed in communication through messages and includes an individual's performed or expressed identity (Hecht and Choi 140-41; Jung and Hecht 266). In this, identity can be performed through social behaviours, social roles, and symbols, such as a fraternity member wearing their letters (Hecht, Jackson, and Ribeau 217).

Next, the relational layer of identity is jointly negotiated and mutually formed within relationships (Hecht, Jackson, and Ribeau 218). To maintain such identities, individuals need to remain in relationship with others—for instance, a mother needs children, and a professor needs students. When people lose or switch their relational identities, they can be more likely to engage in negative health behaviours, such as binge drinking or drug use (Hecht and Choi 141). Michael Hecht and HyeJeong Choi (141) assert that the changing of relational identities can occur as a result of major life changes, and we maintain that going to college for the first time can have a major impact on individuals' relational identities, as students move out of their parents' homes and often leave most of their familiar relationship roles.

Finally, the communal layer of identity deals with how collective groups define their identities through mutual characteristics, histories, and shared memories (Hecht and Choi 142; Jung and Hecht 267). Such identities are sometimes represented through negative stereotypes or cultural codes (Hecht and Choi 142). For example, membership in a fraternity can sometimes be tied to negative stereotypes regarding drinking and sexual assault, yet membership can also provide a social identity and a sense of belonging.

Central to any discussion of CTI are two important concepts: interpenetration and identity gaps (Hecht and Choi 142-43). The four layers described above are not conceptualized as separate from each other but rather as interpenetrated, meaning that identity layers can be identified independently but together constitute a whole (Hecht and Choi 142). For example, an individual interested in examining gender identity (which is a personal identity) must also consider how society defines gender roles (communal) or how others view a person as a man or a woman (relational) (Jung and Hecht 267).

These layers operate collectively, and in some situations, individuals' varying layers of identity may contradict one another (Jung and Hecht 267). In such cases, identity gaps—"discrepancies between or among the four frames of identity" (Jung and Hecht 268)—can occur as a result of inconsistency between the levels. Identity gaps are outcomes of communication and relationships, as people are not always transparent or consistent, resulting in communication imperfections (Jung and Hecht 268). For example, the way in which a person communicates and expresses an enacted identity can differ from their views of self. Such gaps can demonstrate the dialectical tensions between contradiction and coexistence of identity frames, which illustrate the fluid nature of identity (Jung and Hecht 268).

CTI can help higher education administrators to develop messages to promote healthy behaviours during organizational socialization, such as college orientation and welcome week. CTI provides a framework for message design in risk reduction programming by helping administrators reflect on the target individuals' salient identities (Hecht and Choi 146-47).

Memorable Messages

Organizations can use memorable messages to influence during the socialization process. These messages enable organizational members to understand organizations and offer a guide for appropriate behaviour (Stohl 232). New college students can reflect on the messages they have received from family members, mentors, and peers as they prepare to join their university culture (Wang 337). Memorable messages are worth examining because they can provide us with information about ourselves, our society, and our ways of communicating (Orbe et al. 287). Memorable messages about the college experience could have the ability to either perpetuate or diminish rape myth acceptance in individual students.

Although memorable messages have traditionally been identified as direct, oral injunctions, they can also exist in the form of "ambient" messages, which are indirect and implicit socializing messages (Dallimore 217). Whether direct or ambient, messages are considered memorable when they answer an internal conflict or a personal problem, provide a means for self-assessment, or offer a greater understanding of self (Orbe et al. 288; Smith, Ellis, and Yoo 328). The memorable messages students receive could affect decisions about how to behave or intervene in a case of sexual assault.

When faced with troubling situations, college students are able to recall memorable messages from mentors and family members (Nazione et al. 139; Wang 341). These messages have the potential to remain salient throughout a student's college experience and postcollege career (Wang 337). Those messages can result in explicit action from students to better their situation or correct their behaviour (Nazione et al. 137), such as past encouragement to use tutoring services that inspire later behavioural change.

However, college students report memorable messages that lead them in competing and sometimes opposing positions. First generation college students can struggle to manage competing discourses and memorable messages related to home and college commitments (Wang 351). Also, since familial memorable messages about college do not come from firsthand experience for some first-generation students, this can lead them to feel confused about their priorities. For example, two common themes for college students' memorable messages include "do your best in school and try hard" as well as "enjoy your life" (Nazione et al. 138; Smith, Ellis, and Yoo 331). If enjoying life includes heavy drinking and staying up late every night, it could be difficult for that student to do well in class. Additionally, a fraternity brother or student athlete may receive conflicting messages from university personnel—promoting bystander intervention—and from their fraternity brothers or teammates—

promoting sexual conquest and hegemonic masculinity.

Although the majority of students' memorable messages tend to come from family members (Kranstuber, Carr, and Hosek 46), over a quarter of memorable messages college students receive come from academic personnel, including professors, student affairs personnel, and residence hall staff (Nazione et al. 140). Overall, the memorable messages students receive from important figures in their lives are indicators of student success (Kranstuber, Carr, and Hosek 57).

Messages from university personnel not only inform students about important campus resources but also potentially influence students' acceptance of rape myths. In this way, university staff can lessen the impact of rape culture on their campuses. Members of groups with a higher social acceptance of rape myths, such as fraternities and athletic clubs, can benefit from student affairs–led programmatic interventions that provide these students with accurate information (Bannon, Brosi, and Foubert 81-82). To address students' needs and promote crisis prevention, universities should plan and convey consistent messages about significant issues throughout the course of a student's college career (Nazione et al. 138), starting in the training requirements offered during organizational socialization.

In order to test the effectiveness s of one such program, we used two research questions:

Research Question 1: What memorable messages do students recall from their university's sexual assault prevention training?

Research Question 2: What are the shared themes of students' memorable messages?

Methods

Participants included eight students aged nineteen to thirty-six years from a mid-sized, Midwestern university. There were five women and three men. The racial/ethnic makeup of the participants was Caucasian (n=7) and Latino (n=1). Five participants identified as straight or heterosexual, two identified as gay or homosexual, and one identified as bisexual. The participants represented both graduate students (n=4) and undergraduate students (n=4). All participants were new students at the university and completed the online sexual assault prevention training during or before their first semester.

After this study received Institutional Review Board approval, first-year students who had completed the university's online sexual assault prevention training were recruited using an email, which included a transparent overview of the research goals and was sent through the university's communication centre. After students confirmed their interest in participating, they were given a screening questionnaire to ensure their eligibility (eligible participants had to have completed the training program and be at least eighteen years of age). Students who met the eligibility criteria were emailed a digital copy of the online consent form for their records.

Interviews were conducted using a semistructured interview protocol and lasted from eighteen minutes to forty-eight minutes, with an average length of thirty-two minutes. At the end of each interview, participants were sent home with a handout containing resources, including contact information for on-campus counselling services, in case they felt any discomfort in discussing issues related to sexual assault. Following each interview, memos were created (Tracy 196), which noted the descriptions of each interview as well as any initial impressions. These interviews resulted in 108 pages of single-spaced transcriptions and eight pages of hand-written memos. After transcription, the interviews were verified (Tracy 238).

Following the transcription verification process, coding procedures started. Initial coding incorporated a constant-comparative analysis to identify and develop categories and thematic patterns (Strauss and Corbin 67). During the open-coding process, coding categories were combined and revised until they needed no further modification (Strauss and Corbin 224-25). In this phase, existing theoretical models were used to explain the content of field notes and transcription. After the coding analysis, four participants provided respondent validation through member checks (Tracy 238). Keeping participant diversity in mind, member checks were solicited from one male undergraduate, one female undergraduate, one male graduate student, and one female graduate student.

Results: Tensions between Expectations and Experiences

At several points during the interviews, the participants expressed various tensions between the messages they retained from the training and their actual lived experiences, from references to conflicting or contradictory experiences to feeling a sense of otherness from ingroups. Participants noted that while the training's messages could be useful or important, there were sometimes significant differences between their expectations that resulted from the training and their personal experience with those topics. Throughout discussions with each participant, three tensions emerged: (a) important versus uncomfortable, (b) control versus helplessness, and (c) redundant versus. enlightening. These themes will be explained and illustrated through examples of how participants framed these tensions.

Important versus Uncomfortable

One of the memorable messages that students expressed when looking back on their experience with the training was that it is extremely important to discuss sexual assault. However, the participants ex-pressed a level of discomfort when it comes to holding these discussions, and identified that regardless of importance, people are unmotivated to talk about sexuality. Instances of this theme include references to the awkwardness and discomfort that occurs when discussing sex and the avoidance of conversations about sex, especially with important figures. Arvada,[1] a heterosexual graduate student, explained the importance of being able to talk about sexuality/sexual assault: "[Talk-ing about sexuality] helps to normalize what's going on with students' experience ... you can just get more feedback from how to have healthier relationships, or to really get what they want ... like to do what they want in a relationship and being clear about expectation and what happens like, at parties and whatnot."

Arvada explains here that talking about sexuality would help normalize sexual experiences and would also help students to identify what types of behaviours are unhealthy. Being able to name and identify unhealthy sexual behaviours can be liberating for those who have survived a sexual assault and can also help build a culture that is intolerant of rape myths. Additionally, open discussion about sexual behaviours could lead to communal norms that influence the way an individual enacts his or her sexuality.

Similarly, while participants thought it was important to share information about sexual assault and claimed they felt comfortable doing so in an online setting, they did not think it would be a good idea to share that same information in a seminar or group setting. Thomas, a heterosexual graduate student, articulated this tension:

> If it's in person, it's a little bit easier, I think, to ... connect the people and to communicate ... I think the impact, too, would be like way more powerful than it would be just like reading it online. On the other hand, it could be ... sensitive, a sensitive issue for some people. Sensitive like, it could be also like a lot more difficult to get through ... Like I could just imagine if somebody's been raped or something like that ... it might be like more difficult or ... it's like more emotionally problematic for them.

Here, Thomas struggles to grapple with the fact that although face-to-face training could be more effective sexual assault training (Rodriguez et al. 246-247), talking about such issues in person can be a source of discomfort, or even triggering.

Reinforcing the awkward nature of discussions about sexuality, Sara, a heterosexual freshman, shared that it would be very difficult to get students to talk about sexual assault in groups because the topic is culturally taboo, and she expressed some frustration along the way: "Like it is such a taboo topic to most people that it is hard to get that motivated to ... want to know more. I mean the people that I know that want to know more either were or know someone who has been sexually assaulted so that motivated them to learn more, like 'what can I do?' 'What should I do if this happens?'" Sara expresses the extent to which sexual assault is an off-limits topic of conversation for most people, yet when people want to learn more, it is usually due to a personal experience with the issue. If these assaults are treated as such a taboo topic that personal experience is the only feasible motivation for learning more, the silence becomes reified, and space is lost for discussing sexual assault and understanding consent.

Sara later stated that she was personally interested in sexual assault prevention because her mother had been sexually assaulted. Sara's relational identity to her mother motivated her to learn about helping other victims, yet she also believed that group-based training could be problematic: "I think that if you did it with a friend, it would be more of a joke.... You would want to make it more of a light-hearted conversation, and [it] would end up being a joke, and you wouldn't take it as seriously." Sara's prediction that participating in training with a friend could lead to it being taken as a joke can be linked to the use of humour to diffuse awkward or uncomfortable conversations. People often use face-saving and humour to overcome discomfort associated with talking about sex (Miller-Ott and Linder 72). Despite participants' open acknowledgment that talking about sexual issues would be helpful, they all perceived some aversion to discussing these issues.

Control versus Powerlessness

Another tension identified by participants was the idea that individuals can take control of their safety, which was contrasted with remarks about the powerlessness of individuals to prevent sexual assault. In this tension, participants used victim-blaming language—indicating that victims might have been able to prevent sexual assault—and also described sexual assault as something that "just happens" regardless of what steps one couldt take to prevent it. Sara, a heterosexual freshman, told us that sexual assault often happens precisely because people assume it will not, and they fail to educate themselves:

> This does happen basically because some people are like, "well, it doesn't happen, that won't happen to me," and ... I've heard that so many times, like "oh well, that won't happen to me," but if you are putting yourself in that situation—you don't even have to put yourself in the situation—it can happen anywhere, anytime. And it is not your fault, but you have to be knowledgeable about what to do or what you can do to maybe prevent it or stop it or something.

Sara struggles with the idea that sexual assault is not the victim's fault, but she still maintains that if individuals took time to properly educate themselves, they could "maybe prevent it or stop it" from taking place. Although she acknowledges that a victim should not be blamed for being sexually assaulted, she also ascribes some level of responsibility to an individual who was not vigilant in taking action.

Ana, a heterosexual graduate student, explained the complicated role that alcohol can play in consensual sexual activity:

When you put yourself in a situation where you're not being fully aware of what's happening around you, that's like putting your control out of your hands ... I think because of that, it's very easy for people to assume like, "oh, this is when I can get what I want from this person because they're finally gonna say yes to me, because they're not really thinking clearly anymore." And sometimes alcohol, you know... it lets you just do whatever and not really deal with the consequences.... And I think that's why it's so confusing, when it comes to rape. It's such a blurred line because even if both parties are drunk, how does anyone know who said yes or not?

Like Sara, Ana spent some time grappling and backpedaling, careful not to fully place blame on a victim of sexual assault. But she also fails to blame the aggressor and, instead, attributes the cause of the assault to alcohol. Although it is true that alcohol is used to render victims more vulnerable to an assault (Lisak and Miller 79-80), Ana's position is a culturally endorsed rape myth (Burt 225-229), asserting that cooperation equals consent. When victims are blamed for choosing to use a controlled substance, the responsibility of the perpetrator is edadicated. The tension these students experienced while using victim-blaming rhetoric and adhering to cultural codes that enable perpetrators reveals a potential gap between their personal and communal identities.

Redundant versus Enlightening

Another theme that became apparent was the tension participants experienced in viewing the training as being redundant versus enlightening. Within this theme, participants insisted that the training's messages were unnecessary and did not fit their lifestyles, asserted that the training was designed for people with less life experience, and, contrarily, shared descriptions of new information that they were exposed to as a result of the training.

Graduate students, reifying their communal identity frame, claimed that they had already become accustomed to the college experience and, therefore, did not see the need for taking part in the training. Similarly, the undergraduate students seemed to think that they had already learned most of the material covered by the training before they arrived on campus.

Thomas, a graduate student, explained the following: "it seemed to be targeted more toward like, a younger audience. And it seemed to be like, more appropriate for like, incoming freshmen or like new students to college ... I found it like a little redundant coming out of college, for like already having done a bachelor's degree." Ana, also a graduate student, echoed Thomas's aversion: "I don't know if it's that useful for graduate students who have already gone through undergraduate ... now they're—to me, I would think more like adults—I would think that they'd be more careful, at least my perception would be that. So for me, I didn't really find it necessary." In this statement, Ana differentiates herself from undergraduate students, a recurring theme among graduate students, who suggested that their life experience makes them inherently different, wiser, and more experienced. Such an assumption implies that the number of years a person has lived automatically makes them more informed and experienced.

Although the graduate students thought the information covered in the training was most appropriate and useful for undergraduate students, undergraduates did not agree. Despite being new to college, these students still felt that they had enough life experience to render the training material unnecessary. Flower, a heterosexual freshman, noted that "it was like something ... covered in health class in high school ... it's not something you have forgotten... it seemed like there was a lot of going through stuff that didn't seem as important to me." Apart from how redundant and inapplicable they perceived the training material to be, participants frequently also commented that they had, in fact, gained new knowledge from the training.

It is especially important to note that some participants discovered new information about the nature of consent. Lance, a homosexual freshman, shared that he had not previously realized that consent cannot be given by someone who is intoxicated: "I learned a lot about like the sexual assault portion because like I didn't know certain, like—if they're drunk, or like, whatever, like you can't do that. That's against the law. I didn't know that." Correspondingly, Arvada, a graduate student, stated: "If people have been drinking, then they can't consent to, like, sexual activity ... I think that was more clear than it had been in the past." Despite protests from participants about how redundant and unnecessary the training was, it actually imparted some important and brand new information, particularly related to the definition of consensual sex.

Sydney, a bisexual graduate student, seemed to have a good pulse on this tension when she explained conversations she held with her peers regarding the training:

> I think there's some degree of ... like we're above all this because we went through undergrad ... like "Oh I know like how to watch my drink and stuff," but when I have brought up positive aspects of it, they do admit that they've been pretty impressed with that ... and they admit you can always learn more stuff. But I feel like the initial impression, they can't relate; it's like rolling your eyes.

Sydney's summation of this tension was also emphasized by the other participants. No one wanted to be seen as a novice—reinforcing a cultural expectation that everyone should already know the information covered in the training. Such an expectation may prevent students from being vocal about seeking more information in an effort to protect their self-concepts, which could serve to reify harmful communal norms when it comes to speaking openly about sexuality.

Conclusion

These tensions experienced by participants reveal the differences between the expectations the online training created for them and the experiences they went through upon arrival at college. In the tension important versus uncomfortable, participant describe the importance of communicating about sexuality but also expressing a lack of motivation or desire to hold conversations about sex with the people in their lives. When participants touched on the tension of control versus powerlessness, they argued that sexual assault is not the fault of the victim but also placed blame on uncontrollable situational factors, which displaced the aggressor's responsibility. In the tension redundant versus enlightening, participants argued that the training was unnecessary for them while also admitting that it exposed them to new and useful information. Some of the tensions participants identified exemplify the desire of individuals to appear more knowledgeable than, and superior to, their peers. These tensions also highlight some of the ways in which students endorse rape myths.

CTI can be useful for designing messages to spark community-level change. Individuals interested in community-level change can use CTI to develop messages to promote healthy behaviours. However, it can be difficult to develop such messages for an audience as wide as a university because messages aimed at the communal level are most useful for close-knit groups or communities with clear ingroup and outgroup distinctions (Hecht and Choi 146). Using CTI to create cognitive dissonance can be a means for administrators and organizational leaders to promote behaviour change during organizational socialization (Hecht and Choi 146), but messages should be crafted carefully to avoid reifying harmful social norms. For example, individuals who personally do not identify as drinkers may feel cognitive dissonance when they attempt to identify as members of the college community because they recognize that part of the communal college student identity includes the social behaviour of engaging in binge drinking. Such dissonance could prompt individuals to start engaging in unhealthy behaviours in order to fit into their social environment. Communal efforts to increase healthy behaviours often target individuals, relationships, and enactments, and they treat individuals as parts of a whole, collective community (Hecht and Choi 147). Practitioners interested in using this approach should analyze identity formation of their target audience at all four levels and should use a variety of individual appeals to enact a wider community change.

Endnotes

1. Participants selected their own pseudonyms to maintain anonymity.

Works Cited

Bannon, R. Sean, Matthew W. Brosi, and John D. Foubert. "Sorority Women's and Fraternity Men's Rape Myth Acceptance and By-stander Intervention Attitudes." *Journal of Student Affairs Research and Practice*, vol. 50, no. 1, 2013, pp. 72-87.

Banyard, Victoria L., et al. "Unwanted Sexual Contact on Campus: A Comparison of Women's and Men's Experiences." *Violence and Victims*, vol. 22, no. 1, 2007, pp. 53-71.

Burnett, Ann, et al. "Communicating/Muting Date Rape: A Co-cultural Theoretical Analysis of Communication Factors Related to Rape Culture on a College Campus." *Journal of Applied Communication Research*, vol. 37, no. 4, 2009, pp. 465-85.

Burt, Martha R. "Cultural Myths and Supports for Rape." *Journal of Personality and Social Psychology*, vol. 38, no. 2, 1980, pp. 217-30.

Dallimore, Elise. J. "Memorable Messages as Discursive Formations: The Gendered Socialization of New Faculty Members." Women's Studies in Communication, vol. 26, no. 2, 2003, pp. 214-65.

Earle, James P. "Acquaintance Rape Workshops: Their Effectiveness in Changing Attitudes of First Year College Men." *NASPA Journal*, vol. 46, no. 3, 2009, pp. 417-33.

Ellis, Jennifer Butler, and Sandi W. Smith. "Memorable Messages as Guides to Self-Assessment of Behavior: A Replication and Extension Diary Study." *Communication Monographs*, vol. 71, no. 1, 2004, pp. 97-119.

Friere, Paulo. *Pedagogy of the Oppressed: New Revised 20th Anniversary Edition*. Continuum, 1993.

Hecht, Michael L. and HyeJeong Choi. "The Communication Theory of Identity as a Framework for Health Message Design." *Health Communication Message Design: Theory and Practice*, edited by Michael L. Hecht, Sage, 2012, pp. 137-52.

Hecht, Michael L., Ronald L. Jackson, and Sidney A. Ribeau. *African American Communication: Exploring Identity and Culture*. 2nd ed. L. Erlbaum Associates, 2003.

Hust, Stacey J.T., et al. "The Effects of Sports Media Exposure on College Students' Rape Myth Beliefs and Intentions to Intervene in a Sexual Assault." *Mass Communication and Society*, vol. 16, no. 6, 2013, pp. 762-86.

Jung, Eura, and Michael L. Hecht. "Elaborating the Communication Theory of Identity: Identity Gaps and Communication Outcomes." *Communication Quarterly*, vol. 52, no. 3, 2004, pp. 265-83.

Karjane, Heather M., Bonnie S. Fisher, and Francis T. Cullen. *Sexual Assault on Campus: What Colleges and Universities are Doing about It*. National Institute of Justice, 2005.

Knapp, Mark. L., Cynthia Stohl, and Kathleen K. Reardon. "Memorable Messages." *Journal of Communication*, vol. 31, no. 4, 1981, pp. 27-41.

Krakauer, Jon. *Missoula: Rape and the Justice System in a College Town*. Doubleday, 2015.

Kranstuber, Haley, Kristen Carr, and Angela M. Hosek. "'If You Can Dream It, You Can Achieve It.' Parent Memorable Messages as Indicators of College Student Success." *Communication Education*, vol. 61, no. 1, 2012, pp. 44-66.

Lisak, David, and Paul M. Miller. "Repeat Rape and Multiple Offending among Undetected Rapists." *Violence and Victims*, vol. 17, no. 1, 2002, pp. 73-84.

Masters, N. Tatiana. "'My Strength is Not for Hurting': Men's Anti-Rape Websites and Their Construction of Masculinity and Male Sexuality." *Sexualities*, vol. 13, no. 1, 2010, pp. 33-46.

McMahon, Sarah, and Victoria L. Banyard. "When Can I Help? A Conceptual Framework for the Prevention of Sexual Violence through Bystander Intervention." *Trauma Violence Abuse*, vol. 13, no. 1, 2012, pp. 3-14.

Miller-Ott, Aimee E., and Alicia Linder. "Romantic Partners' Use of Facework and Humor to Communicate About Sex." *Qualitative Research Reports in Communication*, vol. 14, no. 1, 2013, pp. 69-78.

Murphy, Michael J. "Can 'Men' Stop Rape? Visualizing Gender in the 'My Strength Is Not for Hurting' Rape Prevention Campaign." *Men and Masculinities*, vol. 12, no. 1, 2009, pp. 113-30.

Nazione, Samantha, et al. "Memorable Messages for Navigating College Life." *Journal of Applied Communication Research*, vol. 39, no. 2, 2011, pp. 123-43.

Orbe, Mark P., et al. "Memorable First Time Sexual Experiences: Gendered Patterns and Nuances." *Communication Quarterly*, vol. 62, no. 3, 2014, pp. 285-307.

Reno, Jenna E., and L.G. McNamee. "Do Sororities Promote Members' Health? A Study of Memorable Messages Regarding Weight and Appearance." *Health Communication*, vol. 30, no. 4, 2015, pp. 1-13.

Rodriguez, Jose I., et al. "Assessing the Impact of Augusto Boal's 'Proactive Performance': An Embodied Approach for Cultivating Prosocial Responses to Sexual Assault." *Text and Performance Quarterly*, vol. 26, no. 3, 2006, pp. 229-52.

Schroeder, Lauren P. "Cracks in the Ivory Tower: How the Campus Sexual Violence Elimination Act Can Protect Students from Sexual Assault." *Loyola University Chicago Law Journal*, vol. 45, no. 4, 2014, pp. 1195-1245.

Schwartz, Martin D. and Walter S. DeKeseredy. *Sexual Assault on the College Campus: The Role of Male Peer Support*. Sage, 1997.

Smith, Sandi W., Jennifer Butler Ellis, and Hyo-Jin Yoo. "Memorable Messages as Guides to Self-Assessment of Behavior: The Role of Instrumental Values." *Communication Monographs*, vol. 68, no. 4, 2001, pp. 325-39.

Smith, Sandi W., et al. "Topics and Sources of Memorable Breast Cancer Messages and Their Impact on Prevention and Detection Behaviors." *Journal of Health Communication*, vol. 14, no. 3, 2009, pp. 293-307.

Stohl, Cynthia. "The Role of Memorable Messages in the Process of Organizational Socialization." *Communication Quarterly*, vol. 34, no. 3, 1986, pp. 231-49.

Strauss, Anselm, and Juliet Corbin. *Basics of Qualitative Research: Techniques and Procedures for Developing Grounded Theory*. 2nd ed. Sage, 1998.

Tracy, Sarah J. *Qualitative Research Methods: Collecting Evidence, Crafting Analysis, Communicating Impact*. Wiley-Blackwell, 2013.

Wang, Tiffany R. "Understanding the Memorable Messages First-Generation College Students Receive from On-Campus Mentors." *Communication Education*, vol. 61, no. 4, 2012, pp. 335-57.

Chapter Seven

Politics of Consent and the Problem with Focusing on Violence

Olga Marques and Jen Rinaldi

September 2017 marked the first academic year wherein all Ontario universities were required to enact mandatory sexual assault policies. These policies not only detail procedural rules but also commit universities to addressing rape culture on campuses throughout the province. Rhetorics of consent are found in these policies' renewed attention to the mantra of "no means no" and the rearticulation of consent as affirmative through a discursive shift towards "yes means yes." Though significant, these reforms still rely on "narrow and problem-focused terms" that conceptualize sex using "biomedical and public health discourses" (Bowleg et al. 588). That is, university policies continue to talk about consent in the context of sex as violence. This chapter explores the following question: How can we recognize violence if we do not know what sex is supposed to—or can—look like?

Ontario university policies feature articulations of sex that continue to focus on cis-heteropenetrative sex acts as the key event of consequence, masking sexual actors and relationships as well as a range of sites and acts of pleasures. The implications of this narrowly conceived version of consent are manifest in, and reinscribed by, mandated policies that derive from existing sociocultural definitions of sex and sexual conduct, without problematizing them. All of the focus on preventing sexual violence—premised on the shared assumption and understanding of what sex is—means that campus communities are not learning about or arriving at any consensus about what they desire, how they are engaging with one another, what a positive sexual experience would or even could look like, and how different configurations of sex can be as long as individuals are conscious of want and comfort.

In this chapter, we seek to rewrite the vocabularies of sex and sexual conduct. We explore the potentialities of sex and what sex means. Rather than discussing sex from the starting point of violence, we advocate for a discursive shift towards sexual conduct and behaviour. To accomplish this, we begin with a critical reading of recent Ontario-based university policies on sexual violence. Then, through recommendations informed by campus campaigns mobilizing around expansive understandings of affirmative consent, we consider what comes next—that is, how to cultivate campus culture related to sexual conduct untethered from sexual violence.

Sexual Violence on Postsecondary Campuses

Increased media reporting of high profile sexual assault cases, the scope of the #MeToo movement, and the broadened platform afforded to survivors and activists, have drawn much attention to the issue of sexual violence on postsecondary campuses across Canada and the United States (U.S.). Media and social media accounts are buttressed by scholarly research that continues to replicate findings that sexual violence on campus is a serious problem. Studies assessing sexual victimization prevalence rates on college and university campuses estimate that between 20 and 25 per cent of women who frequent campuses are at risk of attempted or completed sexual assault (DeKeseredy and Kelly; Fisher et al.; Karjane et al.; Krebs et al.). Despite the implementation of prevention and response initiatives, victimization rates have remained relatively stable for thirty years (Banyard et al., Rozee and Koss). Significantly, these initiatives have not served to change disclosure or reporting rates. In the U.S., national surveys have found that between 5 and 13 per cent of college women who experienced attempted or completed rape report to the police (Fisher et al.). Low rates of reporting have similarly been confirmed in Canadian studies (DeKeseredy and Kelly).

The situational circumstances that surround an experience of sexual violence are often difficult and complicated. Within the context of the postsecondary campus, these complexities are magnified by a shared geographic and living environment, organized social groups, varsity culture as well as a university experience associated with substance consumption, riskier sociosexual expectations and behaviour, and the party scene (Peterson and Muehlenhard; Van Wie and Gross). Experiential accounts and alarming statistics of sexual violence on campus have resulted in provincial mandates requiring postsecondary institutions to implement reporting systems and to formalize procedures for student disclosure.

Policy Developments

In March 2015, the government of Ontario published an action plan to end sexual violence and harassment (*It's Never Okay* 1). In an opening statement to the plan, Premier Kathleen Wynne articulated the motivations for assembling the document: "Above all, we want to challenge and change the deep-rooted attitudes and behaviours that contribute to sexual violence and harassment" (2). The provincial government committed to, among other things, amending legislation to require that postsecondary institutions adopt sexual violence policy; supporting public education programs to facilitate consent culture; and supporting initiatives designed to render postsecondary contexts safe.

The government's action plan led to Bill 132, or the Sexual Violence and Harassment Plan Act, which received Royal Assent in March 2016. The Bill established a framework for colleges and universities to draft or update their sexual violence policies. Respective policies must address sexual violence that postsecondary students experience and establish an institutional process for addressing incidents and complaints of sexual violence (section [sec.] 17[3][a][b]). The Bill required that policies be drafted and reviewed in consultation with students and that postsecondary institutions implement policy and related measures in accordance with legal regulations (sec. 17[4]; sec. 17[6][a][b]).

The policies developed at postsecondary institutions across the province share key definitions in common. Among them, definitions of sexual violence encompass acts of assault, harassment, stalking, sexual exploitation, indecent exposure, and voyeurism (e.g., Brock University Sexual Violence and Harassment Policy, sec. 1.1); more broadly sexual violence refers to "any sexual act or act targeting a person's sexuality, gender identity or gender expression, whether the act is physical or psychological in nature, that is committed, threatened or attempted against a person without the person's consent" (e.g., University of Guelph Sexual Violence Policy, sec. 5[a]; University of Ottawa Policy 67b on Prevention of Sexual Violence, sec. 3.2). Integral to the definition of sexual violence, consent is described in policy as active, affirmative, and direct (e.g., Brock University Sexual Assault and Harassment Policy, appendix 2); ongoing and informed (e.g., University of Guelph Sexual Violence Policy, sec. 5[c]); and unimpaired and conscious (e.g., University of Ottawa Policy 67b on Prevention of Sexual Violence sec. 3.2). Many policies address how consent cannot be assumed or implied, particularly in the absence "no;" cannot be obtained through threat, coercion, or pressure; can be revoked at any time; and cannot be given when the person whose consent is sought is impaired by alcohol or illicit substances (e.g., University of Windsor Policy on Sexual Misconduct, sec. 4.8; University of Guelph Sexual Violence Policy, sec. 5[c]).

Although much of the text in these policies focuses on reporting mechanisms, some policies explicitly identify an institutional responsibility to prevent sexual violence. For instance, the University of Brock identifies the university's twinned obligations to "foster an environment that is free of Sexual Violence" and to "engage with Brock Community Members to establish mechanisms to prevent and respond to Sexual Violence" (Brock University Sexual Violence and Harassment Policy, sec. 5.3). In its policy, York University affirms its "ongoing commitment to foster a culture where attitudes and behaviours that perpetuate sexual violence are rejected, survivors are supported, and those who commit incidents of sexual violence are held accountable" (York University Policy on Sexual Violence, sec. 4.1). York University distinguishes between responsibilities to accountability (e.g., via reporting), to survivors (e.g., via disclosures), and to campus culture (e.g., via educational programs). The University of Windsor Policy on Sexual Misconduct calls upon university members to contribute to prevention by "learning about sexual misconduct [via educational programs];" "modelling healthy and respectful behaviour in personal and professional relationships;" "speaking out against behaviour that encourages sexual misconduct and assault [and] discourages reporting;" "developing the skills necessary to be an effective and supportive ally;" and "intervening in situations that could lead to sexual misconduct [or] to prevent sexual misconduct when it is safe to do so" (sec. 10.1).

Advocacy Groups and Policy Review

Much stock has been put into policy development. As articulated by the Ontario Women's Directorate (see also METRAC 6), effective and clear policies help facilitate "an environment where everyone on campus knows that sexual violence is unacceptable, victims receive the services they need, and perpetrators are held accountable" (ON Women's Directorate 11). The question of whether policies are effective and clear—and indeed, whether they are enough—has, thus, been subject to ample scrutiny. Our Turn, a national student movement first founded at Carleton University, developed an action plan to review postsecondary institutional policies on sexual violence according to a checklist developed through research and in consultation with student groups (Our Turn 38). Highlights from the checklist include mechanisms to ensure procedural fairness, such as an immunity clause for minor drug and alcohol use (such a clause can be found in York University Policy on Sexual Violence, sec. 8.3) and clear timelines (e.g., University of Lethbridge Harassment and Discrimination Policy sec. 1). Policies were critiqued in the Our Turn review for including gag orders (gag order allowances can be found in Carleton University Sexual Violence Policy sec. 8.5[b]) as well as loopholes involving a suspected perpetrator's relationship to the university (e.g., Laurentian University Policy on Response and Prevention of Sexual Violence, sec. 9). Our Turn praised the inclusion of language recognizing the intersectional impacts of sexual violence (e.g., University of Ontario Institute of Technology [UOIT][1] Policy on Sexual Violence for Students and Procedures for Responding to Incidents of Sexual Violence, sec. 7) as well as the language acknowledging the existence of campus rape culture (e.g., University of Ryerson Sexual Violence Policy, sec. V[2])— but it found that few policies included these sorts of passages.

More specific and pointed critiques also abound. Elizabeth Sheehy and Daphne Gilbert criticize Ontario institutional policies adapted and adopted in compliance with Bill 132 for decriminalizing and privatizing sexual violence (293). The authors argue that these robust frameworks for responding to sexual violence consign these incidents to the realm of university administrators, and, in so doing, may foreclose criminal legal action. Further, Elizabeth Quinlan expresses concern that postsecondary schools have been reactive rather than preventative (7). Julie Lalonde concurs, noting that student groups working to prevent sexual violence are more likely to find institutional support only if a scandal has already rocked their campus: "One campus-based expert I spoke with expressed great frustration that their campus was missing a major opportunity to 'get ahead' of the issue. 'We don't have a 'scandal' yet, but it's only a matter of time before we do, so why not focus on prevention now?'" (266). A reactive approach is also embedded in the policies themselves, inasmuch as they cover how to respond to incidents and complaints—that is, policies tend to lack detailed consideration for preventative or even culture-building mechanisms.

In an effort to fill this culture-building gap, student groups have been creatively grappling with campus consent culture notwithstanding, alongside, and beyond policy developments. For example, the University of Guelph built SAFE (Sexual Assault Free Environment), a public education program that promotes healthy sexual relationships (i.e., relationships that respect consent) (*It's Never Okay* 28). At Wilfrid Laurier University, the student group Advocates for a Student Culture of Consent built the Consent is Golden campaign, which promotes ethical sexual practice. They also developed Beyond Consent programming, wherein they consider how gender violence and land violence interrelate, or how consent culture unfolds on lands stolen through processes of white settler colonialism (Berzins). The Canadian Federation of Students' No Means No campaign for twenty years has hosted Consent Culture forums at the federal and provincial levels (Quinlan 8).

These campaigns are not above reproach, however. Norma Jean Profitt and Nancy Ross, for example, caution: "Although these campaigns may potentially help some students negotiate sexual encounters, do they imply that sexual violence is primarily the outcome of ambiguous communication while leaving questions of power and the sociopolitical context of violence unexamined?" (204). Despite vibrant student advocacy, campus sexual violence has remained prevalent and pervasive, so Profitt and Ross ask: "[Does] the emphasis on 'miscommunication,' 'gray rape' (the blurred line between consensual and nonconsensual intercourse), and ignorance about the meaning of consent itself ... add up to a reflection of misogynist culture[?]" (204). Ann J. Cahill explores the problem of the emphasis on consent in sexual violence policy. In her own words: "Focusing on consent hides rather than illuminates sexual inequality" (283). In her example, clear and consistent identification of consent becomes the responsibility of the giver, and a complicated one at that when students receive no sexual education to teach them what consent looks like. She elaborates:

> When consent is used as a hallmark of an ethical sexual interaction, there is almost always an underlying assumption that it is the female-identified partner who is giving or withholding consent; the male-identified partner is assumed to be offering that which can be consented to, or not. This framework assumes a heteronormative sexual narrative in which heterosexual men are the primary desirers of sex, and women do not so much desire sex as concede to it. (282-83).

Conceptualizing Mainstream Sexual Conduct as Heteronormative and Phallocentric

Narratives about sex and sexuality shape the ways sex is spoken about, the ways laws and policies are formulated, as well as the ways in which sexual conduct—and engaging in sexual conduct—is framed within the broader society. The norms that structure gender, sexuality, and sexual conduct place a high premium on compulsory heteropatriarchy. Stevi Jackson writes that heteronormativity is "the normalization of heterosexuality which renders any alternative sexualities 'other' or 'marginal'" (163). Embedded in the whole field of social relations and social life, heteronormativity is a particularly useful concept in understanding how the very acts of sex and sexual conduct are culturally scripted and socially navigated. The denial of women's sexuality is a key component of Adrienne Rich's concept of "compulsory heterosexuality" (638). In heteronormativity, women's sexuality is built upon men's sexuality: without male pleasure, there is no female pleasure. This includes the centrality of the male orgasm to the very definition of sex. More than a simple biological fact, sex has historically been discussed and defined from a man's point of view. Heterosexual sex begins with the male erection and finishes with the male orgasm, framing female sexual pleasure as secondary, lacking, irrelevant, or wholly based on the satisfaction she receives in knowing her male partner was satisfied. Heteronormative understandings of women's sexual pleasure define it as dependent on the male orgasm; it is through knowing, seeing, and experiencing her male partner's orgasm that a woman is able to experience her own pleasure. This is not to say that women do not derive sexual pleasure through penetrative intercourse or that women do not desire to pleasure male partners. The point here is that heteronormative understandings of sex juxtapose male and female sexuality and delineate what constitutes appropriately gendered sexual expressions and expectations.

Another heteronormative aspect of the construction of sexuality and sexual conduct is the passivity of women's sexuality. Men are the initiators of sex and women are waiting to be taken by men (Fassinger and Arseneau). Indeed, the common (gendered) colloquialisms that frame first sexual experiences reiterate heteronormative, cis-centric, and phallocentric normative discourses of sex—that is, women "give it up" and men "get some." Traditional gendered narratives identify women as being not sexual (though sexualized), forbidding women pleasure for its own sake. If women admitted "to taking pleasure from sexuality expressed outside of a 'loving, equal relationship' or in unconventional acts, [they were] perceived to be somehow legitimizing male violence rather than acting assertively" (Assiter and Carol 16). Sex, in heteropatriarchal society, is constructed as something for men.

Sexuality, sexual desire, and sexual conduct—like sex and gender—are cultural and discursive constructions, not immutable or wholly biological. They are learned and constructed through representation (Bhattacharyya; Crawley et al.), although "sexual desire and pleasure are often thought of as belonging to an essentially pre-social, inherent, or 'given' realm" (Mason-Grant 121). The corollary of this position, which is what we posit throughout this chapter, is that ideations of sexual conduct are capable of being constructed and deconstructed. The gendered scripts that shape the practices and possibilities of sexual behaviours, as well as structure our understandings of sexual interactions and what sexed bodies do, merit contemplation. It is social and cultural contexts that give rise to meanings and understandings; thus, the transformation, maintenance, and proliferation of these meanings and understandings must enter into the analysis. It is not enough to merely change the language of consent if the stories we collectively tell ourselves about sex (e.g., who sex is for, whose pleasure is paramount, who is allowed to say "yes," what types of sex there are, and, even, what sex means) remain unchallenged. Sex, for Gargi Bhattacharya "has been revealed as highly historicized, deeply social, always contextual—and as a result, always vulnerable to reworking by other shifts in the terrain of the social." She continues: "However timeless and natural it may feel, sexual expression must bear the impressions of other determinations—otherwise how would we make sense of it (159)?"

Heteropatriarchal discourse uses a lexicon from which individuals draw in the meaning making and understanding of sexual encounters. If sex starts from the male perspective, then so too do understandings of what is not sex. As Nicola Gavey articulates, the "whole question of whether rape is to do with sex or with violence arises from a fixation on the masculine point of view" (33). Heteronormative understandings of male and female sexuality are imbued with an active-passive, or dominant-submissive, dynamic. Normative cultural discourses surr-ounding sexual encounters—and in turn which dismiss coercive, forced, or violent aspects of these encounters—rest upon notions of male sexual persistence and women's sexual resistance and acquiescence. Take for instance, this scenario described by Margaret Wente, columnist for the *Globe and Mail*:

> Here's a mini quiz. Imagine that you are a 26-year-old graduate student. You invite a semi-famous writer to a writing workshop. Some time during the visit, he kisses you against your will. Do you: (a) tell him to cut it out, and quietly spread the word that he's a bit of a jerk? Or do you (b) nurse your grievance for six years and confront him publicly at a writer's festival, from which he is then forced to withdraw because of #MeToo? Naturally, I would answer (a). Back when I was in the publishing business, I did answer (a). Never, never would I have contemplated option (b)—not because I was scared, or feared for my career, but be-cause it's just not that big a deal. So what? That's life. Move on. I've had dozens of conversations with older women who feel the same way.

Margaret Wente reiterates backlash commentary that men should now fear sexual advances and acts with women, that women today are hypersensitive to what is considered part of a so-called normal sexual exchange, and that absent overt acts of physical force or violence, unwanted sexual acts are part and parcel of sexual encounters. Although much time is spent on talking and teaching about sexual violence and rape, there has been less focus, however, on how heteronormative and phallocentric models of sex rest upon rape-supportive discourses and practices. As Gavey poignantly states: "if you tell us that women's accounts of rape are really just accounts of sex, then there is something very wrong with this model of sex" (34). To this she urges us to "call into question the politics and morality of everyday heterosexual sex— including those forms that no one was calling rape" (34).

Awareness campaigns telling us to teach how not to rape abound. But in conversation with both senior high school and university students, in the classroom context, students were adamant with the first author that they knew not to rape. They knew not to pin down and/or physically, to the point of injury, force another person to have sex. They know "stranger danger" rhetoric and risk management, responsibilization, and avoidance strategies. What they knew less of was what sex apart from violence looks like. Discourses on sex that only connect to sexual violence (from unwanted sexual conduct to rape) map on to "broader ideologies of gender and power, revealing how naming remains inextricably intertwined with gender roles, constraints, and expectations" (Fahs 66).

Problematizing Consent

Although sex is socially and culturally posited as cis-heteropenetrative, commencing and ending from the male experience, research indicates that personal definitions of what counts as sex can vary. For instance, Zoe Peterson and Charlene Meuhlenhard outline a ranking system of sexual behaviours, with penile-vaginal intercourse counting as sex, oral/anal sex in dispute (sex to some, not sex to others), and kissing generally not considered sex. Personal definitions of what counts as wanted or unwanted sex, or sexual violence, also vary depending on the nature of the relationship between the individuals involved in the sexual encounter.

Such wide disagreement over what constitutes sex and sexual violence may contribute to underreporting of sexual assault and/or rape. Focused specifically on the campus experience, approximately half of college/university women do not label coercive or unwanted sexual experiences as rape (Bondurant; Kahn et al.). Breanne Fahs explains:

The use of the term "rape" seems contingent on the qualities of both the perpetrator and the victim. Women who labeled their experience as rape more often experienced a forceful assault by an acquaintance, awakening to someone performing a sexual act on them without consent, or experiencing the assault as a child. Women less often called their experience rape if they submitted to a whining or begging boyfriend, gave in to an emotionally needy man, were assaulted by a boyfriend, were severely impaired by alcohol or drugs and unable to resist, were forced to engage in oral or manual sex rather than penetrative intercourse (Kahn 2004), or reported that they initially wanted the sexual intercourse more (Peterson and Muelenhard 2004). Women did not label acts as rape when their scripts about the rape experience did not match the events in which rapes occurred (Little, Rhatigan, and Axsom 2007) or if they had experienced sexual violence during their youth (McCloskey and Bailey 2000). (66).

Research has uncovered many situations and scenarios that lead women not to identify unwanted sexual conduct as rape or sexual violence: feelings of stigma (Littleon and Breitkof), acceptance of rape myths or to protect the male partner (Fahs), an extensive sexual history, or whether the sexual encounter involved foreplay (Flowe et al.). Taken together, "situations that dictate men's sexual access to women—particularly dating and longer-term relations—led more often to underreporting of rape if and when it occurred" (Fahs 66).

If definitions of sex are variable and personal—and the labelling of coercive, nonmutual, or forced sexual interactions is inconsistent and contextual—and both are gendered processes, how then can we cultivate campus cultures of consent when we do not start off with shared understandings and languages of sex and consent? Although campus policies and awareness programming exist on campuses, they are based on administrators' common sense understandings about sex, sexuality, relationships, and consent—not the common sense understandings of students. Policies and campaigns continue to frame sex through the starting point of violence, elevating discussion of risks and sexual assault while subsuming discussions of pleasure, want, and desirability. Research has found that coercion tends to take a more "playful" rather than aggressive turn in adolescent sexual interactions. For instance, researchers have found that adolescent perpetrators of sexual persistence did not categorize their behaviour as coercive but rather "as playful or beneficial, indicating that the behaviours were intended to improve the relationships" (Struckman-Johnson, Struckman-Johnson, and Anderson 85).

The mantra "No Means No" is ubiquitous in sexual violence prevention and awareness programming. Although the verbal or nonverbal evocation of "no" is a pivotal cultural and legal fascination, in social and interpersonal practice blatant declarations of "no" are uncommon. Celia Kitzinger and Hannah Frith explain that in sexual situations, saying "no" is supposed to clearly refuse the sexual advances and solicit the appropriate reaction from the pursing party; however, in typical non-sexual refusal situations, people rarely say no. Rather, cultural conversational norms dictate the provision of an excuse or apology that serves to mitigate any subsequent ill feelings of the rebuffed friend or acquaintance. It is only in communications with strangers when people are more likely to assert a no. What then does this social convention tell us about the infallibility accorded to the outright verbal refusal of unwanted sexual behaviour, particularly when statistics continue to suggest that date, acquaintance, and relationship rape and sexual violence are more prevalent than stranger rape? What does it mean for the success of policy and programming that we continue to teach students to say no when it goes against social convention, particularly gendered social conventions?

Looking beyond Policy

What does this discussion mean for campus sexual violence policies and prevention strategies that focus exclusively on articulations of scenarios absent consent, particularly when research indicates that consent, and its communication, is complex and relies on common-sense heteronormative and patriarchal binaries? Our answer here is twofold. First, following organization mandates like Our Turn's, we suggest that there are places in policy that can be improved. There are substantive, affirmative components to consent that could be identified in policies in order to clarify campus cultural understandings of the term, its significance to sexual encounters, and its impact on responsibility and desire. Furthermore, policy could commit universities to community- and culture-building work endeavours to approach sexual violence proactively rather than reactively. Even if the nature of that commitment remains vague, policy language on preventative and educational strategy opens potential spaces in campus contexts for discussion on sex politics.

Second, we could look beyond policy. Given the objective of university and college policies, (i.e., to prevent sexual violence), there will inevitably be reactive components. Also, the focus on sexual violence carries a logic within the parameters of the document. Policy can provide a framework and recourse when a person has experienced sexual violence. It may be the case, then, that policies are limited and disappointing tools when it comes to supporting the shift in understandings about sex away from the violent and towards the pleasurable.

Research and social media have increased public awareness of the scope of sexual violence occurring on postsecondary campuses, which has triggered polarized responses towards the demand for increased transparency of sexual assault disclosures, incidents, and reporting practices, increased attention to campus adjudication measures, and increased movement towards affirmative consent prior to engaging in sexual conduct. While such renewed attention to sexual violence presents a positive movement forwards, it is also narrowly conceived. The push away from classic rape rhetoric, such as the "stranger danger" scenario, for instance, has not been without vitriolic resistance, which seeks to heighten and further entrench women's responsibilization for any sexual misconduct or violence incurred. That we continue to talk about sexual violence without first talking about what sex is and is not—and about how sex is understood by participants and is socially and culturally positioned—is cause for concern. That we focus all attention to the presence of a "no"—or a "yes"—without unsettling basic assumptions about who can say "no" or "yes" to sex, about whose words or actions are scripted into hegemonic scripts of sexual conduct, and about whose retelling of accounts is afforded primacy should also give us pause.

Endnotes

1. The University of Ontario Institute of Technology is now known as Ontario Tech University.

Works Cited

Assiter, Alison, and Avedon Carol. *Bad Girls and Dirty Pictures: The Challenge to Reclaim Feminism*. London: Pluto Press, 1993.

Banyard, Victoria, L., et al. "Revisiting Unwanted Sexual Experiences on Campus: A 12 Year Follow-Up." *Violence against Women*, vol. 11, no, 4, 2005, pp. 426-46.

Berzins, Taylor. "We Believe Survivors Expert Panel Abridged." *YouTube*, 2018, www.youtube.com/watch?v=Iu6Q5JlUPwA. Accessed 29 Apr. 2020.

Bhattacharyya, Gargi. *Sexuality and Society. An Introduction*. Routledge, 2002.

Bondurant, Barrie. "University Women's Acknowledgement of Rape. Individual, Situational, and Social Factors." *Violence against Women*, vol. 7, no. 3, 2001, pp. 294-315.

Bowleg, Lisa, et al. "Intersectional Epistemologies of Ignorance: How Behavioral and Social Science Research Shapes What We Know, Think We Know, and Don't Know about U.S. Black Men's Sexualities." *Journal of Sex Research*, vol. 54, no. 4-5, 2017, pp. 577-603.

Brock University. Brock University Sexual Violence and Harassment Policy. Policy Owner Office of the President. Approval Authority Board of Trustees. 2016.

Cahill, Ann J. "Why Theory Matters: Using Philosophical Resources to Develop University Practices and Policies Regarding Sexual Violence." *Sexual Violence at Canadian Universities: Activism, Institutional Responses, and Strategies*, edited by Elizabeth Quinlan et al. Wilfrid Laurier University Press, 2017, pp. 275-89.

Carleton University. *Carleton University Sexual Violence Policy*. Responsible Departments Office of the Vice-President (Students and Enrolment) and Equity Services. Approval Authority Board of Governors. 2016.

Crawley, Sara, et al. *Gendering Bodies*. Rowman and Littlefield, 2008.

DeKeseredy, Walter, and Katherine Kelly. "The Incidence and Prevalence of Woman Abuse in Canadian University and College Dating Relationships." *Canadian Journal of Sociology*, vol. 18, no. 2, 1993, pp. 137-59.

DeKeseredy, Walter, and Katherine Kelly. "Sexual Abuse in Canadian University and College Dating Relationships: The Contribution of Male Peer Support." *Journal of Family Violence*, vol. 10, no. 1, 1995, pp. 41-53.

Fahs, Breanne. "Naming Trauma. On the Political Necessity of Nuance in Rape and Sex Offender Discourses." *Critical Trauma Studies: Understanding Violence, Conflict and Memory in Everyday Life*, edited by M. J. Casper and E. Wertheimer, New York University Press, 2016, pp. 61-77.

Fassinger, Ruth, E., and Julie R. Arseneau. "Diverse Women's Sexualities." *Psychology of Women: A Handbook of Issues and Theories*, edited by F. L. Denmark and M. A. Paludi, Praeger Publishers, 2007, pp. 484-6.

Fisher, Bonnie, S., Francis T. Cullen, and Michael G. Turner. *The Sexual Victimization of College Women: Research Report*. National Institute of Justice. 2000.

Flowe, Heather, D., and Ebbe B. Ebbesen. "Rape Shield Laws and Sexual Behaviour Evidence: Effects of Consent Level and Women's Sexual History on Rape Allegations." *Law and Human Behaviour*, vol. 32, no. 2, 2007, pp. 159-75.

Gavey, Nicola. *Just Sex? The Cultural Scaffolding of Rape*. Routledge, 2005.

Government of Ontario. *It's Never Okay: An Action Plan to Stop Sexual Violence and Harassment*. Government of Ontario. March 2015.

Government of Ontario. *Sexual Violence and Harassment Plan Act (Supporting Survivors and Challenging Sexual Violence and Harassment)*. S.O. 2016, c. 2. 2016.

Jackson, Stevi. *Heterosexuality in Question*. Sage, 1999.

Kahn, Arnold, S., Virginia A Mathie, and Cyndee Torgler. "Rape Scripts and Rape Acknowledgement." *Psychology of Women Quarterly*, vol. 18, no. 1, 1994, pp. 53-66.

Karjane, Heather, M., Bonnie S. Fisher, and Francis T. Cullen. *Sexual Assault on Campus: What Colleges and Universities Are Doing about It*. Washington DC. 2005.

Kitzinger, Celia, and Hannah Frith. "Just Say No? The Use of Conversation Analysis in Developing a Feminist Perspective on Sexual Refusal." *Discourse & Society*, vol. 10, no. 3, pp. 293-316.

Krebs, Christopher P., et al. "College Women's Experiences with Physically Forced Alcohol- or Drug-Enabled, and Drug-Facilitated Sexual Assault Before and Since Entering College." *Journal of American College Health*, vol. 57, no. 6, 2009, pp. 639-47.

Lalonde, Julie. "From Reacting to Preventing: Addressing Sexual Violence on Campus by Engaging Community Partners." *Sexual Violence at Canadian Universities: Activism, Institutional Responses, and Strategies*, edited by Elizabeth Quinlan et al., Wilfrid Laurier University Press, 2017, pp. 257-74.

Laurentian University. *Laurentian University Policy on Response and Prevention of Sexual Violence*. Policy Owner Office of Administration President and Vice-Chair. Approval Authority Board of Governors. 2016.

Littleton, Heather, and Carmen R. Breitkopf. "Coping with the Experience of Rape." *Psychology of Women Quarterly*, vol. 30, no. 1, 2006, pp. 106-16.

Mason-Grant, Joan. *Pornography Embodied: From Speech to Sexual Practice*. Rowman and Littlefield, 2004. Print.

METRAC. *Sexual Assault Policies on Campus: A Discussion Paper*. 2014.

Ontario Women's Directorate. *Developing a Response to Sexual Violence: A Resource Guide for Ontario's Colleges and Universities*. Queen's Printer for Ontario, 2013.

Our Turn. *A National, Student-Led Action Plan to End Campus Sexual Violence*. Student Society of McGill University. 2016.

Peterson, Zoe D., and Charlene L. Muehlenhard. "Conceptualizing the 'Wantedness' of Women's Consensual and Nonconsensual Sexual Experiences: Implications for How Women Label Their Experiences with Rape." *Journal of Sex Research*, vol. 44, no. 1, 2007, pp. 72-88.

Profitt, Norma Jean, and Nancy Ross. "A Critical Analysis of the Report Student Safety in Nova Scotia: Co-Creating a Vision and Language for Safer and Socially Just Campus Communities." *Sexual Violence at Canadian Universities: Activism, Institutional Responses, and Strategies*, edited by Elizabeth Quinlan et al., Wilfrid Laurier University Press, 2017, pp. 193-218.

Quinlan, Elizabeth. "Violence Bodies in Campus Cyberspaces." *Sexual Violence at Canadian Universities: Activism, Institutional Responses, and Strategies*, edited by Elizabeth Quinlan et al., Wilfrid Laurier University Press, 2017, pp. 117-37.

Rich, Adrienne. "Compulsory Heterosexuality and Lesbian Existence." *Women: Sex and Sexuality*, vol. 5, no. 4, 1980, pp. 631-60.

Rozee, Patricia, D., and Mary P. Koss. "Rape: A Century of Resistance." *Psychology of Women Quarterly*, vol. 25, no. 4, 2001, pp. 295-311.

Sheehy, Elizabeth, and Daphne Gilbert. "Responding to Sexual Assault on Campus: What Can Canadian Universities Learn from US Law and Policy?" *Sexual Violence at Canadian Universities: Activism, Institutional Responses, and Strategies*, edited by Elizabeth Quinlan et al. Wilfrid Laurier University Press, 2017, pp. 291-327.

Struckman-Johnson, Cindy, David Struckman-Johnson, and Peter B. Anderson. "Tactics of Sexual Coercion: When Men and Women Won't Take No For an Answer." *Journal of Sex Research*, vol. 40, no. 1, 2003, pp. 76-86.

University of Guelph. *University of Guelph Sexual Violence Policy.* Policy Owner Provost and Vice-President (Academic), Vice-President (Finance, Administration and Risk). Approval Authority Board of Governors. 2017.

University of Lethbridge. *University of Lethbridge Harassment and Discrimination Policy.* Responsible Office Human Resources. Approval Authority Board of Governors. 2016.

University of Ontario Institute of Technology. *UOIT Policy on Sexual Violence for Students and Procedures for Responding to Incidents of Sexual Violence. Policy* Owner Provost and VP Academic. Approval Authority Board of Governors. 2016.

University of Ottawa. *University of Ottawa Policy 67b on Prevention of Sexual Violence.* Approval Authority Senate and Board of Governors. 2016.

University of Ryerson. *University of Ryerson Sexual Violence Policy.* Policy Owner Provost and Vice President; Vice-President, Administration and Finance. Approval Authority Board of Governors. 2016.

University of Windsor. *University of Windsor Policy on Sexual Misconduct.* Responsible Office President and Vice-Chancellor. Approval Authority Board of Governors. 2016.

Van Wie, Victoria E., and Alan M. Gross. "The Role of Woman's Explanations for Refusal on Men's Ability to Discriminate Unwanted Sexual Behavior in a Date Rape Scenario." *Journal of Family Violence,* vol. 16, no. 4, 2001, pp. 331-44.

Wente, Margaret. "The #MeToo Generation Gap." *Globe and Mail,* 18 May 2018, www.theglobeandmail.com/opinion/article-the-metoo-generation-gap/. Accessed 29 Apr. 2020.

York University. *York University Policy on Sexual Violence.* Policy Owner Secretariat. Approval Authority Board of Governors. 2016.

Chapter Eight

Rape Culture: The Need for an Intersectional, Comprehensive Social Justice Movement

Leigh Gaskin

Current political and social conversations concerning rape and sexual assault are enveloped in combating gender-based violence on college campuses nationwide. There are still groups working to fight sexual violence beyond the university campus, but the focus seems to have shifted to college women. Although fighting these forms of sexual violence on campuses is critical to becoming a rape-free society, legislation and social justice initiatives often disregard larger populations of women, girls, men, and boys who are routinely sexually assaulted and raped. This trend is not new. There are multilayered historical contexts that have shaped political, legal, and societal expectations for claims and prosecutions of rape and sexual assault. These circumstances involve significant connections to race, class, gender, and sexuality, among other factors, which shape the perception of who is a believable victim and which kinds of people deserve justice for sexual crimes committed against them. All of these concerns are part of rape culture, which is prevalent in the United States (U.S.), and will be the geographic centre of this analysis.

To better understand the mechanisms involved in creating and perpetuating rape culture, it must be defined. Rape culture is a social, political, economic, and governmental system that allows and continues the normalization of rape and sexual assault within a society (Buchwald, Fletcher, and Roth 5-8; Field 174-75; Ferguson). The specific actions, behaviours, and societal ideas that encompass rape culture include trivializing rape, rejecting the extensiveness of rape and sexual assault, and victim blaming (Freedman 1-32; Buchwald, Fletcher, and Roth 5-8; Field 174-75; Ferguson). In addition to the sexual objectification of women and girls, rape culture dismisses the psychological and physical effects that stem from sexual violence and perpetuate myths and untruths about sexual assault and rape (Freedman 1-32; Buchwald, Fletcher, and Roth 5-8; Field 174-75; Ferguson). The unification of these principles allows a culture of rape to remain invisible to most (Freedman, 1-32; Buchwald, eta-all. 5-8; Field, 174-175; Ferguson). Furthermore, rape culture is closely linked to sexism, racism, classism, homophobia, ageism, ableism, religious intolerance, and citizenship status, among other forms of oppression.

Rape culture is rooted in white supremacy, imperialism and colonization, patriarchy, and racism. The formation of white supremacy includes a racialized, gendered, sexualized, and classed sociohistorical order—one that continues to be evasive, yet indiscernible, for the majority of American society (Holland 1-39). Those are ways that both rape culture and white supremacy continue to dominate and control people within the American nation-state. Moreover, white supremacy assumes default heterosexuality (i.e., heteronormativity) and strict conformation to gender binaries (Holland 41-64). Both of which are homogeneous and severe punishments are given for any perceived or actual threat to their formation to forge social order based on identity.

Rigid gender roles trigger a social code based on appropriate positions and places for binary gender identity, which pre-dates white supremacist ideology, and led to the establishment of patriarchy. The basis of patriarchy is a system that automatically values men and boys over women and girls and seeks to base worth in society on the traits associated with masculinity and manhood, while devaluing feminine characteristics. The configuration of patriarchy, white supremacy, gender, class, and heteronormativity—prior to and after colonization and the subsequent transition to capitalism—is the underlying foundation of rape culture (Freedman 2-11). A culture of rape supports, condones, and furthers the sexual assault and rape of people in society, and it promotes structures that institutionalize victim/survivors (Buchwald, Fletcher, and Roth

295-99). Methods for control and punishment for victims and survivors are administered from varying locations within society, which include but are not limited to government, education, church, community, family, and the individual. These establishments are all hierarchical power structures that conform to and reinforce patriarchy. The infiltration of patriarchy in every aspect of society provides a safe haven for men and boys, who have the ability to move freely and openly in society without punishment for their behaviours, actions, and ideas related to rape and sexual assault.

Girls and women do not have the freedom to move and think without limits placed on them by society and the individual. In the context of sexual assault, rape, or the threat of either, these boundaries are used to manage the population by the white supremacist, capitalist, and heteropatriarchal government (Collins 218-28; A. Smith 1-33). The aim of which is to create a type of social and governmental code of conduct for girls and women, including strict gender roles, a cult of white womanhood as well as western beauty ideals that prize virginity, control sexuality, and must be adhered to (Freedman 6-18). Conforming to these demands confines girls and women to a subordinated status and makes them easier to control. At the same time, the benefit for those who do conform is that they are considered worthy of saving—paradoxically from a system deliberately created to keep them vulnerable.

It will never be enough for girls and women (predominately Caucasians) to be alleviated of the fears and actions associated with sexual violence. A. Smith explains: "Sexual violence is a tool by which certain peoples become marked as inherently 'rapable.' These peoples then are violated, not only through direct or sexual assault, but through a wide variety of state policies, ranging from environmental racism to sterilization abuse" (3). Society must work together for a common good, to end rape and sexual assault within our lifetimes. This goal should be facilitated through abolishing prisons, through aiding movements of formerly colonized peoples to decolonize their psyches, and supporting the sexual expression of people living with dis/abilities (Collins; Gutiérrez; Roberts; A. Smith). Society needs to address the violent hypermasculinity that confines boys and men to rigid gender standards, to support the reproductive freedoms of women of colour, and to demand a ceasefire to end all wars. All of the issues listed here are related to rape culture and, ultimately, must be resolved to end rape culture itself

(Collins; Gutiérrez; Roberts; A. Smith). The objective to end rape culture is not confined to stopping individual acts of rape and sexual assault, it is a commitment to identify, address, and rethink all aspects of society that condone and encourage rape and sexual assault in the U.S. One mechanism that supports and enforces rape culture is state-sanctioned violence (Collins 215-24).

In the U.S., state-sanctioned violence is the way in which the American government, as a nation-state, inflicts violence on specific groups of people for the purpose of regulating their activities through the threat, or the actual use, of violence (Collins 215-24). As Patricia Hill Collins writes, "In American society, sexual violence has served as an important mechanism for controlling African Americans, women, poor people, and gays and lesbians, among others" (216). These claims are echoed by Andrea Smith: "It is clear that the state has a prominent role in perpetrating violence against Native women in particular and women of colour in general" (5). With further examination of the historical legacies and legal sanctions placed on people of colour and women, it becomes apparent that state-sanctioned violence—centred upon raced, classed, and gendered characteristics that work in relation to one another and in a hierarchical manner that supports rape culture—condones sexual assault and rape as well as purposefully ignores the overall social problems associated with sexual violence.

Concurrently, the cult of white womanhood has constructed specific and rigid standards for public and private appropriateness, purity, submissiveness, and adherence to male authority. Beyond outlining behaviours of girls and women, the cult of white womanhood established a code of white Western Eurocentric beauty standards—which includes preferences such as hair texture and styles, particular body shapes and sizes, facial features, and petite stature. All women and girls are judged according to their bodies and their ability to embody fragile white femininity, obligated to a chaste life (Freedman 6-18). All women are exiled from freely expressing their own sexual desire and pleasure and are seen primarily as objects of desire for heterosexual men (Freedman 10).

In addition, the cult of white womanhood has promoted the proper place of white women as birthers of the nation-state and insisted they promote the values of white supremacy to their children as keepers of the republic (Freedman 2-15; M. Smith 1-15). This privileged yet confined middle-to-upper class white women to domestic pursuits; however, this status was rarely ever afforded to women of colour in American society. The standards associated with the cult of white womanhood continue to be the way that all women are judged; their lives validated by their ability to conform to societal expectations of white femininity. Thus, gender dynamics, the embodiment of a range of masculine and feminine characteristics and forms of sexuality are critical in understanding white supremacy and whiteness as power structures (Collins 25-69; Freedman 10). The valuation of white lives over those of people of colour in the U.S. supports institutional oppression and condones various structures of white supremacy, which are crucial to understanding American society and rape culture.

The reward for fitting into the confines of hegemonic white femininity is the illusion of safety and protection vis-à-vis the law and justice system. Such a situation creates an internal-external dialogue that continues to reinforce the code of conduct through individual discipline, victim blaming, slut shaming, and using intimidation to persuade victims not to report sexual assault. Grounding this contemporary example through historical context, Estelle Freedman writes that "Narratives of conquest and empire, which tended to naturalize sexual violence as part of historical processes, also significantly influenced American definitions of rape" (5). Accordingly, the narrative of rape disciplines girls and women as a group as well as individuals, and it controls their bodies and their ability to move freely throughout society. Thus, beyond being acts of sexual violence, the threat of rape and sexual assault also acts as a fear mechanism that regulates the behaviour of girls and women. The perpetuation of rape myths and common knowledge about the types of people who are raped creates a dialogue that supports a "master rape narrative" about who can and cannot be raped.

A master rape narrative creates and reinforces the illusion of the perfect victim—an attractive, white, cis-gendered, heterosexual, thin, abled-bodied, middle-class woman, who does not drink too much, wears the right clothing, is neither sexually provocative nor promiscuous, vocally says no, fights back during a sexual assault or rape event, and so on. Any person who falls beyond those parameters is typically told their case will not be good enough to go to trial, if, of course, the victim even decides to press charges or pursue a civil case. Thus, the majority of people who are sexual assault/rape survivors are rendered as "unrapeable";

their experiences are rejected as illegitimate, undeserving of support and help, ineligible for justice or retribution (A. Smith 1-23; Collins 215-24; Freedman 6-10). At the same time, however, national antirape and sexual assault organizations use the totalled number of all victims—those who report and the estimated numbers of those who do not—to advocate for justice that primarily impacts Caucasians. Again, it is the "be seen but not heard" rhetoric that has held true for so many identity groups in America, as they labor to gain equal rights that white Americans possess. It is no wonder that national activist and advocacy groups who address sexual assault and rape organize around college women and their victimization. College women embody what Americans value, adherence to the cult of white womanhood and the ability to fit within the master rape narrative.

The master rape narrative allows an individualized course of action to address the perceived causes and effects of rape and sexual assault in the U.S. In the current social, political, and economic climate, matters that are categorized as individual issues are in need of correction—rape and sexual assault are no different. The idea of a master rape narrative can be useful for three reasons: 1) it provides a funded outlet for victims to seek help regarding their experiences after a sexual assault/rape event has occurred; 2) it allows survivors of sexual assault and rape the opportunity to speak their truths, creating a visible community space for support; 3) it can provide a tangible, human story to a topic that is rarely discussed. However, the master rape narrative fails victims/survivors of sexual assault and rape by hiding the actual institutional, social, economic, and political reasons that the U.S. is not a rape-free country. The master rape narrative is convincing enough to elicit many types of programs at local, state, and national levels aimed at rape and sexual assault prevention and advocacy, but it does not strike at the heart of rape culture.

The purpose of a master rape narrative is transforming a statistical probability for girls and women, that they will be raped or sexually assaulted in their lifetime, into a monolithic one-off event, that the victim is an exception and not the rule. The reality is that a significant number of people, from all different groups, including people who are currently and formerly incarcerated, women of colour, men and boys, people from the trans community, undocumented peoples, aging populations, children, people living with disabilities, and far too many others are or will become victims/survivors of sexual assault. Girls and women living with disabilities are the most likely group to be sexually assaulted or raped in their lifetimes. Specifically, "83% of women with disabilities will be sexually assaulted in their lives," but only 3% of sexual abuse is reported (Disability Justice). However, there is little public outcry over the despicable amounts of rape and sexual assault perpetrated upon women living with disabilities. Those women deserve for their stories to be heard and to receive the justice they are far too often denied. Instead, there are national conversations about college women who will be sexually assaulted.

The Centre for Disease Control (CDC) estimates that nationally, "37.4% of female rape victims were first raped between ages 18-24." This CDC fact sheet is circulated to a wide audience of advocates, activists, medical professionals, and government officials. Within the fact sheet, that statistic is paired with another equally as horrifying fact, "In a study of undergraduate women, 19% experienced attempted or completed sexual assault since entering college" (Centre for Disease Control). In our society, one rape or act of sexual assault is far too many. Although college women only make up 19 per cent of sexual assault and/or rape victims, according to the CDC, the Obama administration and national victim advocacy groups, focus much of their prevention efforts on the group. Collectively, the subtle messaging is that college women should be the primary concern and their rapes matter. In the widely circulated CDC fact sheet, interestingly there is no mention of the rates of sexual violence among people living with disabilities. Focusing on one group, in this case, cis women enrolled in higher education, implicates those women are worthy of protecting and saving from a potential rape and conceals and silences others who are equally in need of help and assistance.

The ability to turn an epidemic of sexual violence into an isolated individual incident is the way that government and society elect to ignore the legacies of race, class, sexuality, dis/ability, and gender in society in addressing rape culture. Freedman argues that "The history of repeated struggles over the meaning of sexual violence reveals that the way we understand rape helps determine who is entitled to sexual and political sovereignty" (11). The reality is that not all women and girls will attend college due to systemic oppressions, such as race, class, dis/ability, nationality, citizenship status, age, and carcerality, among others. Such a focus on college students says to other groups of girls and women that the national conversation about sexual assault does not include them. It says that society is not concerned about providing legal protection to women of colour, trans women, women who lack citizenship status, women who are presently incarcerated, and women living with dis/ abilities. Their rapes do not seem to count, a reality that supports white supremacist heteropatriarchy—which signifies that only white women who possess economic privilege are valuable and worthy of protection and saving, which is situated in the cult of white womanhood.

This worthiness is defined by government and society, and it is troubling in the context of programming and funding for victim support agencies. Frequently, aid offered by government is administered through competitive grants or through contracts. A large portion of funding is funneled into the private or non-profit sectors, which offer support services, at market value, for sexual assault and rape victims. Yet both government-sponsored programs and non-profit organizations only emphasize how to prevent rape and sexual assault not on how to actually deal with the culture of rape. Such programming is turned into a product, much like educational services, and it is concerning for a number of reasons, especially considering the intensified efforts to contain sexual assault and rapes on college and university campuses. Often turning a service into a product, to productize is due to financial and public relations reasons. In the context of rape culture, is specifically the need for fewer lawsuits and less monetary payouts, now that students are suing universities and colleges under violation of Title IX legislation, all of which amount to negative publicity. In order for the educational product, for example the college experience, to sell there must be an image projected to student consumers, including aspects of safety. Thus, rape and sexual assault prevention programming on college campuses nationwide is at an all-time high due to those needs, not because of an actual concern for student safety or for a safer learning environment.

Moreover, colleges and universities can claim to be addressing and leading the response to campus-based sexual violence by adding prevention programming aimed at stalking, intimate partner violence, sexual harassment, and dating violence (Know Your IX), as those forms of gender-based violence were not previously included and connected to sexual violence. Other campus-based prevention programming includes Green Dot, It's On Us, Know Your IX, No More, Where Is Your Line?, and Stop Rape Now. Know Your IX, which was featured in a campus sexual assault awareness documentary film, *The Hunting Ground*, has gained many supporters and has helped victims/survivors of sexual assault and rape to sue their university based on Title IX violations. The institutionalization of not only the university, as a standardized product, but also sexual assault and rape creates a dialogue that provokes national debate that around saving college women. The point of including these programming organizations in this conversation about the foundations of rape culture, master rape narratives, and in an intersectional analysis of rape culture is not to say these programs do not work. It is, rather, to point out the historical, social, and political contexts that are rarely addressed in popular culture nor are they acknowledged in governmental action to quell sexual violence.

Activists and advocates who work within the field of rape culture have said that in order to combat rape culture, they must continue existing programming to create a culture of consent that lasts from birth until death, which includes all genders and sexualities; provides information about sexuality and sexual orientations, gender expression, sex education; and stresses affirmative consent, in which only "yes" means "yes" in all sexual activities. Society is in need of a cultural shift that understands rape and sexual assault as unacceptable. We must overcome social and cultural taboos about sexuality and create a non-patriarchal model for its expression.

Most importantly, activists and advocates must develop an inter-sectional and collaborative coalitional movement uniting against rape and sexual assault in American society. Freedman has highlighted the uneven social justice movements that previously addressed sexual assault and rape among girls, boys, women, and men:

> The struggle to redefine rape in America has remained historically invisible, in part because the disparate critics considered here never formed a unified social movement. No single organization, such as those focused on achieving suffrage or temperance, addressed sexual violence. Thus, there is no collection of national conference proceedings or a periodical devoted to the subject of exposing rape as a social and political problem. (8)

While many national organizations currently work on these issues—such as the Rape, Abuse & Incest National Network, the Date Safe

Project, End Rape on Campus, Rape Prevention and Education Program (a CDC project), SOAR | Speaking Out About Rape, and the National Alliance to End Sexual Violence—these groups have not drastically reduced the number of rapes and sexual assaults in the U.S. These groups, at minimum, emphasize and make visible the experiences of rape/sexual assault victims and advocate for justice on their behalf through the legal framework. We must be wary, however, of saying that these are the only needed and desired programs for sexual assault victims and survivors. Sometimes, programming groups combine rape and sexual assault victims' experiences and assemble them as a monolithic, homogenous group, which, in many ways, function as an identity marker.

The ways that diverse groups of women experience and recover from sexual assault and rape vary based on social location. An intersectional method for ending rape culture and sexual violence must involve multiple approaches, from grassroots organizations, national advocacy groups, governmental bodies, and people becoming anti-rape culture activists, and be expected to involve consensus leadership to end rape culture. We must demand more than rights-base legislation, legal protections, and public acknowledgments that forms of sexual violence occur. We must understand that flattening various experiences concerning rape and sexual assault into a master rape narrative does little to address the causes of rape. Formulating a plan to address and combat rape culture—which is a social, political, economic, psychological, and historical crisis—on a local, state, and national level is imperative and urgent. We must move forwards in an intersectional movement that demands a society free of rape and sexual assault. Nothing less will do.

Works Cited

Buchwald, Emilie, Pamela R. Fletcher, and Martha Roth, editors. *Transforming a Rape Culture.* Milkweed, 2005.

Center for Disease Control. "Sexual Violence Facts at a Glance" *CDC*, 2012, www.cdc.gov/ViolencePrevention/pdf/SV-DataSheet-a.pdf. Accessed 30 Apr. 2020.

Collins, Patricia Hill. *Black Sexual Politics: African Americans, Gender, and the New Racism.* Routledge, 2005.

Disability Justice. "Sexual Abuse." *Disability Justice*, 2016, disability justice.org/ sexual-abuse/. Accessed Apr. 30 2020.

Ferguson, Sian. "8 Appalling Examples of How Rape Culture Shows Up on College Campuses." *Everyday Feminism*, 2016, everyday feminism.com/2016/09/rape-culture -on-campuses/. Accessed 30 Apr. 2020.

Freedman, Estelle B. *Redefining Rape: Sexual Violence in the Era of Suffrage and Segregation.* Harvard University Press, 2013.

Gutiérrez, Elena R. *Fertile Matters: The Politics of Mexican-Origin Women's Reproduction.* University of Texas Press, 2008.

Holland, Sharon Patricia. *The Erotic Life of Racism.* Duke University Press. 2012.

Know Your IX. "Title IX." *Know Your IX*, 2016, http://knowyourix. org/title-ix/. Accessed 30 Apr. 2020.

Roberts, Dorothy. *Killing the Black Body: Race, Reproduction, and the Meaning of Liberty.* Vintage Books, 1997.

Smith, Andrea. Conquest: *Sexual Violence and American Indian Genocide.* Duke University Press, 2005.

Smith, Merril D., editor. *Encyclopedia of Rape.* Greenwood Press, 2004.

Chapter Nine

Online Rape Culture and Bystander Intervention

Jodie Bowers and Carolyn M. Cunningham

A number of controversial events have sparked conversations about how to address rape culture on college campuses. Rape culture can be defined as "an environment in which rape is prevalent and in which sexual violence against women is normalized and excused in media and popular culture" (Marshall). Thus, rape culture has two dimensions: one that includes actual violence and one that promotes violence through popular culture. It should be noted that although rape culture is primarily discussed in terms of women, men also experience rape culture.

In recent years, there have been several high profile events that have brought attention to college students' experiences with rape culture. For example, the documentary *The Hunting Ground* chronicles the high number of incidents of rape on college campuses and the difficulty of using university channels to address it. Robin Thicke's song "Blurred Lines" also sparked conversations about the normalization of women as victims of sexual aggression. Additionally, there have been a number of online efforts to counter rape culture and encourage victims to go public about sexual violence, such as the hashtag activism around #YesAllWomen—in which victims are encouraged to publicly share their experiences about sexual harassment and rape.

Online activism around rape culture seems a natural fit with the current generation of college students, who are considered digital natives tethered to their electronic devices. They use social media, such as Facebook and Twitter, to extend their networks and access popular culture. Due to always being online, students are more likely to witness or participate in discourses that can perpetuate rape culture. They also likely witness or become bystanders to instances of aggressive comm-unication that could be, and often is, considered cyberharassment which often happen in emotionally charged online communication. Thus, cyberharassment, bystanders, and their connection to perpetuating and challenging rape culture become important issues for colleges and universities.

This chapter provides tools for addressing aggressive communication and cyberharassment, especially in connection with rape culture, and outlines what steps college administrators, students, and faculty can take to counteract this growing problem. These new ways people experience rape culture call for the development of educational programs that not only address how society accepts these beliefs but it can begin to augment the status quo. We believe this change can be bolstered by teaching the importance of bystander intervention. Previous research in this area suggests that in face-to-face (FTF) situations, when bystanders intervene on behalf of a bullying victim, the bully tends to back off. Therefore, we argue that if bystanders intervene in hostile online conversations, then we can address online rape culture.

Rape Culture Online

In general, rape culture is defined as an environment in which sexual assault is normalized. The term first emerged in the 1970s during the second wave of feminist activism (Connell and Wilson 105), yet, more recently, the term has been used to describe a range of activities, including pervasive sexual assault on college campuses, rape jokes, victim blaming, and popular culture texts that promote rape.

In recent years, attempts have been made to address and change rape culture. Jessalyn Keller, Kaitlynn Mendes, and Jessica Ringrose argue that the reemergence of rape culture in public discourse can be linked in part to the rise in feminist online content. In their study of online feminist activism, they found that many of the young feminists became familiar with the term "rape culture" through their participation in online communities, such as Facebook, Tumblr, and Twitter. Through these media, girls and women can show support for victims of sexual assault and violence, send counter messages, and interrupt rape culture through creative interventions, such as the SlutWalk movement.

Victims are increasingly speaking out against sexual assault and victim blaming. For example, in 2011, after a Toronto police officer stated that "women should avoid dressing like sluts in order not to be victimized" (qtd. in Carr 24), feminist activists formed the social movement SlutWalk, which is designed to address slut shaming and victim blaming. SlutWalk hosts events to draw attention to the stigma of rape. In these events, women often reclaim the stigma around female sexual agency through dressing provocatively and reclaiming the term "slut".

Social movements like SlutWalk have not been without their criticisms. In a viral letter titled "An Open Letter from Black Women to SlutWalk Organizers" a number of African American women criticized the movement for not addressing the specific issues that they face, especially since Black women experience concerns about sexual assault differently. Thus, for Black women to call themselves "sluts" in an attempt to reclaim the word does not account for the specific concerns about sexual objectification that Black women have, and it would, in fact, perpetuate white privilege.

SlutWalk is just one example of how discourses of rape culture are negotiated and discussed. In recent years several online movements—including hashtag activism like #YesAllWomen, in which women are encouraged to share their own stories of misogyny and sexual assault—have offered different ways to address rape culture and have led to broader discussions about sexual assault and victimization (Rodino-Colocino 1113).

New forms of communication technologies can reinforce rape culture through victim blaming, but they may also provide new avenues for victims to speak and be heard. As Carrie Rentschler argues, online rape culture and feminist activism becomes a site for young women's activism (65). Here, social media offers young women not only platforms to speak out against online violence but also ways to participate in a feminist counterpublic (Sills et al. 1).

In their study of feminist online efforts to counteract and address rape culture, Keller, Mendes, and Ringrose found that Twitter may offer a safe way for victims of sexual assault to share their experiences. Posting to the Twitter handle #BeenRapedNeverReported, for example, can allow survivors of sexual assault to connect with a community of survivors. They can also feel a sense of solidarity and raise feminist consciousness.

College Students' Use of Social Media

In the current media landscape, it is no longer adequate to think of online life as separate from F2F life. People meet and communicate in a variety of forums; thus, aggressive forms of communication can occur anywhere. Additionally, social media platforms promote interactivity. These newer forms of communication allow users to comment on photos and posts or share a variety of media and events with larger audiences by sharing their posts as well as others' on their own accounts.

Whereas Facebook, Twitter, and Instagram require that users create a profile and thus the identity of the perpetrators or victims of cyberharassment may be tracked, newer forms of social media, such as Yik Yak and Snapchat, promote an element of anonymity. On Snapchat, user-generated content disappears after a specified amount of time, which makes it almost impossible to display the content again, whereas Yik Yak (now defunct) messages were posted anonymously and were then voted upon by other users for their popularity. Posts, or "yaks," were intended for "herds," or groups who were within a ten-mile radius of each other. Snapchat, in contrast, is a form of social media in which posts disappear once they are viewed by users unless they are shared on an individual's story. A Snapchat story is a series of snaps that can be added to by a user and remain available to be seen by that user's friends for a full twenty-four hours. It should be noted that at the time of this research, Yik Yak had ceased operation, but its absence does not diminish the significance of the platform's promotion of rape culture or the harassment users saw or experienced while using it. There are other apps that allow anonymous posting of content (e.g., whisper) and more are likely to be developed. For this reason, in this section of the chapter, we will look at several case studies that show how Yik Yak and Snapchat have promoted aggressive communication, cyberbullying, and rape culture.

Upon its release in 2013, Yik Yak was rapidly adopted by college students across the U.S. The appeal of being able to publish whatever one wanted, without being attached to the content, was a novel idea, thus spurring the app's initial success. The developers behind Yik Yak stated their inspiration for the app was to "level the playing field and connect everyone" (Mahler 8) while giving a voice to the disenfranchised individuals in a given physical location. The intent was that instead of only a select population of vocal students or individuals (such as popular college athletes, club members, etc.) having their voices heard, that those who were more introverted or perhaps hold a historically marginalized social status could also be heard through their anonymous communication on the app. According to TechCrunch blogger, Josh Constine, Yik Yak hit its peak usage in October 2014 with 2,067,000 active monthly users. Downloads of the app slowly declined, and the company saw several changes in leadership throughout its short lifespan. In April 2017, Yik Yak announced they would shutter their app and remove it from the app marketplace (Statt).

Unfortunately, due to the unique design of the app, Yik Yak gained notoriety for something other than evening the playing field. Users took advantage of the anonymity and location-based features the app offered and created an especially hostile environment on school campuses across the U.S. Due to the unique location-based usability of the app, the hostility did not remain online, victims were left wondering who around them was responsible for posting hateful comments and who around them was participating in the cyberharassment. Due to the app's popularity among harassers, it soon became accessible to middle and high school students across the U.S., places where instances of cyberbullying are rapidly increasing. Thanks to geo-fences, or virtual barriers—developed by the Yik Yak's creators (Mahler 8) as a means to combat cyberbullying and cyberharassment—the app was no longer accessible on middle school and high school campuses. Although such action was a step in the right direction, the app was still extensively used on college campuses, and for college administrators, determining what action they could take (if they took any at all) to curtail the cyber-harassment was hindered by questions surrounding free speech, which is outside the scope of the present chapter.

Another heavily used social networking app is Snapchat. According to a 2017 article by Zephoria Digital Marketing, Snapchat has over 200 million daily active users in the U.S., Canada, and the United Kingdom ("The Top 10"). Mediakix reported that 70 per cent of those users were under the age of thirty-five. Of that, 37% per cent are between the ages of eighteen and twenty-four (DeMers). Snapchat is a messaging app that allows users to chat as well as send pictures and videos, which can be edited with fun, daily-updated filters and text. However, Snapchat's main selling feature is that a "snap" is only available for a limited amount of time (up to ten seconds) and then disappears from the viewer's phone. This setup makes it easy for people with negative agendas to send out messages to specific individuals or to all of their followers with little, if any, repercussion. This feature leaves victims of harassment and cyber-bullying with no proof of the snap unless they capture it with another device.

Both public and anonymous forms of social media can lead to what John Suler calls an "online disinhibition effect" (321). Disinhibition occurs when people self-disclose more than what they normally would in a F2F context. In online situations, the level of disinhibition can be increased in an individual due to the anonymity computer-mediated communication affords its users. Disinhibition can also be experienced when people post and comment in a manner different than if their identity were known, which becomes problematic when social media users act in this manner and use the anonymity Snapchat provides to post hateful and aggressive comments. When others witness this type of behaviour, they may be more inclined to do the same, thereby perpetuating and normalizing the behaviour. By witnessing others participating in negative forms of communication—such as cyber-harassment, trolling, or flaming—they may see these forms of behaviours as acceptable because they are unlikely to be countered.

This is where bystander intervention is important. Bystanders have the ability to sway how a conversation plays out because studies indicate that when an aggressor is confronted in a F2F situation, he or she is likely to back down. Therefore, it is reasonable to theorize that the aggressor would also back down in an online situation if they were confronted by others or noticed others standing up for and supporting the victim. More outwardly displayed support for rape victims and supporters of antirape movements could produce the small changes necessary for larger shifts in what is deemed acceptable and normal by society.

However, as Holly Jeanine Boux and Courtenay Daum point out, smartphones and social media have changed the way society thinks about rape (149). Several sexual assaults have been documented through the use of smartphones, such as the Steubenville, Ohio, case. In this case, a thirteen-year-old girl was filmed by bystanders as she was sexually assaulted, and the case became well-known because of its documentation on social media, especially through Facebook, Twitter, and text messages. This is just one of the many ways that rape culture is perpetuated both in person and online. In this case, the assault occurred F2F, was witnessed and documented by bystanders, and was then spread virally online. Understanding how interventions can address bystander apathy, such as in this case, becomes especially crucial to changing rape culture.

Cyberharassment

As mentioned previously, rape culture has received increased attention due to its proliferation through social media platforms. This harmful online behaviour can occur through cyberharassment, a form of aggression in which perpetrators harass people online. There are a variety of forms of cyberharassment, including unwanted posts on social media sites, photoshopping pictures to depict graphic scenes, or unwanted and frequent emails and texts. One disturbing aspect of cyberharassment is rape threats targeted towards women.

In the United States (U.S.), there have been attempts to pass legislation against cyberharassment. These laws recognize the unique nature of cyberharassment: posts can come from victims who may not know the perpetrators and can occur beyond the U.S. border, which makes pros-ecuting cyberharassment more difficult.

Despite the difficulty of formal laws against perpetrators, it is important to recognize how victims may respond to cyberharassment. In her article "Why Women Aren't Welcome on the Internet," Amanda Hess argues that the prevalence of online rape threats against (primarily) women have become so normalized that it is difficult for victims to find help in the current legal system.

As previously mentioned, cyberharassment can be found throughout various social media channels. There are guidelines that each site sets, but some are more lax than others. For example, community standards on Facebook and Twitter allow for blocking users if they participate in cyberaggression, and when yak's were down voted five times, they were deleted from the bulletin board. However, even when social media accounts are blocked for violating community standards, perpetrators may find other outlets to bully or harass their victims. Equally problematic is the belief that individuals will self-police the content of their posts thus believing civility will persevere. Unfortunately, this does not always happen. Recently, there have been several cases of individuals being harassed anonymously via Yik Yak and Snapchat to such an extent where several of them have attempted suicide. Several of these instances also directly perpetuate our acceptance of rape culture. Here are just a few examples of cyberharassment perpetuated through Snapchat and Yik Yak as well as their aftermath:

- A Minnesota family took to YouTube to vent their frustrations concerning the harassment their adopted daughter had been experiencing through Snapchat. The harassers thought they could get away with these hurtful messages they were sending because of the disappearing design of the app, but one of the messages was recorded by another smartphone before it disappeared, which allowed her parents to bring attention to their daughter's situation (Suhay).

- A fourteen-year-old British girl reportedly attempted suicide after hateful snaps were sent to her after already enduring torment on Facebook and Twitter over several months (Suhay).

- At Eastern Michigan University, three female professors who were all coteaching a class together became the topic on Yik Yak during their class lesson. The comments constituted cyber-harassment, since they contained "demeaning ... crude, sexually explicit language and imagery" (Mahler). Even though one of the professors sought restitution for the harassment she received, nothing much was done after the situation, and no one was held accountable—namely, because of the anonymity of the posters.

And, finally, here is most extreme example.

- In 2015, at the University of Mary Washington in Fredericks-burg Virginia, a group of female students filed a complaint with the United States Department of Education claiming "the school failed to protect them after they reported assault and death threats on the 'cyberbully' network Yik Yak" (International Business Times). This complaint came just a week after the feminist group on campus, Feminist United, had one of their board members murdered by her male roommate after she spoke out against the university rugby team's crude chant and was target-ed on Yik Yak, along with the feminist group, in more than sev-en hundred yaks. According to the same article, the university refused to block Yik Yak on the campus Wi-Fi connections and responded to the complaints by indicating they had no means to deal with the cyberharassment the women were experiencing. The university merely told them to submit future complaints to Yik Yak.

These are just some examples of how users felt it was okay to post hurtful and potentially demeaning content about women, perpetuating rape culture, on Yik Yak and Snapchat, as well as other social networking sites. These examples also show the actions taken, or not taken, by authority figures when dealing with the issues, and they are clear examples of the need to address online rape culture as well as to encourage bystanders to speak up.

Online rape threats and cyberharassment reflect larger U.S. cultural morals about gender. In her book *This Is Why We Can't Have Nice Things*, Whitney Phillips conducts an ethnography of trolling, which is another form of aggressive communication. Trolling is a form of cyberharassment in which anonymous users meet in anonymous chat rooms, such as 4chan. In these chatrooms, users post content that then becomes fodder for trolls. Trolls may engage in online rape threats or attack different websites. Phillips argues that some trolling behaviours are not new and should be understood within larger contexts of popular culture discourses that promote sensationalism, as can be seen in such outlets as Fox News (51). Indeed, rape jokes, a form of rape culture, have become normalized in popular culture.

Research is now beginning to look at how cyberharassment affects college students (Melander 263). Tanya Beran and her colleagues found that in the U.S. and Canada, 33.6 per cent of high school students and 8.6 per cent of college students reported being cyberharassed (562). Even though the number was lower for college students, the growing trend among high school students suggests that as this group moves into college, that numbers may also increase.

In a study of cyberharassment among college students, Sheri Bauman and Angela Baldasare found malice, deception, public humiliation, and unwanted online contact as common forms of cyberaggression used among college students (320). Cyberharassment occurred both in and

JODIE BOWERS AND CAROLYN M. CUNNINGHAM

out of the classroom. For example, students cited different forms of media in which harassing communication was posted, such as on Facebook, a website called *The Dirty*, Twitter, email, and online gaming sites.

Baumand and Baldasare offer some insight to how students were psychologically affected by cyberharassment. They found differing responses to cyberaggression based on the medium used as well as demographics of the victims. In their study, they highlight that cyber-harassment on Facebook had a higher predictor of distress, possibly because of Facebook's large network of users (325). Additionally, they found that students in sororities and fraternities, as well as those in the LGBT community, felt high levels of distress when experiencing cyberharassment (323).

In another study, Lisa Melander found that cyberharassment was increasingly common among college students (263). She examined intimate partner violence and identified different forms of violence that can occur through online cyberharassment, which often included monitoring behaviour and aggressive forms of communication (265). One difference she found in online harassment as opposed to F2F harassment was that private conversations and private information can quickly become public, especially when messages can be spread quickly (267). This is important because forms of harassment that were previously seen as private, can become public causing more harm to victims.

Maeve Duggan found that there are six different forms of online harassing behaviours, including offensive names (27 per cent), having someone personally embarrass them (22 per cent), physically threatened (8 per cent), stalking (8 per cent), being harassed for a sustained period of time (7 per cent), and sexual harassment (6 per cent). She found that young women experienced more sexual harassment and stalking, forms of cyberharassment that perpetuate a societal acceptance of rape culture.

Given that cyberharassment can occur both anonymously and knowingly, it is important that solutions and interventions are sensitive to these nuances and that interventions are designed accordingly.

Solutions

Bystander Intervention

Much of the discourse that perpetuates rape culture and aggressive communication takes place online through social media apps, such as Facebook and Snapchat, which are highly public forums. Therefore, it is likely that a large number of individuals are able to witness this behaviour and could report it if they chose to do so. However, the majority of these witnesses do nothing. Bibb Latané and John M. Darley, leading researchers on the bystander effect, have developed a theoretical framework for why bystanders do not intervene in crisis situations. They show that when there is more than one witness to an emergency situation, the likelihood of bystander intervention is low. Their research explores a woman's murder in 1964, which was witnessed by thirty-eight individuals, yet none of them reported the crime to the police or aided the victim. Although the witnesses' failure to react could certainly be explained by apathy, Latané and Darley looked for other reasons. The theory the researchers developed, the bystander effect, attempts to explain the phenomenon of how bystanders react during an emergency or in particularly distressing situation. The researchers argue that bystanders must go through a series of steps before deciding whether or not to intervene, and their results show that instances of intervention were markedly lower when there was more than one witness present. They theorize that this reaction is due to individuals entering a "state of pluralistic ignorance" (249)—that is, people try to appear calm while looking for cues to see that others also appear calm. People gauge their reactions based on the reactions of those around them. If other bystanders are communicating (verbally or nonverbally) that the situation is not an emergency, then others will not likely intervene.

Pluralistic ignorance, then, is a type of bystander apathy and "refers to a collective perception or definition of the emergency situation as not being a real emergency as an effect of social comparison between the passive bystanders" (Thornberg 5). If during a cyberharassment incident, no one comes to the aid of the victim, it is reasonable to assume that other witnesses will not intervene either, since the situation was not interpreted as an emergency due to the lack of communicated responses. It is also possible that since the online world is vastly public, individuals fall prey to the fear of appearing that they are engaging in social blunders (Thornberg 5). According to Thornberg, "the mere presence of other bystanders can also inhibit a witness from intervening or helping in an emergency situation because he or she is afraid of looking foolish or behaving in an embarrassing way in front of others" (5).

Pluralistic ignorance directly ties into the diffusion of responsibility (Thornberg 6). The more people witnessing an act of cyberharassment, the less likely someone is to step up and intervene. In such a situation, responsibility is shared by all of the witnesses, which results in no one acting. Each witness assumes that someone else will intervene. Defeating pluralistic ignorance is an important factor for getting bystanders to start speaking up in online environments, especially when it comes to stopping the perpetuation of rape culture.

Bystander intervention requires an understanding of pluralistic ignorance and the diffusion of responsibility. Despite the promising potential of bystander intervention, research shows that bystanders are unlikely to intercede in cyberbullying or cyberharassment because they believe they are not responsible, they think the situation is trivial, or they fear their intervention will result in their embarrassment. A study of bystander behaviour in traditional F2F bullying situations, conducted by Susan Easton and Amanda Aberman, highlights that although bystanders regularly remained silent when observing bullying, they understood that their lack of action did send particular messages to the aggressor and the victim (61). Messages sent to the aggressor ranged from users stating that they were afraid of the bully to supporting the message the bully was putting forth (Easton and Aberman 61). In terms of the victim, they received few messages of support. (Easton and Aberman 61). By simply engaging in responsible civil digital citizenry, bystanders could potentially help end the cycle of aggression and cyberharassment.

Educational programs, which are discussed later in this chapter, can encourage students to intervene when they witness cyberharassment and other forms of aggression. Learning how to be a better citizen in person and online will help shift our society from one that shames victims to one that embraces and supports them.

Digital Citizenship

In addition to increasing bystander intervention, teaching students digital citizenship can also curb the spread of online rape culture. To date, the concept of digital citizenship has mostly focused on K-12 education, but the rise of cyberharassment and online rape culture suggests the need for it to be taught in higher education as well. In general, digital citizenship is about being an "effective member of digital communities" (Hollandsworth, Dowdy, and Donovan 38). This term can be used to refer to one's behaviour in online communities as well as to understand how one's own information is used or received by others.

College students may come across online rape culture in their classes or in their other online forms of communication, thus making the concept of digital citizenship more relevant. Therefore, it is important to make students aware of the many ways in which they can address or avoid cyberharassment.

Addressing online rape culture needs to be part of a larger conversation of civility and online communication, which is part of becoming responsible digital citizens. Media literacy, an important part of digital citizenship, becomes a crucial component to teaching students how to critically examine the information they come across.

Whitney Phillips provides concrete ways that users can be more responsible contributors to online content. In her online article in *Quartz*, she argues that it is important to highlight negative communication and protect private information. It may be difficult to get those engaging in cyberharassment to change their behaviours. Instead, she advocates for users to highlight the harm posed by the communication. Highlighting the harm of cyberharassment can lead to empathy and take focus away from those who are creating the messages.

If someone is engaging in misogynistic communication or cyberharassment, she encourages users to talk about the harm that the communication causes, not what the person intended. This would create a "rhetorical shift" in which the focus is on the impact of the communication, not intent ("We're the Reason"). Being responsible also requires that users do not share negative forms of communication but instead ignore it and move on.

One of the challenges of addressing online rape culture is protecting free speech. The Internet is typically understood as a free marketplace of ideas, where good ideas will reign over poorer ones. However, cyberharassment can lead its victims becoming silenced in cyberspace. Thus, there is a need to create a more inclusive space for free speech, which can happen through the rhetorical shift.

Students should also understand how to protect their private information to avoid being victims of cyberharassment. One strategy is to find what information is publicly available on websites that list personal addresses or emails. If these websites have the option to remove personal information, this is one way students can be more in control of their information. Avoid using geographic location software.

Passwords are another way that users can protect their identity. Change passwords often and avoiding using those that are easy to find out. There are also online services that can help users find more secure passwords.

"A DIY Guide to Feminist Cybersecurity" has a number of tips that students can use to protect their private information and avoid being victims of cyberharassment. These include the following:

- Using privacy extensions on web browsers like Firefox to stop web trackers and encrypt browsing;
- Being aware of phishing scams;
- Encrypting your phone and computer to protect private files;
- Refraining from using social media sites to log into other websites;
- Reporting violations to the social media company;
- Spreading positive messages; and
- Joining online activist communities.

Campaigns for Teaching Empathy and Tolerance

In order to create change, empathy as well as tolerance must be taught in the classroom. A 2015 study published by the journal *Social Forces* discusses how Americans have generally become more tolerant of all disenfranchised groups, which is the first step in curbing societal passive acceptance of aggressive communication and rape culture (Twenge, Carter, and Campbell 379). However, being tolerant does not translate into being empathetic towards the struggles faced by the members of those disenfranchised groups. This attitude can be equated with bystander inaction in cyberharassment instances. This laissez-faire approach to hoping that civility and respect will win out is no longer acceptable. The following antibullying campaigns, though directed towards youth, could potentially create an atmosphere in the college level that is more empathetically inclined because they focus on encouraging bystanders to act instead of remaining silent. They would need to be altered to fit this more diverse and dynamic group of college students.

Think Kindness—This positivity campaign was founded by Brian Williams, who is considered one of America's top youth speakers. The program is aimed towards elementary school students and is focused on engaging in random acts of kindness. According to the organization's website, the program's goal is to have participating schools reach five thousand random acts of kindness in just fifteen days. This program, with a little adjustment to meet different audience dynamics, could potentially be used for college-level programs. The program itself is easily adaptable to fit into the service that campus organizations already provide their institutions. Implementing such a program as Think Kindness may result in changes in the college atmosphere that could be transcendental to individuals and eventually spill over into other areas of their lives, which could create smaller ripple effects that could possibly result in societal shifts. For more information, visit *www.thinkkindness.org*.

I Am A Witness Campaign—This antibullying campaign is aimed towards "activating the 'silent majority' of kids who witness it each day, transforming them from passive bystanders into an active collective that speak up against bullying" ("Press Release") all through a simple emoji. The heart of this campaign is the witness emoji. Shaped like a speech bubble with an eye in the centre, this emoji enables teens to take a stand against bullying and show support for someone who is being bullied by posting it online or through a text message. This is a simple yet effective way of letting a victim know they are not alone as well as letting the bully know that the messages they send are being seen by people who find them irresponsible and hurtful. This type of campaign could be used on social media applications similar to Yik Yak and on Snapchat, Instagram, Twitter, and Facebook.

Although these are just two examples of programs that could be expanded or adapted to fit within the college setting, they have the potential to create smaller changes that may result in larger changes overtime.

Administrative Levels of Addressing Cyberharassment

Digital citizenship can be addressed at the administrative level. In his article on cyberharassment, Josie Ahlquist argues that higher education administrators need to become leaders to lay out expectations and become role models for students. Increasingly, colleges and universities are crafting policies to address cyberbullying and cyberharassment. These policies can be a part of the acceptable use policies that many universities already have in place. For example, Missouri University defines cyberharassment and cyberstalking broadly to include such activities as, trolling, harassing, releasing personal information, mobbing (sending multiple texts), stalking and masquerading (making fake accounts). The university also offers insight into what students should do if they are victims of cyberharassment, including documenting the behaviour and taking screen shots of the bullying in order to trace it. Once the evidence is collected, students can report it to Office of Student Conduct.

Professional development training for faculty to identify and address these forms of communication could also be helpful. Moreover, university-wide policies about the acceptable use of a campus's Internet network could also fight cyberharassment. For example, the University of West Alabama bans cyberbullying and cyberharassment, examples of which include "harsh text messages or emails, rumors sent by email or posted on social networking sites, and embarrassing pictures, videos, websites, or fake profiles" ("Cyberbullying"). In order to make these efforts effective, universities need to have policies and systems in place to address offenders.

Addressing Cyberharassment at the Classroom Level

In the Bauman and Baldarese study, they found that students were in favour of university involvement in curbing this cyberharassment (325), including syllabi explaining these harmful forms of communication. They also found the LGBT community as well as those involved in sororities and fraternities may need different types of interventions (328). These syllabi would outline the rules for online forms of communication, similar to how teachers try to create a safe space in the classroom. They could also encourage students to tell instructors when they are experiencing harassing communication. Many universities are requiring teachers to put information about sexual misconduct on their syllabi, and adding a section on acceptable use policies related to online and F2F classroom discussions would also be helpful.

There are several ways that teachers can address cyberharassment in their classrooms, and the website *Teaching Tolerance* has tips and activities for the classroom.

Conclusion

The suggestions presented here are not intended to be a cure-all for the larger societal issue of online rape culture. They are only mean to offer some strategies for college administrators, teachers, and students to help address the problem of online rape culture, and they also show how teaching empathy and tolerance as well as getting witnesses to speak up can curtail the problem of cyberharassment from growing larger. We navigate between online and offline worlds seamlessly, and the boundaries between the two often become blurry. The boundary between our public and private lives has also become blurred. What might be said in the classroom can now easily be posted on social media and quickly shared with large groups of people. As such, it is important to teach students about online rape culture and how to address it.

Works Cited

Ahlquist, Josie. "Infusing Digital Citizenship into Higher Education." *Josie Ahlquist*, 2014, www.josieahlquist.com/2014/01/27/infusing-digital-citizenship-into-higher-education/. Accessed 1 May 2020.

"A DIY Guide to Feminist Cybersecurity." *Hack Blossom*, hackblossom. org/cybersecurity/. Accessed May 1 2020.

Bauman, Sheri, and Angela Baldasare. "Cyber Aggression among Coll-ege Students: Demographic Differences, Predictors of Distress, and the Role of the University." *Journal of College Student Development*, vol., 56, no. 4, 2015, pp. 317-30.

Beran, Tanya N., et al. "Evidence for the Need to Support Adolescents Dealing with Harassment and Cyber harassment: Prevalence, Pro-gression, and Impact." *School Psychology International*, vol. 33, no. 5, 2012, pp. 562-76.

Black Women's Blueprint. "An Open Letter from Black Women to the Slutwalk". *Gender & Society*, vol. 30, no. 1, 2015, pp. 9-13.

Boux, Holly Jeanine, and Courtenay W Daum. "At the Intersection of Social Media and Rape Culture: How Facebook Postings, Texting and Other Personal Communications Challenge the 'Real' Rape Myth in the Criminal Justice System." *Journal of Law, Technology & Policy*, vol. 2015, no. 1, 2015, pp. 149-86.

Carr, Joetta L. "The SlutWalk Movement: A Study in Transnational Feminist Activism." *Journal of Feminist Scholarship*, vol. 4, 2013, pp. 24-38.

Carson, Biz. "The Yik Yak App Is Officially Dead." *Business Insider*, 28 Apr. 2017, www.businessinsider.com/yik-yak-shuts-down-2017-4. Accessed 1 May 2020.

Connell, Noreen, and Cassandra Wilson, editors. *Rape: The First Sourcebook for Women*. New American Library, 1974.

Constine, Josh. "Yik Yak's CTO Drops Out As the Hyped Anonymous App Stagnates." *TechCrunch*, 6 Apr. 2020, beta.techcrunch.com/ 2016/04/06/yik-yuck/?_ga=2.241031235.1776298204. 1528760535 -1060122462.1528409995. Accessed 1 May 2020.

DeMers, Jason. "A Sneak Peek Into Snapchat's Advertising Revolution." *Forbes*, 15 Apr. 2016, www.forbes.com/sites/jaysondemers/2016/ 04/15/a-sneak-peek-into-snapchats-advertising-revolution/#43a1e 5b0772e. Accessed 1 May 2020.

Duggan, Maeve. "Online Harassment." *Pew Research Center*, 2014, www.pewinternet.org/2014/10/22/online-harassment/. Accessed 1 May 2020.

Easton, Susan S., and Amanda Aberman. "Bullying as a Group Communication Process: Messages Created and Interpreted by Bystanders." *Florida Communication Journal*, vol. 26, no. 2, pp. 46-73.

Hess, Amanda. "Why Women Aren't Welcome on the Internet" *Pacific Standard*, 6 Jan., 2014, psmag.com/why-women-aren-t-welcome-on-the-internet-aa21fdbc8d6#.34flvkm8y. Accessed 1 May 2020.

Hollandsworth, Randy, Lena Dowdy, and Judy Donovan. "Digital Citizenship in K-12: It Takes a Village." *TechTrends*, vol. 55, no. 4, 2011, pp. 37-47.

Keller, Jessalyn, Kaitlynn Mendes, and Jessica Ringrose. "Speaking 'Unspeakable Things': Documenting Digital Feminist Responses to Rape Culture." *Journal of Gender Studies*, vol. 27, no. 1, 2018, pp. 22-36.

Latané, Bibb, and John Darley. "Bystander "Apathy." *American Scientist*, vol. 57, no 2, 1969, pp. 244-68.

Mahler, Johnathan. "Who Spewed That Abuse? Anonymous Yik Yak App Isn't Telling." *The New York Times*, 8 Mar. 2015, www.nytimes.com/2015/03/09/technology/popular-yik-yak-app-confers-anonymity-and-delivers-abuse.html. Accessed 1 May 2020.

Marshall University. "Rape Culture." *Marshall*, www.marshall.edu/wcenter/sexual-assault/rape-culture/. Accessed 1 May 2020.

Melander, Lisa. "College Students' Perceptions of Intimate Partner Cyber Harassment." *Cyberpsychology, Behavior and Social Networking*, vol. 13, no. 3, 2010, pp. 263-68.

Phillips, Whitney. *This is Why We Can't Have Nice Things. Mapping the Relationship Between Online Trolling and Popular Culture*. MIT Press, 2015.

Phillips, Whitney. "We're the Reason We Can't Have Nice Things on the Internet." *Quartz*, 29, December 2015, qz.com/582113/were-the-reason-we-cant-have-nice-things-online/. Accessed 1 May 2020.

"Press Release." *Ad Council*, 2020, www.adcouncil.org/News-Events/Press-Releases/Ad-Council-Debuts-Twitter-Custom-Emoji-for-I-Am-A-Witness-Bullying-Prevention-Campaign. Accessed 8 May 2020.

Rentschler, Carrie. "Rape Culture and the Feminist Politics of Social Media." *Girhood Studies*, vol. 7, no. 1, 2014, pp. 65-82.

Rodino-Colocino, Michelle. "#Yesallwomen: Intersectional Mobilization against Sexual Assault is Radical (Again)." *Feminist Media Studies*, vol. 14, no. 6, 2014, pp. 1113-15.

Sills, Sophie, et al. "Rape Culture and Social Media: Young Critics and a Feminist Counterpublic." *Feminist Media Studies*, vol. 16, no. 6, 2016, pp. 935-51.

Statt, Nik. "Yik Yak, Once Valued at $400 million, Shuts Down and Sells Off Engineers for $1 million." *The Verge*, 28 April 2017, www.theverge.com/2017/4/28/15480052/yik-yak-shut-down-anonymous-messaging-app-square. Accessed 1 May 2020.

Suhay, Lisa. "Fatal Stabbing after Snapchat Message: How to Respond to Online Abusers and Bullies." *The Christian Science Monitor,* 21 Jan. 2015, www.csmonitor.com/The-Culture/Family/2015/0121/Fatal-stabbing-after-Snapchat-message-How-to-respond-to-online-abusers-and-bullies. 1 May 2020.

Suler, John. "The Online Disinhibition Effect". *Cyberpsychology & Behavior,* vol. 7, no. 3, 2004, pp. 321-26.

Thornberg, Robert. "A Classmate in Distress: Schoolchildren As Bystanders and Their Reasons for How They Act." *Social Psychology of Education,* vol. 10, no. 1, 2007, pp. 5-28.

"The Top 10 Valuable Snapchat Statistics-Updated April 2017. *Zephoria Digital Marketing,* zephoria.com/top-10-valuable-snapchat-statistics/. Accessed 11 June 2018.

Twenge, Jean M., Nathan Carter, and Keith Campbell. "Time Period, Generational, and Age Differences in Tolerance for Controversial Beliefs and Lifestyles in the United States, 1972-2012." *Social Forces,* vol. 94 no. 1, 2015, pp. 379-99.

University of West Alabama. "Cyberbullying and Cyber Harassment Policy Statement." *University of West Alabama,* catalog.uwa.edu/content.php?catoid=34&navoid=1566. Accessed 1 May 2020.

Chapter Ten

American Rape Culture: The Circulation of Affect, Victim Blaming, and Cyborg Vaginas

Erin R. Kaplan

"Hi. Have you ever been out walking at night alone wishing you could feel safer? And you, parents and friends; how often have you worried about a loved one? We want to provide a product that will make women and girls feel safer when out on a first date, or a night of clubbing, taking an evening run, travelling in another country, or other potentially risky situations. Our product line provides a layer of protection in case of assault. It is, in fact, anti-rape-wear."

—AR-Wear

Thus begins the Indiegogo fundraising video for the bionic undies of AR-Wear, a company, which believes that fitting women and girls with their products will "provide a substantial barrier to sexual assault." The company raised over fifty thousand dollars in only a few weeks of soliciting donations in late 2013, and as of 2016, it has begun the process of transitioning from making prototypes to manufacturing in bulk. I would like to note here that I use the terms "women" and "woman" throughout this chapter to classify any woman-identified individual regardless of their assigned sex at birth.

So, one may ask, what exactly is antirape wear (AR-Wear)? According to AR-Wear, they are a line of products that provide protection from sexual assault, but are also "elegant" and "able to be worn comfortably during normal activities." Not only will they protect the modern-day potential rape victim who is out on the town or going for a run, but they even protect women who have "had too much to drink, [were] drugged, or [were] asleep." The founders believe that AR-Wear "will give women and girls additional power to control what happens to their bodies in case they are assaulted" (AR-Wear "Confidence & Protection").

The next question is obviously how? AR-Wear's stylish but effective product comes with locking waist and thigh straps, coupled with a combination-style lock on the waistband, and the company uses materials resistant to cutting and pulling, which the advertisers demonstrate by pulling and slashing at the material, tugging at it while on the body of a svelte young model. The best part, however, is the "skeletal structure," which is placed on the "waistline, thighs, and central areas" (AR-Wear, "Confidence & Protection"). There is no comfort quite like having a skeletal structure around your vagina when you are out for a run! Talk about the cyborg effect!

Upon the launch of the campaign, dozens of women were quoted on the fundraising platform, Indiegogo, praising the makers of this product for attempting to protect women from assault. Personally, my initial reaction was a mixture of hilarity and horror. But then as I allowed myself to think about what this campaign was about, why the creators behind these bionic panties identified a market for this product, and why nearly 2,500 people contributed to funding it. There seemed to me something much more significant at stake in these undies.

This chapter uses AR-Wear's "chastity belt" to ground a discussion of American culture's commodified, inscribed, and omnipresent fear of rape; its role in the production of affect and self-regulation; and the countless myths about rape, rapists, and sexual violence. Engaging with affect theory, specifically with the work of Sara Ahmed and Brian Massumi, I probe how rape fear is promulgated through affective means as well as engage with specific incidents that serve as modes of affective production to both debunk and demystify the current rape culture as disseminated by the media, our elected leaders, and by people such as the designers of AR-Wear.

The possibility of violence always exists. Whether it is burglars breaking into your apartment, drunken fights in pubs, roadside bombs, vandals keying a car, terrorist threats, or men in dark alleys, there is no question that American culture is violent. People only need to watch a few minutes of the local news each night to be convinced that they or someone they love will be the next victim. This is particularly true for women, who from a very young age are taught to perpetually be on the lookout for a potential rapist creeping out from the shadows. We, woman-identified individuals, come to think of rape as a part of our natural environment. Something that we want to avoid at all costs, but that is also inevitable. At some point, someday, each of us will be a victim. For Susan Brownmiller, rape "is nothing more or less than a conscious process of intimidation by which all men keep all women in a state of fear" (14-15), and, therefore, we must always be on the lookout. Although it is with the best of intentions that our parents, teachers, doctors, and friends instill this fear, it is not without a cost. The present fear of future violence created by the ubiquitous present terror produces a climate in which women are incapable of moving though the world uninhibited. For Sara Ahmed, "The object of fear is not simply before us, or in front of us, but impresses upon us in the present, as an anticipated pain in the future" (*Cultural Politics* 65). Brian Massumi looks at this present-future fear in regards to terrorism and state violence and he asks, "How could the nonexistence of that which has not happened be more real than what is now observably over and done with?" ("The Future Birth" 52). I believe this question can easily be asked about American rape fear as well.

If the past is prologue, then one should assume that having walked down a street one hundred times would prove that the street is safe. In the culture of rape fear, however, this is not the case. Instead of looking at what has actually happened to us on that particular street countless times, we, as humans, will look for what has not, but definitely will happen on that street at some point in the future. For Massumi:

Threat is from the future. It is what might come next. Its eventual location and ultimate extent are undefined. Its nature is open-ended. It is not just that it is not: it is not in a way that is never over. We can never be done with it. Even if a clear and present danger materializes in the present, it is still not over. There is always the nagging potential of the next after being even worse, and of a still worse next again after that. The uncertainty of the potential next is never consumed in any given event. There is always a remainder of uncertainty, an unconsummated surplus of danger.[...] The future of threat is forever ("The Future Birth" 53).

If the future of threat is forever, then there is no avoiding it; it becomes a part of us whether it is real or not. Because it feels real, it is real, and as long as the threat does not materialize, it does not mean that it is not valid, only that it has not yet happened. If an actual instance of violence does eventually occur—even days, weeks, months, or years after the threat is perceived—then the feeling was always, already correct (Future Birth 54). Thus Americans of all genders create an atmosphere in which all women are moving thorough the world experiencing a real fear, which is affectively produced not necessarily by actual reality but by a perceived future reality, creating "the mass affective production of felt threat-potential [which] engulfs the (f) actuality of the comparatively small number of incidents where danger materialized. They blend together in a shared atmosphere of fear" (*Future Birth* 61), until we are all finally purchasing underwear with skeletal frames protecting our vaginas ... just in case.

The reality is that the perceived fear is not located in a specific time, place, or body; rather, it exists in the cumulative experiences of all women. Each story of assault, each anecdote, sediments a history wherein the future rape becomes inevitable. For Ahmed, each new "encounter is mediated; it presupposes other faces, other encounters of facing, other bodies, other spaces, and other times" (*Strange Encounters* 7). Therefore, my interaction with a stranger/ potential rapist does not exist in the vacuum of that time, place, and moment; rather, it exists as an accumulation or assemblage all the narratives and material encounters of assault I have ever heard or experienced, both real and fictional.

Giles Deleuze and Félix Guattari's theory of assemblage posits that objects on all scales of measurement, from individual cells to world economic systems, cannot truly be analyzed without looking at the structures, elements, and other objects which make them. Thus, as assemblage is an aggregation of all of the component parts of an object, system, or structure.

Rape exists as an assemblage as well. There is the material reality of rape and the physical assault that occurs, but rape is also a part of an oppressive and ongoing culture of fear. If one is lucky and the assault does not occur, it not just fails to negate the perceived fear but rather heightens it, as the fear can now be projected into a future time and place so that no woman can ever be truly unafraid. By fixing the fear onto a specific person or object, one can confront and contain it, even if to do so means being the victim of an assault. When the fear does not have an object with which it is associated, one must fear all possible objects of association. Ahmed explains this by saying that:

the passing by of the object of fear does not mean the overcoming of fear; rather, the possibility of the loss of the object makes what is fearsome all the more fearsome. If fear had an object, then fear could be contained by the object. When the object of fear threatens to pass by, then fear can no longer be contained in an object. Fear in its very relationship to an object, in the very intensity of its directness towards that object, is intensified by the loss of its object. One could characterize this absence as about being not quite present rather than, as with anxiety, being nowhere at all (*Cultural Politics* 65).

It is, therefore, not the event of a rape that is the most fearsome, it is the possibility of that event in our future, which creates the knowledge for women that "rape has always already occurred and women are always raped or already rapeable" (Marcus 386); it is not a matter of if a rape will occur but rather when. It is the anticipation of the violence in the future, because of women's inherent rapeability, that creates an atmosphere of constant fear as well as the necessity to always be ready and awaiting a violent assault. For Martin Heideigger what produces human fear is

something that threatens us, is not yet within striking distance, but it is coming close.... As it draws close, this 'it can, and yet in the end may not' becomes aggravated. We say, 'It is fearsome.' This implies that what is detrimental as coming-close, close by carries with it the patent possibility that it may stay away and pass us by; but instead of lessening or extinguishing our fear, this enhances it. (179-80)

In essence, the only way to really overcome the constant yet latent, affective though often not material fear of rape, is actually to be raped. Even then, the fear is never completely removed, as it always exists as a future possibility. Therefore, women must suit up to defend themselves against this inevitability.

In an effort to protect oneself, without the aid of a combination lock on one's waistband, women are put in the position of having to limit where their bodies can be present in public spaces so as to avoid a potential encounter with an assailant. Ultimately, such an approach hinders the woman's agency to move about freely in space, further restraining her bodily movement. This is certainly not a new concept for women, since it is understood that to be seen implies that one is 'available'. As Joanna Bourke states, "sexually active women have become 'common property'" (9); thus, the only guarantee of safety is not to leave the sanctuary of domestic space, for fear of being blamed for what may occur outside it. Ahmed adds to this configuration that "the relationship between movement, occupation, and ownership is well documented in feminist work: for example, women's restricted movement within public spaces is a result, not only of the fear of crime, but of the regulation of femininity, in which 'being seen' in certain spaces becomes a sign of irresponsibility" (*Strange Encounters* 33).

This sense of (ir)responsibility for one's physical location extends to the responsibility for one's future attack. As long as "safety for women is [...] constructed in terms of not entering public spaces, or staying within the home" (*Strange Encounters* 33), then women who leave must be accountable for the actions of the other people with whom they come in contact. This, too, is a familiar trope in the history and production of rape culture, in which the victim/survivor is blamed for her own rape. Much research has gone into analyzing the mechanics of this thinking; according to Bourke, "An ICM [a social research firm] poll in October 2005 found that one in every three women believe that women who acted flirtatiously are partially or totally responsible if they end up being raped and one in four women believe that women who wear sexy clothes are also partially or totally responsible if they are raped" (406). These assumptions of responsibility lead to the vast majority of rapes going unreported because in addition to the trauma of the event itself, the victim must perform her victimhood on an endless loop for medical experts, lawyers, juries, and judges. She must look forward to her entire life being put on trial.

The stigma attached to any person claiming to have been raped is significant and [...] the victim faces an ordeal that is often described as approaching a second assault" [...] rape trials resemble "degradation ceremonies" for the victim[...].Unlike other criminal trials, the rape victim becomes the focus of attention. Her life is placed under intense scrutiny[...]. Her cloths, hairstyle, posture, accent and tone of voice all take on immense significance. The woman is reduced to her body: what she was wearing, how she walked and her sexual attractiveness. Consent is inferred though the female victim's body, rather than the male perpetrator's actions. In this reduction of the woman to her body, she is diminished as not a full person under law and, indeed, within society. Few women are able to bear the burden of performance. (Bourke 398-99)

Thus, in order to avoid the "second assault" at a trial, many women do not report at all. According to the Rape, Abuse, and Incest National Network (RAINN), approximately 60 per cent of rapes go unreported, and 97 per cent of rapists will never spend a day in jail because, in part, our culture often believes that the rape is not entirely the rapist's fault. In questioning what the survivor was wearing, how she walked, what her sexual history is, and how attractive she may be, it is implied that some part of the rape was in some way asked for. Thus, the justice system makes the argument that women are responsible not only for their own rapes but also the prevention thereof.

This notion of women's role in preventing rape once again brings us to AR-Wear, which claims its goal is to help women and girls feel safe. However, if the present legal system is focused on what a rape victim wore, offers a detailed account of her sexual history, forces her to acknowledge any and all sexual indiscretions in her past, and, ultimately, assaults her once again, I cannot help but wonder whether the next question we ask her will be "Why weren't you wearing your anti-rape wear?" Does it become just another thing that women are supposed to do to prevent violence against them instead of addressing the violence itself? Additionally, if they do not wear antirape wear, does it become another piece of evidence for blaming them for their own assaults?

If women take up this responsibility of preventing rape for fear of being held responsible for it both socially and legally, they are fundamentally being asked to change the way they move about in the world. Whether that means not going out alone, not going out at night, or not going out at all—or wearing assault-prevention undergarments when they do leave their home—women are forced into limiting the ways in which they operate in the world.

I borrow from feminist disability theory to further problematize this issue. Disability theory has worked to deconstruct the so-called natural dichotomy of able bodies versus disabled bodies in a way that challenges thinkers to look critically at how that false dichotomy is produced, both through social constructions and material experiences, in a manner that is productive for an analysis of rape culture. In Susan Wendell's foundational piece on the subject, "Toward a Feminist Theory of Disability," she asks her readers to query who is physically disabled based on the) definitions of impairment, disability, and handicap provided by the United Nations (UN). She quotes extensively from the UN:

> *Impairment* Any loss or abnormality of psychological, physiological, or anatomical structure or function. *Disability* Any restriction or lack (resulting from an impairment) of ability to perform an activity for a human being. *Handicap* A disadvantage for a given individual, resulting from an impairment or disability, that limits or prevents the fulfillment of a role that is normal, depending on age, sex, social and cultural factors, for the individual. (106)

If women and girls, being female, are inherently rapeable and, thus, must amend their actions, limit their exposure in public spaces, and buy antirape protection, they are prevented from fulfilling "a role that is normal," which creates a handicap where once there was none. Women are handicapped from fully engaging in the world because they are disabled by their rapeability and are, thus, impaired by having bodies that can be raped (i.e., having vaginas). This singular body part then comes to stand in for the whole body of the individual. Sharon Marcus places this narrative of the female-body-as-vagina into the larger rape discourse: "The entire female body comes to be symbolized by the vagina, itself conceived of as a delicate, perhaps an inevitably damaged and pained inner space" (398). Adding to that definition is Bourke, who contends the following: "The female body is often portrayed as already, always, violated. Before any penetration (consensual or not) the woman's body 'precipitates' attack. By virtue of being female, the woman is already 'victim,' the wounded, suffering, gendered subject. She is defined in relation to 'it,' the penis" (421). Thus, she is handicapped by having a female-presenting body and then held responsible for said handicap.

These ideas taken to their logical conclusions creates a world in which women self-correct and remove themselves from public society in an effort to avoid the punishment of having transcended the public-domestic border. This is, in effect, Foucauldian bio-politics at work. Patricia Clough analyzes rape culture through a Foucauldian lens and looks at how individual experiences are made statistically material, such as "one in three women in the world have been raped" and are cast onto all women: "The linking of control and political command with the risk factors of statistically produced populations is a form of power that Michel Foucault calls biopolitics. In contrast to disciplining, biopolitics turns power's grasp from the individual subject to 'life itself'" (222). For Foucault, the body is taken over, individuated, and then "massified" until the threat is "directed not at man-as-body but at man-as-species [or in this case, woman-as-species]" (243). For Clough, "biopolitics is not without any interest in the individual; biopolitics individualizes as it massifies" (222). Analyzing rape culture through biopolitics produces a clear pattern: the attack is individuated through reports on the news about a specific incident that has happened to a specific individual with a specific history, and then the story is massified, such that all women become that individual; women fear that what happened to that one woman could happen them all, thus increasing the circulation of fear and affect. Ahmed points out that "signs increase in affective value as an effect of the movement between signs: the more signs circulate, the more affective they become" (*Cultural Politics* 45). Thus, the more the story is massified, the more women must fear and the more they increase an "anticipation of hurt of injury" (65). This constant "fear projects us from the present into a future" (65), such that women must inevitably change the way they engage with the world in the present—staying indoors, never talking to strangers, and becoming patrons of AR-Wear.

Ultimately, then, AR-Wear plays deeply into the commonly held belief that women are responsible for their rapeability; moreover, this ideology presupposes that all men are "sexual machines that cannot be controlled, even by themselves" (Cahill 23). Thus, men need women to limit their public exposure so as not to tempt them thus taking responsibility for men's internal rapist.

Of course, men's so-called uncontrollable sexual appetites are also produced by rape culture, which naturalizes and massifies male aggression. It is well documented that the discourse of rape culture is intrinsically racist and classist—the myth of the Black male rapist is as present today as it was fifty, one hundred, or two hundred years ago. During the Jim Crow era in American history, "the most common justification for lynching was that white women had to be protected from black men intent on corrupting their virtue" (Bourke 101). Presently, this desperate need to protect white female virtue is played out in the American justice system, wherein juries are likely to find a Black man guilty of assaulting a white woman, whereas "complaints by African-American women are often simply dismissed by the police" (Bourke 396). Sharon Marcus corroborates such a finding:

The notorious racism and sexism of the United States police and legal systems often compromise the feminist goals of a rape trial. Interracial rape cases constitute a minority of rapes committed and rapes brought to trial, but when the rapist is white, exhibit significantly lower rates of conviction that interracial rape cases, and much higher rates of conviction when the rapist is Afro-American. In both intra- and interracial rape trials, rapes African -Americas often do not obtain convictions even in the face of overwhelming evidence of brutalization; raped white women have great difficulty in obtaining convictions against white rapists. In the relatively smaller percentage of cases where they have been raped by African Americas, white women often obtain legal victories at the cost of juries' giving currency to racist prejudices and to patronizing ideologies of female protection. (388).

This narrative then plays out in the media, creating a feedback loop in which the myth of the Black male rapist is produced. More Black men are found guilty as a result, which buttresses the assumption that they are more prone to committing violent sexual attacks in the first place. Helen Benedict, in her analysis of American rape culture argues the following: "This essentially racist perception leads to widely held misconceptions that more rapes are committed by black men against white women, or by lower class men against higher class women—a conception bolstered by the press, which tends to give these stories more play than other kinds of rapes" (15) Such discourses produce an affective fear in white women of Black men.

The fear that is felt by white women when confronted by the presence of Black male bodies is complex and complicated. While the fear may be inherently racist and not at all based in factual reality, it is real because it is experienced affectively and thus genuine for the individual experiencing the fear, regardless of its legitimacy or the likelihood of it being borne out in practical terms. The realness of the fear can be explained by Ahmed's notion of "stickiness," wherein my projected fear becomes "stuck" onto a body that I experience as fearsome, thus making it so. "Ahmed explain this in further detail: "While the signs of affect seem to pass between bodies ... what passes is not the same affect, and it depends on (mis)reading the other's feelings.... The other is only felt to be fearsome through a misreading, a misreading that is returned by the other through its response of fear" (*Cultural Politics* 63). This projection comes from the historicity of encounters, which appear similar to the one that an individual is experiencing in the moment but actually has little to no connection to that experience and is created via the massifying effects of rape fear and the production of affect. For Ahmed:

Stickiness is an effect of surfacing, *as an affect of the histories of contact between bodies, object, and signs.* To relate stickiness with historicity is not to say that some things and objects are not sticky in the present. Rather, it is to say that some stickiness is an affect. Stickiness depends on histories of contact that have already impressed upon the surface of the object. (*Cultural Politics* 90)

Thus, I impress my fear onto another body, leaving my own trace or imprint on that body, much the same way my fear of that body leaves an imprint on mine. In this way, affect circulates, or slides, between bodies in proximity to one another, without the intentionality of either party involved. Affect is always precognitive; it is the unconscious feeling that exists before thought. Ahmed explains:

The slide of affect means that it does not come from a subject, nor an object, but involves the sociality of encounters, or the intensity of what it means to live with and by others, whereby "withness" involves the differentiation between others. In other words, the circulation or slide of affect has sticky effects, a stickiness that surfaces as skin [or gender, or race] on the surface of bodies ("The Skin of the Community" 104).

Despite the very real fear of assault that is felt in many such encounters, statistical evidence about rape more often than not should debunk such fear but does not. According to RAINN, "approximately 2/3 of rapes were committed by someone known to the victim." Within that statistic, 73 per cent are committed by a nonstranger: 38 per cent are committed by friends or acquaintances of the victim; 28 per cent are committed by intimate partners; and 7 per cent by relatives. What these data show is that stranger rape only accounts for approximately 35 per cent of all sexual assaults, yet it is one of the most ubiquitously experienced fears for women and girls. What may look like a rational fear on its face is indeed a cultivated menace, propagated by the media and by society at large and fundamentally changes women's experience in the world. Instead of women being taught to fear people they know, they are educated in "stranger danger" and taught to fear those whom they do not. As Ahmed notes, "The stranger is here figured as the violent monster whose elimination would mean the safety for women and children. Such a figuration allows the home to be imagined as a safe haven" (*Strange Encounters* 36). Even though, in reality, it is not.

What AR-Wear then is selling is protection against a mythicized assailant, who is statistically unlikely to exist. Marketing the product for "women and girls [who want to] feel safer when out on a first date, or a night of clubbing, taking an evening run, travelling in another country, or other potentially risky situations" is incredibly misleading and contributes to the notion that rape is inevitable (AR-Wear, "Confidence & Protection"). In reality, AR-Wear actually cultivates rape culture. Through its advertising campaign, the company brilliantly offers both the supply and the demand for its own product. Moreover, they do not argue that the product will actually make anyone safer; they claim it will make its wearer *feel* safer. Essentially, what they are selling is peace of mind. What they are selling is an affect. Although one could argue that this marketing strategy is just that—smart marketing— thoughtful consumers must ask ourselves what this kind of thinking can do. As Marcus reminds us, "Various theories have recognized that rape causes fear, but have ignored the other half of the vicious circle— that often rapes succeed as a result of women's fears" (394). Is it possible that all of the talk about rape, rape prevention, rape trials, rapists, etc. is actually, in part, responsible for rape? This is not to say that antirape feminists, or feminists writ large, are responsible for rape. Sexual assaults are physically material experiences; however, they are affective events as well. Because rape fear gains power through the circulation of affect, both feminist (self-defence and otherwise) and non-feminist (AR-Wear) campaigns promoting awareness of rape cultivate a fear that can, in many ways, reify the threat and produce a culture in which rape is expected; thus, the act of rape as well as the fear of it becomes legitimized.

Because American rape culture is developed in and by the media, it is almost entirely unavoidable for modern young women; it becomes a kind of performance with a script, familiar characters, and often predictable outcomes which we, as its audience, absorb. By constantly speaking about rape, it becomes reified rather than dismantled. In saying that all women should fear rape, a culture is created in which this is true via the mass production of affect. I would like to close this chapter by looking at recent incidents in which the combination of fear, affect, the media, and the question of responsibility have all intersected.

Who is Really Rapeable?

On August 11, 2012, a sixteen-year-old girl in Steubenville, Ohio, did what most teenage girls at one point or another do during high school: she told her parents that she was sleeping at a friend's house and instead went to a party full of teenagers, alcohol, football players, and no parents in sight. She was drunk to the point of vomiting and blacked out at some point during the course of the evening. When she woke up, she had no idea what had happened to her the previous night, but thanks to social media her ignorance did not last long. Trent Mays and Ma'lik Richmond (seventeen and sixteen, respectively) "used their fingers to penetrate the girl in the early hours of Aug. 12" (Oppel). Mays was quarterback of the high school football team, and Richmond played wide receiver. Both were admired by their teammates, who documented the assault. They took photos and videos during the rape and then posted them to social media, which later served as evidence in the trial. Both boys were found guilty of the rape of a minor. Richmond was sentenced to at least one year, and Mays was sentenced to two, as he was also found guilty of disseminating photographs of the event under child pornography laws. In November 2013, Ohio's attorney general, Mike DeWine, charged four additional culprits, adults this time, for failing to report the assault to police, of which they were aware, in an effort to protect the young assailants. Just a few months later on January 5, 2014, Richmond was released from juvenile detention, and Mays followed in January 2015.

Whereas the crime against the young woman served as a first assault, the second assault came from the media. Instead of focusing on this young woman's attack, its delayed prosecution, and the subsequent humiliation—not mention the threats of bodily harm to her and her family—news media from all sides sympathized with Mays and Richmond, two all-star student athletes whose lives would be ruined forever. One particularly offensive report on the verdict against the two boys came from CNN, whose legal analyst, Poppy Harlow, said this of the trial:

> It was incredibly emotional, incredibly difficult, even for an outsider like me, to watch what happened as these two young men that had such promising futures—star football players, very good students—literally watched as they believed their lives fell apart ... when that sentence came down, [Ma'lik] collapsed in the arms of his attorney.... He said to him, "My life is over. No one is going to want me now." Very serious crime here, both found guilty of raping the sixteen-year-old girl at a series of parties back in August. Alcohol fueled parties; alcohol is a huge part of this. (qtd. in Beck).

To which anchor, Candy Crowley, responded as follows:

> You know, Paul, a sixteen-year-old now just sobbing in court, regardless of what big football players they are, the other one just seventeen, a sixteen-year-old victim, they still sound like sixteen-year-olds.... The thing is what's the lasting effect, though, on two young men being found guilty in juvenile court of rape, essentially? (qtd. in Beck).

This is quintessential victim blaming. The statement "alcohol is a huge part of this" is meant to explain away the actions of the rapists and possibly blame the victim for her attack. Because of her irresponsibility and drunkenness, they, the two assailants, should not have to suffer. She was drunk, and boys will be boys—so goes the familiar refrain. This individuated encounter will most certainly end up as a cautionary tale for all young women, massifying this one girl's experience as something that will probably happen to all young women, should they find themselves drunk. Ultimately, the event reifies "the women's responsibility to act as gatekeeper to sex by assuring that men act 'correctly' [and] the men themselves [are] excused as mere victims of their irrepressible sex organs" (Bourke 44). Victims indeed.

Most of the trial's coverage focused on how tragic Mays's and Richmond's stories were, so much so that the girl at the centre of the trial was all but forgotten. The media focused on how the two young men will spend at least the next year of their lives in juvenile detention, will be unable to get football scholarships for college, and will be registered sex offenders upon their release. The assault of a drunk and unconscious sixteen-year-old girl was hardly remarked upon.

Whereas most rape trials centre on the victim's word against her assailant, in the Steubenville case, the prosecution had graphic Twitter photos and YouTube videos as concrete evidence of assault. Moreover, the girl in question was only sixteen and had no previous record of illicit sexual activities. As a result, the media painted the young woman as an innocent victim. Although she did make the ill-advised decision to drink, her innocence, demonstrated in the photos and videos (many of which depict her being dragged about, head lolling from her neck, unconscious) that were taken that night, attest to her rapeability. She was young, sweet, white, and naïve, and she did not deserve what happened to her, bad choices or not.

That was not the case for the hotel maid, Nafissatou Diallo, who in 2011 accused Dominique Strauss-Kahn (at the time the director of the International Monetary Fund) of trying to rape her and then forcing her to perform oral sex in a luxury suite of the Sofitel in New York. Diallo's told her lawyer, Kenneth Thompson, the story, who then relayed its details to *The Telegraph*'s Jon Swaine, who then published the following:

> Mr. Thompson claimed prosecutors had photographs of bruises on the maid's crotch that were inflicted by Mr. Strauss-Kahn.... He had also torn a ligament in the woman's shoulder and ripped her stockings, Mr. Thompson said. "After he finished, she got up and started to run to the door and started spitting Dominique Strauss-Kahn's semen out of her mouth in disgust all over that hotel room."

As the case mounted and the press swarmed, credibility issues began to surface for Diallo, including filing an exaggerated application for asylum, having a phone discussion about potential benefits of pressing charges, and having had contact with a man who was being held in jail for the possession of four hundred pounds of marijuana. She also reportedly changes her story: "Having repeatedly claimed that after the alleged attack, 'she fled to an area of the main hallway' of the Sofitel and hid until Mr. Strauss-Kahn left his suite, she now admits she 'proceeded to clean a nearby room' [for fear of losing her job] before reporting the incident to her supervisor" (Swaine).

A legal team, hired by Strauss-Kahn to investigate Diallo's past, discovered all this information in an effort to destroy her credibility. In a *New York Times* piece by John Eligon and Joseph Goldstern about the defence's case, the authors interview Jeffrey Lichtman, a Manhattan defence attorney, about the process of defending a case such as this. Lichtman is quoted as saying the following

> You really have to attack the witness's credibility.... While it may seem morally unseemly to the public, it's legally appropriate and we have to do the best we can for our clients.... You have to make this into a money thing at the end. Has she defaulted on loans or bounced checks? ... More often than not, what you have to do is badger a witness in a way that doesn't necessarily make them break, but makes them either not credible or less credible or puts in doubt something that they have said.... That's a really good cross-examination.

For Diallo, the case never even made it to trial. Once the credibility issues came to light, the media attacked Diallo as a lying, scheming, and money-hungry immigrant, who probably lured Strauss-Kahn into having sexual relations with her—DNA samples confirm that a sexual encounter did take place—and lied about it to the press for money. Diallo's gender, race, ethnicity, class, and immigrant status meant that even if the incident was, in fact, rape, she was, in reality, unrapeable: "Confident, articulate, white women are in a stronger position to make claims and insist that they are taken seriously, as are women with a supportive family, partners, or friends" (Bourke 394-95). In contrast, women of colour, poor women, queer women, trans women, sex workers, women with sexually promiscuous pasts, and other marginalized women are not thought of as people who can be raped. Their status in society is such that any sexual assault committed against them is seen as a product of the women's own doing. The way in which cases such as Diallo's are portrayed in the media further establishes this notion by continually disregarding the accusations of the women in question, by attacking their credibility, or by claiming that they got what they deserved. As a result, women in these stigmatized groups often do report their rapes, thus making the sexual violence experienced by these women even more invisible. Bourke concludes: "Stigmatized groups within society, such as prostitutes and the poor, are most reluctant to report rape, believing (often correctly) that they will be reproached for lying and that their sexual history will be widely broadcast" (394-5). Thus further sedimenting the false notion that it is only white women of means who are 'rapable.'

What to Do?

Had the sixteen year-old-girl or Ms. Diallo been wearing AR-Wear's protective panties, there may not have been vaginal penetration (in the case of the Steubenville victim), but the assaults would still have occurred. Ms. Diallo would still have allegedly been attacked and forced to perform oral sex, and the young girl in Steubenville, Ohio, would likely still have been dragged around, photographed, and exploited. Why does protecting the sanctity of the vagina become the central—indeed the only point—at which a woman's body should be protected? AR-Wear reduces sexual violence exclusively to vaginal assault and, thus, reduces women's bodies to merely vaginas waiting to be assaulted. Moreover, even if AR-Wear might have stopped those attacks, asking either of these women to take responsibility to have prevented their future assault before it had even occurred is ludicrous. These panties serve as a passive, antifeminist strategy to avoid attack, much in the same way that 1970s antirape feminists thought self-defence classes could work as an active strategy. Ultimately, however, the self-defence feminist answer to the question of rape is insufficient for the same reason I argue these antifeminist panties are—they put all the responsibility for rape onto women, without ever considering the responsibility of the rapist. Nicola Gavey reminds us that even in the 1970s, asking women to take self-defence classes "evoked some degree of cautiousness within more contemporary anti-rape circles due to concerns that it may be seen as unreasonably imputing responsibility for rape (and rape prevention) onto women" (113). Nevertheless, that is exactly what American rape culture does, both in individual cases and in larger legal trends.

For example, in December 2013, Michigan passed a law forbidding nearly all public and private insurance companies to include abortion services in their plans for enrollees. If a woman is worried about possibly needing an abortion in the future, she will need to purchase additional insurance to do so. According to Kathleen Gray of the Detroit Free Press, "The initiative would require most private and all public health insurance plans to offer a separate rider for an abortion. And a person would have to buy that rider before knowing if they needed an abortion. They would not be able to buy the rider after getting pregnant by any means, including rape or incest." Critics of the bill called it "rape insurance," and Senate Minority Leader (now Governor) Gretchen Whitmer argued during the debates on the bill that "This tells women who were raped ... that they should have thought ahead and planned for it" (qtd. in Bassett). And Michigan is not alone: at least twenty-one states require similar riders for insurance customers.

In each of these instances, women are held responsible for their own assaults, and those assaults feed rape fear, which increases the affective production of that fear and makes rape more threatening, more dangerous, and more the fault of the victim. Such fear is debilitating. The fear of future violence creates violence in the present—both the future violence produced by affect as well as and the real violence of existing in a society in which one is always on the verge of being attacked. Living in this way is living with violence. Turing once again to Ahmed:

> Fear of the world as the scene of a future injury works as a form of violence in the present, which shrinks the bodies in a state of afraidness, a shrinkage which may involve a refusal to leave the enclosed spaces of home, or a refusal to inhabit what is outside in ways that anticipate injury (walking alone, walking at night, and so on). Such feelings of vulnerability and fear hence shape women's bodies as well as how those bodies inhabit space. Vulnerability is not an inherent characteristic of women's bodies; rather, it is an effect that works to secure femininity as a delimitation of movement in the public, and over inhabitance in the private. (*Cultural Politics* 70)

Feminists know that the answer is not victim blaming, hiding oneself in their home, learning self-defence, or even locking-up their vaginas. The answer cannot be found in the responsibility of the victim; it has to come from men and from society as a whole. The question is how to get there.

Nicola Gavey, who has written extensively on 1970s antirape and self-defence feminisms offers the following notion: "In order to stop rape, we would need to sidestep assertions of its overwhelming horror and of women's vulnerability. This is not to deny the truth of these assertions, when applied in specific circumstances, but to refuse them as generalized truth claims that take on an over-determined power" (97). Though less than ideal for some, the notion that we should stop speaking about rape as an all-encompassing horror that all women should always fear has its merits. Maybe if we stop aggregating, massifying, and cultivating our own fear of rape, there would actually be less to fear.

Works Cited

Ahmed, Sara. *Strange Encounters: Embodied Others in Post-Coloniality.* Routledge, 2000.

Ahmed, Sara. *The Cultural Politics of Emotion.* Routledge, 2004.

Ahmed, Sara. "The Skin of the Community: Affect and Boundary Formation." In *Revolt, Affect, Collectivity: The Unstable Boundaries of Kristeva's Polis*, edited by Tina Chanter and Ewa Plonowska Ziarek, SUNY Press, 2005, pp. 95-112.

AR-Wear. "AR Wear—Confidence & Protection That Can Be Worn." http://www.indiegogo.com/projects/ar-wear-confidence-protection -that-can-be-worn. Accessed 4 Nov. 2013.

Bassett, Laura. "Michigan 'Rape Insurance' Bill Passes tnto Law." *The Huffington Post*, 12 Dec. 2013. http://www.huffingtonpost.com/2013 /12/11/michigan-rape-insurance_n_4428432.html. Accessed 2 May 2020.

Beck, Laura. "Here's What CNN Should Have Said About the Steubenville Rape Case." *Jezebel*, 18 Mar. 2013. jezebel.com/5991018/ heres-what-cnn-shouldve-said-about-the-steubenville-rape-case. Accessed 2 May 2020.

Benedict, Helen. *Virgin or Vamp: How the Press Covers Sex Crimes.* Oxford University Press, 1993.

Bourke, Joanna. *Rape: Sex Violence History.* Shoemaker & Hoard, 2007.

Brown, Steven D., and Ian Tucker. "Eff the Ineffable: Affect, Somatic Management, and Mental Health Service Users." *The Affect Theory Reader,* edited by Melissa Gregg and Gregory J. Seigworth, Duke University Press, 2010, pp. 229-49.

Brownmiller, Susan. *Against Our Will: Men, Women, and Rape.* Ballantine Books, 1993.

Cahill, Ann J. "Sexual Violence and Objectification." *Theorizing Sexual Violence,* edited by Renée J. Heberle and Victoria Grace, Routledge, 2009, pp. 14-30.

Clough, Patricia T. "The Affective Turn: Political Economy, Biomedia, and Bodies." *The Affect Theory Reader,* edited by Melissa Gregg and Gregory J. Seigworth, Duke University Press, 2010, pp. 206-228.

Deleuze, Gilles, and Felix Guattari. *A Thousand Plateaus.* Translated by Brian Massumi, University of Minnesota Press, 1987.

Eligon, John and John Goldstern. "The Strauss-Kahn Case: Sizing Up a Legal Clash's Many Facets." *The New York Times,* 5 Jun. 2011, www.nytimes.com/2011/06/06/nyregion/the-strauss-kahn-case-sizing-up-a-legal-clashs-many-facets.html?pagewanted=1&ref=dominiquestrausskahn&_r=0. Accessed 2 May 2020.

Foucault, Michel. *Society Must Be Defended: Lectures at the College de France, 1975-1976.* Translated by David Macy, Picador, 2003.

Gavey, Nicola. "Fighting Rape." *Theorizing Sexual Violence,* edited by Renée J. Heberle and Victoria Grace, Routledge, 2009, pp. 96-124.

Gray, Kathleen. "Michigan Legislature OKs Initiative to Require Insurance Rider for Abortion Coverage." *The Detroit Free Press,* 12 Dec. 2013, ww.freep.com/article/20131211/NEWS06/312110143. Accessed 2 May 2020.

Heberle, Renée J. and Grace, Victoria. "Introduction." *Theorizing Sexual Violence,* edited by Renée J. Heberle and Victoria Grace, Routledge, 2009, pp. 1-13.

Heidegger, Martin. *Being and Time.* Translated by John Macquarrie and Edward Robinson, Harper & Row, 1962.

Hess, Amanda. "The Comfortable, Elegant Chastity Belt For the Modern Rape Victim." *Slate*, 4 Nov. 2013. www.slate.com/blogs/xx_factor/ 2013/11/04/ar_wear_these_anti_rape_shorts_update_the_chastity_ belt_for_the_rape_culture.html. Accessed 2 May 2020.

Marcus, Sharon. "Fighting Bodies, Fighting Words." *Feminists Theorize the Political*, edited by Judith Butler and Joan W. Scott, Routledge, 1992, pp. 385-403.

Massumi, Brian. "The Future Birth of the Affective Fact: The Political Ontology of Threat." *The Affect Theory Reader*, edited Melissa Gregg and Gregory J. Seigworth, Duke University Press, 2010, pp. 52-70.

Murphy, Ann V. "Reality Check." *Theorizing Sexual Violence*, edited by Renée J. Heberle and Victoria Grace, Routledge, 2009, pp. 55-71.

Oppel, Richard A., "Ohio Teenagers Guilty in Rape That Social Media Brought to Light." *The New York Times*, 17 Mar. 2013, www.nytimes. com/2013/03/18/us/teenagers-found-guilty-in-rape-in-steubenville -ohio.html?pagewanted=all&_r=0. Accessed 2 May 2020.

Rape, Abuse, and Incest National Network, www.rainn.org/statistics/ criminal-justice-system. Accessed 8 May 2020.

Swaine, Jon. "Dominique Strauss-Kahn Walks Free after Maid Rape Case Crumbles." *The Telegraph*, 1 July, 2011, www.telegraph.co.uk/ finance/dominique-strauss-kahn/8611957/Dominique-Strauss- Kahn-walks-free-after-maid-rape-case-crumbles.html. Accessed 2 May 2020.

Wendell, Susan. "Toward a Feminist Theory of Disability." *Hypatia*, vol. 4 no. 2, 1989, pp. 104-124. Accessed 2 May 2020.

Chapter Eleven

Unrapeable?: Rape Myths and Fat Women

Tracy Royce

"That woman is in as much danger of being raped as I am of being
sliced in half by a real life light saber."
—One of the many Internet trolls who besieged fat feminist
writer Lindy West after she publicly critiqued male comics for
telling offensive rape jokes (West, "If Comedy Has No Lady
Problem, Why Am I Getting So Many Rape Threats?")

I n early September 2015, almost two and a half years before enter-
tainer Bill Cosby's April 2018 conviction on three counts of sexual
assault (Roig-Franzia), comedian and actor Damon Wayans sparked
controversy during a recorded radio interview for New York hip hop
station Power 105's *The Breakfast Club* (Edwards). Asked to weigh in on
the allegations against Cosby, Wayans defended the veteran comic using
a well-worn approach: he denigrated Cosby's accusers and undermined
their credibility by proclaiming them insufficiently attractive to rape.
Referring to Cosby's accusers as "bitches," Wayans stated, "And some
of them, really, is unrapeable ... I look at them and go, 'No he don't
want that. Get outta here!'" (*The Breakfast Club*, Power 105.1 FM).
    Of course, rape apologia and the concept of "unrapeability" predate
Wayans's appalling interview. Feminist scholars, activists, and survivors
have decried rape culture and the prevailing myths that are used to
excuse and normalize the acceptance of rape (Harding 22) since the
1970s (Grubb and Turner 445). The intervening decades have seen much

in the way of antirape scholarship and activism, with #MeToo and related movements bringing worldwide attention to allegations of sexual harassment and assault perpetrated by powerful men in a variety of professional industries. As the many revelations of 2017 suggest, rape culture and rape myths still remain salient in the twenty-first century (Buchwald, Fletcher, and Roth; Harding; West, *Shrill* 190).

Recent decades have also evinced heightened scrutiny and social control of fat bodies, as the media frenzy surrounding the so-called "obesity epidemic" foments what sociologists refer to as a moral panic about fat people (Campos et al. 58-59), particularly fat women (Boero 55). Numerous empirical studies indicate that women are disproportionally affected by antifat bias across multiple domains of life, including employment, education, romantic relationships, and healthcare (Fikkan and Rothblum 557-58). However, the intersection of antifat bias and violence against women, including sexual violence, has received scant attention from researchers and fat studies scholars alike (Royce, "The Shape of Abuse" 151).

This chapter explores the relationship between rape myths and antifat bias. Following a brief discussion of rapes myths and rape culture, I argue that antifat bias and myths about rape interact and amplify each other. I examine personal accounts of women caught at the intersection of rape myths and antifat bias, including the case of fat feminist writer Lindy West, who endured years of online harassment by trolls after publicly confronting rape culture in standup comedy (West, *Shrill* 195-212). I conclude with recommendations for ways to meaningfully integrate material relevant to fatness into college and organizational antirape curriculum, thereby undermining rape culture and fat oppression alike.

Rape Myths

Psychologists Kimberly Lonsway and Louise Fitzgerald define rape myths as "attitudes and beliefs that are generally false but are widely and persistently held that serve to deny and justify male sexual aggression against women" (134). Rape myths include such troubling beliefs as "she asked for it" and "she wanted it" (Harding 22), implying sexual consent when none has been given. Surfacing and circulating within various forms of media (Bonnes 222-23; Garland et al. 57-62;

West, *Shrill* 195-212), rape myths also affect social action at both the individual and institutional level (Conaghan and Russell 26). Rape myths influence not only perpetrator behaviour and the commission of sexual assault, but also victims' reporting behaviour and the decision-making behaviour of investigators, prosecutors, and jurors (Conaghan and Russell 26). Damaging attitudes and beliefs thereby contribute to a pervasive rape culture that excuses, normalizes, and even condones rape.

Despite some cultural and societal variation, rape myths nonetheless "consistently follow a pattern whereby, they blame the victim for their rape, express a disbelief in claims of rape, exonerate the perpetrator and allude that only certain types of women are raped" (Grubb and Turner 445). In particular, this latter theme suggests that some women's (purported) behaviour or social category membership protects or excludes them from the dangers of rape experienced by other, more rapeable women. Of course, this is pure myth. And this is where fat women come in.

Women, Fatness, and Antifat Bias

A Brief Word about Language

But why use the term "fat" to refer to large women and girls who have survived the trauma of sexual assault? Isn't "fat" an insult? A slur? Indeed, speakers, writers, and Internet trolls alike may display malice in labeling someone "fat." Nonetheless, advocates of fat pride, such as Marilyn Wann, have reclaimed the term "fat" (xii-xiii), rescuing it from the realm of insults and reframing it as a value-neutral adjective that accurately describes the bodies of large women and men. "Fat" is preferable to more frequently used descriptors such as "overweight" and "obese," which are considered to be derogatory and to reinforce dominant cultural assumptions about the normalcy and superiority of thin bodies. According to fat pride advocate and writer Marilyn Wann:

> "Overweight" is inherently anti-fat. It implies an extreme goal: instead of a bell curve distribution of human weights, it calls for a lone, towering, unlikely bar graph with everyone occupying the same (thin) weights. If a word like "overweight" is acceptable and even preferable, then weight prejudice becomes accepted

and preferred...[Further,] calling fat people "obese" medicalizes human diversity. (xii-xiii)

As such, rejection of these stigmatizing "O-words" (Wann xii-xiii) and self-identification as "fat" (Saguy and Ward) have been important practices for academics and activists associated with fat liberation. It is for this reason that I embrace the use of "fat." Similarly, where context demands (such as with discussion of the so-called "obesity epidemic"), I adopt fat studies scholars' customary use of scare quotes to cordon off the terms "obese," "obesity," and "overweight" to "indicate their compromised status" (Wann xii).

Additionally, some fat studies scholars use the terms "fatphobia" and "fatphobic" to describe the antifat attitudes, beliefs, social practices, and policies that negatively affect fat people (Boero 103; Herndon 12). Although I have used "fatphobia" in earlier writing (Royce, "The Shape of Abuse" 154), more recently, I have come to regard the term as problematic because it "implies that anti-fat utterances and writings arise from fear, rather than emotions that are less easy to excuse" (Royce, "Fat Invisibility, Fat Hate" 26). "Fat hatred," "fat oppression," and "antifat bias" may better capture the negative experiences of weight-based prejudice and discrimination endured by many people whose body size exceeds the limits of social acceptance.

Fat Women, Sexuality, and Social Control

As previously noted, antifat bias is pervasive across multiple domains of life, and this is especially true for fat women (Fikkan and Rothblum 557-558). In her Pulitzer Prize–nominated classic *Unbearable Weight*, cultural studies scholar Susan Bordo emphasizes that body size entails a gendered experience, whereby women in Western patriarchal societies are subjected to more weight-related and appearance-related pressures than men are (166). More recently, sociologist Natalie Boero contends that the current media furor over the "obesity epidemic" is "at its most basic level...about women" (55).

Fat women's experience is understood as being characterized by invisibility (Boero 113; Goodman 1; Royce, "Fat Invisibility, Fat Hate" 21-23, 28) and even "hyper(in)visibility" (Gailey 12-19), whereby fat women are subjected to heightened surveillance and social control on the one hand, and erasure on the other (Gailey 58). Sociologist Jeannine Gailey posits that fat women occupy both ends of this extreme spectrum, sometimes simultaneously (18), which results in "othering" them both structurally and in person-to-person interaction (58).

Similarly, fat women are frequently characterized as occupying one or both ends of an extreme spectrum of sexuality. Fatness, often considered unfeminine and/or associated with asexuality, is sometimes understood as a willing retreat from (hetero)sexuality, whereby women hide behind their fat. Conversely, fat women are, at times, also associated with "excess and desire" and thereby believed to be "insatiably sexual" (Boero 106).

Gailey explains the relevance and impact of such contradictory and damaging discourses upon fat women:

> The dominant cultural discourse and framing of large bodies as unattractive serves as a form of social control that reinforces stereotypes and mistreatment of fat women. Messages stating that fat people (especially women) are lazy, gluttonous, lacking willpower, and nonsexual or hyper-sexual are repeated so frequently, and often without criticism, that many people assume they are true. (134)

Furthermore, Gailey argues, social control of fat women and their sexuality emerges not merely as stigma, but also as "shaming, abuse, and victimization" (Gailey 117).

Rape Myths, Fat Women, and Unrapeability

Of course, fat women are not the only social category to have been labelled "unrapeable." In particular, African American women have been treated as unrapeable, both under slavery and subsequently. As with the stereotype of the sexually insatiable fat woman, African American women are often stereotyped as hypersexual and, therefore, are believed to be always sexually available and consenting (Gross). African American women are further rendered unrapeable by the American justice system, wherein prosecutors are significantly less likely to file rape charges if the victim is Black than if the victim is White (Pokorak 41-42). Even when cases do move forward and convictions are won, disproportionately short sentences are meted out for perpetrators who rape Black women (Sharpley-Whiting 56).

Just as African American women's experiences of rape have been shaped not only by rape myths but by institutionalized racism, fat women who claim to have been raped have to contend with both rape myths and antifat bias. These can interact to undermine fat victims' credibility, rendering them essentially unrapeable in the eyes of others, including institutional actors who are tasked with providing protection or justice for victims.

One prevalent myth is that rape, rather than being an act of brutality and violence, is instead an act of sex and desire. But within mainstream society, fat women are not legitimate objects of desire. Instead, they are considered undesirable, even asexual, because their size exceeds the strictures of mainstream beauty norms (Gailey 111-12). Therefore, if rape is (understood to be) an act of desire and fat women are (considered) undesirable, fat women are (believed to have been) disqualified as credible victims of rape. This troubling (but all too common) line of reasoning harkens back to the mistaken belief that "only certain types of women are raped" (Grubb and Turner 445).

If this seems simplistic, consider the anecdotal reports of a few survivors. Some fat rape survivors have disclosed that police officers have responded to their attempts to report rape with incredulity, mockery, and a refusal to take down a report (Goodman 81; Mabel-Lois and Aldebaran 53). One fat woman, writing anonymously to *Big Beautiful Woman Magazine*, discloses attempting to report a home invasion and rape to the police. Rather than receiving assistance and solace, instead she overheard one officer exclaim to the other, "Who would want to rape her?" (qtd. in Goodman 81). W. Charisse Goodman laments: "While the fat woman is probably not accused of 'asking for it' by flaunting her supposed non-existent charms, she may, incredibly, have to endure the world's wonderment at a rapist's selection of her for a victim" (81).

Writer Ashleigh Shackelford's account suggests that her rapist not only endorsed this warped logic, but may have also deliberately exploited it to silence her:

I was raped when I was 18 by a man who subsequently told me that I should feel grateful that anyone would want to touch me. "You should feel so lucky, you fat bitch," he said. I never told anyone because why would anyone believe that a fat Black girl like me could be assaulted, when my own attacker made sure to mention that I was fortunate to even be considered for such violence.

Here, rape is framed not as violence but as a favour or compliment, which is typically reserved for women who are considered sufficiently desirable. The fat victim is overtly instructed to feel gratitude for having been selected for violation. Her supposed unrapeability as a young woman who is both fat and Black is used against her as an additional form of abuse and control.

Such arguments are deployed not only by rapists themselves but also by those who defend them. In 2007, three teenaged boys from Catford, South-East London faced trial for the alleged gang rape of two teenaged girls. Although the defendants denied any wrongdoing, the girls detailed a brutal and terrifying ordeal, claiming that the three boys stole their cell phones, repeatedly raped them in a park, and threatened to kill them if they reported the attacks to the police. Nonetheless, during closing arguments to the jury, a female barrister defending one of the accused teens played upon antifat bias to undermine the credibility of one of the alleged victims. Noting also that the girl had "slimmed down a lot" since the alleged assault, the barrister stated, "She was 12 stone 6 pounds [174 pounds]—not quite the swan she may turn into. She may well have been glad of the attention" (metrowebukmetro). Surely such statements, especially when made by institutional actors, reinscribe the violence for which the fat survivor seeks remedy.

Lindy West versus Online Misogyny and Fat Hatred

Women need not have survived an actual, physical rape in order to be targeted by such rhetoric, however. Fat feminist writer Lindy West got caught in a vitriolic online firestorm after critiquing male comics' propensity for telling offensive rape jokes. West tackled rape culture in comedy both in an article on *Jezebel* and in a televised debate with comic Jim Norton on W. Kamau Bell's FX show *Totally Biased*. What followed was years of online harassment by trolls, whose rhetoric inadvertently served to shore up West's arguments. West received a barrage of misogynist and antifat comments on *Jezebel*, as well as hateful emails, tweets, Facebook entries, and other online posts (West, *Shrill* 195-212).

West fought back powerfully, both online, where she posted a video of herself reading a portion of her backlash comments aloud, and in her 2016 memoir, *Shrill: Notes from a Loud Woman*, wherein she concludes that her efforts eventually helped change standup culture for the better

(203-7). Nonetheless, the trolls' tweets, comments, and posts are instructive in their naked embrace of rape myths and antifat bias. The comments appear to fall into several main categories.

Comments trended towards assertions that West's critique of rape jokes was motivated by her bitterness or disappointment that "no one would rape her":

> I bet she's just jealous nobody would rape her. (West, "If Comedy Has No Lady Problem")

> That big bitch is bitter that no one wants to rape her do some laps lardy holly [sic] shit her stomachs were touching the floor. (West, *Shrill* 197)

At the heart of the backlash was the collusion of antifat bias and rape myths that conflate rape with sexual desire and insist upon the unrapeability of fat women:

> I appreciate you take preventative anti-rape measures like being so dumb and obese no one will want to sleep with you ever. (West, "If Comedy Has No Lady Problem")

> No one would want to rape that fat, disgusting mess. (*West, Shrill* 197)

> You're fat, ugly, and unfuckable. You don't have to worry about rape! (West, *Shrill* 198)

> Jabba has nothing to worry about, not even a prison escapee would rape her. (West, *Shrill* 200)

And, unsurprisingly, West also received direct and indirect rape threats:

> There is a group of rapists with 9000 penises coming for this fat bitch. (West, *Shrill* 198)

> Holes like this make me want to commit rape out of anger, I don't even find her attractive, at all, I just want to rape her with a traffic cone. (West, *Shrill* 202)

Considered together, the comments form a disturbingly contradictory pattern. Rape myths conflating desire, sex, and rape combine with antifat bias, which positions West outside of mainstream heterosexual desirability. Being considered undesirable, she is therefore invulnerable to sexual violence, which she is paradoxically believed to desire, as it has apparently been denied her. Nonetheless, her punishment for speaking out should be the very thing to which she, as a fat woman, is supposedly immune: rape.

Moving Forwards

How can academics and advocates address the intersection of rape myths and antifat bias? To start, I'll provide a personal anecdote that illustrates some of the potential problems associated with failing to adequately account for the gendered relevance of body size when interceding with rape culture, rape myths, and related practices used to control women's bodies and/or sexuality, such as slut-shaming.

As an undergraduate, I participated in a weekend-long antirape seminar on my university campus. As with similar trainings I had previously taken within the community, this program sought to increase participants' knowledge about rape while deconstructing and countering prevalent rape myths. One of the facilitator's exercises—I'll refer to her as "Colleen," since that isn't her real name—had students arranged in an inward-facing circle surrounding her. Colleen then issued a series of statements, pausing after each so that participants who endorsed any particular statement could make their position visible to everyone else. Participants did so literally—by stepping towards the centre of the circle. When Colleen eventually uttered, "I have been called a 'slut,'" I, along with some of the other students, stepped forwards.

The second part of the exercise encouraged discussion of what had just transpired: students were provided the opportunity to ask questions or simply offer their own observations about the experience. When a young, blond woman stated, "I was surprised by some of the people who stepped forwards and admitted to having been called a 'slut,'" I (and likely others) knew she must have been referring to me: as a nontraditional student, I was a decade older than the others, but perhaps more importantly, I was also quite a bit fatter. What followed was some generic discussion of slut-shaming and its relationship to rape culture (Tanenbaum xx, 241-42), but the issue of body size was never explicitly addressed, either then or later on.

Facilitator Colleen's silence on the issue of fatness (specifically the student's implication that as a fat woman I was somehow insufficiently attractive and/or sexual to warrant slut-bashing) put the onus on me to broach the subject and educate my younger undergraduate peers. I now regret that at that particular time, I found myself unable to do so. But a failure to overtly address the issue of size in this teachable moment had the additional effect of reifying some of the very rape myths that we were tasked with dismantling: only girls and women who are considered conventionally attractive (a component of which is being sufficiently slim) are vulnerable to having our sexuality and/or bodies scrutinized, controlled, and violated. In the eyes of this young woman, and possibly others, I was safely removed from the types of aggression we were there to discuss and confront.

I was left with the following question: if I were raped today and encountered this seminar participant as a professional tasked with helping me in a legal, medical, counselling, or other capacity, would she find me credible? Or, for her, would my body size render my account unbelievable and me as unrapeable?

What the facilitator could have done differently right from the start was to undertake an intersectional approach that included an analysis of size. Given the myth of the Black rapist, coupled with the fact that African American women are also often represented or treated as unrapeable, feminists of colour have made a convincing case for considering violence against women through an intersectional lens (Crenshaw). Over the years, the campus and community antirape and antidomestic violence trainings in which I have participated typically embraced a model of intersectionality that incorporated not only race, class, and gender, but also sexual identity, immigration status, and religion. But without exception, they neglected to address how rape and other forms of violence against women may be differently experienced by women with larger bodies.

Needless to say, an approach that incorporates an analysis of size would entail engaging with content exploring the confluence of rape myths and antifat bias. Despite the vitriolic tone of the comedy fans' (i.e., the trolls') comments included therein, Lindy West's memoir, *Shrill: Notes from a Loud Woman*, is humorous and relatable. Assigning brief excerpts as background reading—particularly relevant chapters are "Death Wish" (165-194) and "It's about Free Speech, It's Not about Hating Women" (195-212)—could provide a foundation for thoughtful discussion about how rape myths and antifat bias interact.

Furthermore, antirape trainings, especially those conducted on college campuses, can include modules about a form of sexual coercion and humiliation that specifically targets women deemed to be unattractive, particularly fat women: "hogging." Jeannine Gailey and Ariane Prohaska's research on "hogging" shows how college men participate in the degradation and coercion of women that they believe to be "easy targets" and "desperate," precisely because such women have "violated traditional gender norms by being unattractive or overweight" (Gailey and Prohaska 38). Again, this practice never surfaced as a topic of discussion in any antiviolence training I have attended, even those that have been led by fat facilitators.

Finally, trainings (and organizations and institutions) themselves can create a climate that is either hostile or hospitable for fat people. Have chairs with constricting sides or arms? See if you can rustle up some without arms so that those of us with wider "seats" don't get squashed (Hetrick and Attig). Eschew "fat talk" (Nichter) and instead commit to disrupting fat disparagement. Diet culture belongs in the feminist studies classroom as a topic of critical analysis, not within feminist organizations as a matter of practice.

As the editors of the revised edition of *Transforming a Rape Culture* posit, "We will continue to live in a rape culture until our society ... chooses to eradicate the beliefs and practices that beget sexual violence" (Buchwald, Fletcher, and Roth 8). But challenging the rape myths that permit rape culture to flourish also entails careful consideration of the very bodies we inhabit, as well as the antifat biases that can make surviving rape all that more painful.

Works Cited

Boero, Natalie. *Killer Fat: Media, Medicine and Morals in the American "Obesity Epidemic."* New Brunswick, NJ: Rutgers University Press, 2012.

Bonnes, Stephanie. "Gender and Racial Stereotyping in Rape Coverage." *Feminist Media Studies*, vol. 13, no. 2, 2013, pp. 208-27.

Bordo, Susan. *Unbearable Weight: Feminism, Western Culture, and the Body.* Tenth Anniversary Edition. University of California Press, 1993/2003.

Breakfast Club Power 105.1 FM. "Damon Wayans Interview at The Breakfast Club Power 105.1 FM (09/04/2015)." *YouTube*. 4 Sept. 2015, www.youtube.com/watch?v=n52uSXCKdLs. Accessed 3 May 2020.

Buchwald, Emilie, Pamela R. Fletcher, and Martha Roth. "Are We Really Living in a Rape Culture?" *Transforming a Rape Culture*, edited by Emilie Buchwald, Pamela R. Fletcher, and Martha Roth, Milkweed Editions, 2005, pp. 5-9.

Campos, Paul, et al. "The Epidemiology of Overweight and Obesity: Public Health Crisis or Moral Panic?" *International Journal of Epidemiology*, vol. 35, no. 1, 2006. pp. 55-65.

Conaghan, Joanne and Yvette Russell. "Rape Myths, Laws, and Feminist Research: 'Myths about Myths?'" *Feminist Legal Studies*, vol. 22, no. 1, 2014, pp. 25-48.

Crenshaw, Kimberle. "Mapping the Margins: Intersectionality, Identity, Politics, and Violence against Women of Color." *Stanford Law Review*, vol. 43, no. 6, 1991, pp. 1241-99.

Edwards, Stassa. "Damon Wayans Defends Bill Cosby, Calls Victims 'Unrapeable.'" *Jezebel*, 6 Sept. 2015, jezebel.com/1729067609. Accessed 3 May 2020.

Fikkan, Janna L. and Esther D. Rothblum. "Is Fat a Feminist Issue? Exploring the Gendered Nature of Weight Bias." *Sex Roles* vol. 66, no. 9, 2012, pp. 575-92.

Gailey, Jeannine A. *The Hyper(in)visible Fat Woman: Weight and Gender Discourse in Contemporary Society*. Palgrave Macmillan, 2014.

Gailey, Jeannine A., and Ariane Prohaska. "'Knocking Off a Fat Girl': An Exploration of Hogging, Male Sexuality, and Neutralizations." *Deviant Behavior*, vol. 27, no. 1, 2006, pp. 31-49.

Garland, Tammy S., Kathryn A. Branch, and Mackenzie Grimes. "Blurring the Lines: Reinforcing Rape Myths in Comic Books." *Feminist Criminology*, vol. 11, no. 1, 2016, pp. 48-68.

Goodman, W. C. *The Invisible Woman: Confronting Weight Prejudice in America*. Gurze Books, 1995.

Gross, Kali N. "The Criminal Unrapeability of Black Women." *Ebony*, 30 Sept. 2014. Accessed 22 Nov 2016.

Grubb, Amy R., and Emily Turner, Emily. "Attribution of Blame in Rape Cases: A Review of the Impact of Rape Myth Acceptance, Gender Role Conformity and Substance Use on Victim Blaming." *Aggression and Violent Behavior*, vol. 17, no. 5, 2012, pp. 443-52.

Harding, Kate. *Asking for It: The Alarming Rise of Rape Culture—And What We Can Do about It.* Da Capo Press, 2015.

Herndon, April Michelle. *Fat Blame: How The War on Obesity Victimizes Women and Children.* The University Press of Kansas, 2014.

Hetrick, Ashley, and Derek Attig. "Sitting Pretty: Fat Bodies, Classroom Desks, and Academic Excess." *The Fat Studies Reader*, edited by Esther Rothblum and Sondra Solovay, New York University Press, 2009, pp. 197-204.

Lonsway, Kimberly A., and Louise F. Fitzgerald. "Rape Myths: In Review." *Psychology of Women Quarterly*, vol. 18, no. 2, 1994, pp. 133-64.

Mabel-Lois, Lynn, and Aldebaran. "Fat Women and Women's Fear of Fat." *Shadow on a Tightrope: Writings by Women on Fat Oppression*, edited by Lisa Schoenfielder and Barb Wieser, Aunt Lute Books, 1983, pp. 53-57.

Metrowebukmetro. "Lawyer: 'Rape' Girl Should Be 'Glad of Attention.'" *Metro UK.* 17 May 2007, metro.co.uk/2007/05/17/lawyer-rape-girl-should-be-glad-of-attention-369735/. Accessed 3 May 2020.

Nichter, Mimi. *Fat Talk: What Girls and Their Parents Say about Dieting.* Harvard University Press, 2000.

Pokorak, Jeffrey J. "Rape as a Badge of Slavery: The Legal History of, and Remedies for, Prosecutorial Race-of-Victim Charging Disparities." *Nevada Law Journal*, vol 7, no. 1, 2006, pp. 1-54, scholars.law.unlv.edu/cgi/viewcontent.cgi?article=1418&context =nlj. Accessed 6 May 2020.

Prohaska, Ariane, and Jeannine A. Gailey. "Achieving Masculinity through Sexual Predation: The Case of Hogging." *Journal of Gender Studies*, vol. 19, no. 1, 2010, pp. 13-25.

Roig-Franzia, Manuel. "Bill Cosby Convicted on Three Counts of Sexual Assault." *The Washington Post*, 26 Apr. 2018, www.washington-post.com/lifestyle/style/bill-cosby-convicted-on-three-counts-of-sexual-assault/2018/04/26/d740ef22-4885-11e8-827e-190efaf-lflee_story.html. Accessed 3 May 2020.

Royce, Tracy. "The Shape of Abuse: Fat Oppression as a Form of Violence against Women." *The Fat Studies Reader*, edited by Esther Rothblum and Sondra Solovay, New York University Press, 2009, pp. 151-57.

Royce, Tracy. "Fat Invisibility, Fat Hate: Towards a Progressive Pedagogy of Size." *The Fat Pedagogy Reader*, edited by Erin Cameron and Constance Russell. Peter Lang Publishers, 2016, pp. 21-29.

Saguy, Abigail C. and Anna Ward. "Coming Out as Fat: Rethinking Stigma." *Social Psychology Quarterly*, vol. 74, no. 1, 2011, pp. 53-75.

Shackelford, Ashleigh. "Society (and My Rapist) Says I'm Too Ugly to Be Raped." *BGD: Black Girl Dangerous*, 17 Sept. 2015, www.bgdblog. org/2015/09/society-and-my-rapist-says-im-too-ugly-to-be-raped/. Accessed 3 May 2020.

Sharpley-Whiting, T. D. "When a Black Woman Cries Rape: Discourses of Unrapeability, Intraracial Sexual Violence, and the State of Indiana v. Michael Gerard Tyson." *Spoils of War: Women of Color, Cultures, and Revolutions*, edited by T. Denean Sharpley-Whiting and Rene T. White. Lanham, Maryland: Rowman & Littlefield, 1997, pp. 47-58.

Solovay, Sondra, and Esther Rothblum. 2009. "Introduction." *The Fat Studies Reader*, edited by Esther Rothblum and Sondra Solovay, New York University Press, 2009, pp. 1-7.

Tanenbaum, Leora. *I Am Not a Slut: Slut-Shaming in the Age of the Internet.* HarperCollins, 2015.

Wann, Marilyn. 2009. "Foreword: Fat Studies: An Invitation to Revolution." *The Fat Studies Reader*, edited by Esther Rothblum and Sondra Solovay, New York University Press, 2009, pp. xi-xxv.

West, Lindy. *Shrill: Notes From a Loud Woman.* Hachette Books, 2016.

West, Lindy. "If Comedy Has No Lady Problem, Why Am I Getting So Many Rape Threats?" *Jezebel*, 4 June 2013, jezebel.com/if-comedy-has-no-lady-problem-why-am-i-getting-so-many-511214385. Accessed 3 May 2020.

Chapter Twelve

The Indian Film Industry: Feeding Rape Culture in India

Kirthi Jayakumar

Introduction

Every crime has a motivating factor or an enabling environment that allowed for it to happen. Enabling environments are a combination of passive and active factors that include a range of beliefs, attitudes, actions, legislations and policies, responses, and security sector structures. Although enabling environments by themselves cannot cause a crime, it is important to understand that they still do affect, encourage and provide the justification for the crime.

Rape culture is essentially an enabling environment; it blames victims of sexual assault and normalizes male sexual violence. What feeds and keeps rape culture alive is a mosaic of different factors that includes culture, interpretations of religion, patriarchal attitudes, and historically held and endorsed values of antagonism towards women, among other things.

This chapter looks at the Indian film industry, including music and music videos from films, as being crystallizing elements that inform and feed rape culture in India. I argue that by not making sensitized cinema, the Indian film industry is creating content that feeds rape culture. This chapter accounts for the fact that insensitive content is normalized by the educated masses and is internalized as acceptable and permissible by those with little to no sensitized education.

The Indian Film Industry: The Phenomenon

The Indian film industry is a blend of many subfilm industries—namely, the Hindi film industry or Bollywood, the Tamil film industry, the Malayalam film industry, the Telugu film industry, the Kannada film industry, the Marathi film industry, the Bengali film industry and the Bhojpuri film industry, among others (Suroor). Of these, Bollywood is easily the largest in terms of revenue, production, and reach, a fact that is evident from the inadvertent confusion that Bollywood is synonymous with the Indian film industry. With 3.7 million movie tickets being sold in 2006 and 84 per cent of Bollywood revenue coming from the box office, the influence of these films stretches from the smallest village to the largest city (Bamzai). In general, it has been calculated that Indian movies have an audience of 1.38 billion people worldwide (Statista).

The audience for Indian-language films in India totals 1.2 billion people, including rural and urban populations. It is a given that the film industry is a large mainstay of pop culture, which influences and informs social attitudes among different groups in India. According to the 2013 Annual Report of the National Crime Records Bureau (NCRB), 24,923 rape cases were reported across India in 2012. Out of these, 24,470 were committed by someone known to the victim. By 2013, the number of reported rapes in India had jumped to 33,707, according to the NCRB.

Although it is important to recognize that a myriad of factors have caused sexual violence and rape to become so rampant, it is also true that certain aspects of popular culture have been instrumental in keeping rape culture alive in India. In terms of film, the Indian film industry has never glorified rape in its product and cannot be alone held responsible for the increasing number of rapes across the country. Yet the film industry has promoted certain behaviours that tend to normalize rape culture and has normalized ideas of toxic masculinity among men.

The Portrayal of Women: One Part of the Problem

One of the biggest drawbacks in the Indian film industry is its portrayal of women. From idolizing the goody-two-shoes woman as the ideal type, to presenting a woman who has been raped as having no future, to objectifying women as an object to lust after, and to completely disregarding the notion of consent its films, the Indian film industry's portrayal of women is underscored by dehumanization.

The goody two shoes: Indian culture is not homogenous, given the many building blocks that constitute the nuanced concept; however, certain things are given a hefty premium within it, especially the role of a woman. The body of the woman is made the de facto carrier of cultural signs. The insignia of marriage in the form of a necklace, a smattering of vermillion on her hairline, and the bindi, or the red dot, on her forehead, where her third eye is, are all considered a hallmark of a good wife. The clothing she wears determines where her values lie.

Stigmatization: There are countless films in the eighties and nineties that use a plotline in which a female character is either raped or sexually harassed. Invariably, her brother becomes the one to avenge her defilement, while the woman herself is presented as having no future. She remains confined in the house or is portrayed as depressed and broken, and her family laments repetitively that she has no life what-soever. Her family sees her rape as a black mark on its social standing, and the ascribed stigma is thrust upon the girl like a cross for her to bear.

Objectification: This remains one of the most common and enduring modes of portrayal of women, regardless of the genre, storyline, or era in which the film was made. Arguably, the deployment of the "item number" may have something to do with the cultural ethos of hiring court dancers or courtesans for entertainment. In most films, regardless of whether the story is benefitted by its inclusion or not, there is an item number—a raunchy song and dance involving a woman dancing while a horde of lewd and lecherous men drool over her. The earliest recorded item number goes back to 1954. Although this trend is indeed disturbing, since the objectification of women is promoted as acceptable, it is also a bit of a paradox: women are empowered in their choice of what to wear, sing, and dance, but they do so purely for male attention. A woman dressing skimpily in these films and the lecherous behaviour it elicits from the men normalizes such behaviour outside the film realm, where women dressed skimpily are seen as asking for men's often aggressive attention. In most films, the woman is framed around the man, and her portrayal is often tied to his perception of her

Regardless of which of these four is chosen as the mode of portrayal, one common notion that continually rings true is that "Men act, women appear. Men look at women; women watch themselves being looked at" (Berger 47). Women become merely props in creating the ethos that sets the context of the story. In Indian cinema, women remain in one way or the other as holders of a passive position, in which they function merely as "bearers and not the makers of meaning, merely an appendage to the man, the wielder of power" (Mulvey 34). Most often, stories are centered on the male lead: their perceptions shape the entire film. Women are built around the male character: the hero's mother, the hero's sister, the hero's love interest, or the one the hero dances with and lusts after. Women are very rarely showcased as being independent agents or primary decision makers for themselves; they rarely defy or question authority. A few exceptions do exist, but even in some of these exceptions, the female characters' defiant actions are contextualized within the framework of the male gaze.

Consent has no value in these films, as most of them refute the notion. The projection of women and their roles represent a proclivity to dismiss the value of what women say in response to their sexual overtures. For instance, the wooing or courtship of women on screen is carried out through harassment, teasing, molestation, and the pursuit of women until they give in to the man. This portrayal suggests that it is okay for a man to stalk, abuse, harass, and molest a woman in the name of wooing her. In many films, women themselves willingly participate in such acts, which reinforces the stereotype that consent can be dismissed. Some women go so far as to seek out item numbers as a career milestone in their lives—to the point that certain films are even coveted, as ideal avenues to be an item number in. The irony lies in the fact that Indian society, with few exceptions, is fraught with a plethora of rules that govern interactions between men and women. The norm is that a good girl and a good boy do not talk to each other. Society is strictly heterosexual, and homosexuality is seen not only as an anomaly but as a crime by some. Arranged marriages are the norm, but the films do slightly disrupt these ideals. The man in these films is the ideal but of a different standard. He does anything to get the girl, who at first dismisses him and refuses his harassing advances; she then suddenly throws away all her apprehensions and ends up with him. This is a common occurrence across the film industry, regardless of the language.

The Portrayal of Men: The Other Part of the Problem

Although the portrayal of women in Bollywood is flawed, it is only one part of the problem that accounts for the fuelling of rape culture. The portrayal of the man—in any capacity, be it the hero or the villain, or even the father of the heroine—is often tied to a sense of toxic masculinity, in which the male characters dominate through violence. Films often centre on a lead narrative that stems from the men: their conflicts, their ambitions, their revenge, their desires, and their macho heroic antics. All of these films put a premium on masculinity. Although much has been written about how these films promote an unhealthy body image for women, the films also project a negative one for men through their idealizing of the muscular male body. The hypermasculinity on display in these films suggests that men should be aggressive, violent, and macho; they should also be capable of fighting the bad guys with their hands, dancing like a pro, being an ideal son, and being a heartthrob for every woman he passes.

Such portrayals of masculinity suggest an ethos that equates manhood with violence, which, in turn, translates into a terribly high amount of violence against women in India. Masculinity is continually equated with aggression, which forces young Indian men to set unrealistic and outrageous masculine standards for themselves. Furthermore, regardless of whether they fit the physical standards, men still choose to demonstrate their masculine dominance over women. On-screen portrayals of men harassing, stalking, and mistreating women are often imitated off screen. The underlying notion is that if a man harasses and stalks a woman enough, he will eventually win her over—even if she initially says no, she will eventually say yes. Such an understanding encourages men to be brutish in their behaviour—actions that are perpetually reinforced by the images they see in these films.

How Does This Feed Rape Culture?

The Indian film industry is not the sole cause of rape culture in India. However, it still promotes antagonism against women in society. The Indian film industry portrays characteristics of toxic masculinity—most often in an exaggerated fashion—and glorifies them in order to encourage mass consumption. These behaviours augment a social climate that is already poised against women, and they feed into the rape culture.

Figures from India's National Crime Records Bureau suggest that a rape takes place every twenty-two minutes in the country. The portrayal of women in Bollywood tends to reiterate the same old stereotypes. A woman is made an object, and she is often seen gyrating among lewd and lecherous men, set to songs that are filled with lewd and obscene lyrics (Brook). Men are also portrayed in a stereotypical fashion: the hero is a macho man, with a well chiselled body, who is ready enough to assert his dominance. He uses violence to get what he wants. Villains are almost always portrayed as completely terrible human beings with no sense of humanity; they are steeped in debauchery, mindless violence, and a tendency towards sexual violence. These stereotypes tend to dehumanize men as well, as they only presented masculinity one dimensionally—submerged in machismo.

Rape is about dominance. By celebrating toxic hegemonic masculinity and objectifying women as well as ignoring their consent, the film industry promotes rape culture in India. As a result, these films support the notion that a woman's resistance to men's advance can be ignored in real life as well (Jaikiran).

The Indian film industry reflects an undercurrent of institutionalized sexism that prevails in India. These elements emerge from a social setting in India in which homosexuality is criminalized, sex is not spoken about, and sex education is discouraged and even banned in some of the largest cities and states. The combination of the disavowal these important conversations, which must be had, as well as the misogyny and patriarchy that are reasserted time and again on screen is one of the biggest factors that contribute to a constant cycle of violence in India.

Works Cited

Bamzai, Kaveri. *Bollywood Today.* Lustre Press Roli Books, 2007.

Berger, John. *Ways of Seeing.* Penguin, 1972.

Brook, Tom. "Does Bollywood Incite Sexual Violence in India?" BBC, Oct. 21, 2014, www.bbc.com/culture/story/20140205-does-bolly wood-incite-sex-crimes. Accessed 4 May 2020.

Jaikaran, Elizabeth. "What Are Our Favorite Bollywood Films Teaching Us about Rape Culture and Consent?" *Brown Girl Magazine,* 30. Dec. 2015, www.browngirlmagazine.com/2015/12/what-bolly wood-films-teach-us-about-rape-culture-and-consent. Accessed 10 May 2020.

Mulvey, Laura. "Visual Pleasure and Narrative Cinema." *Film Theory and Criticism,* edited by Leo Braudy and Marshall Cohen Oxford University Press, 1999, pp. 803-816.

Statista. "Target Audience for Hindi and Other Indian Regional Language Films in 2012, by Region (in Millions)." *Statista,* 2012, www.statista.com/statistics/259315/bollywoods-target-audience-size-by -region/. Accessed 4 May 2020.

Suroor, Hasan. "Sharmila Tagore Honoured by Edinburgh University." *The Hindu,* 26 Oct. 2012, www.thehindu.com/arts/sharmila-tagore-honoured-by-edinburgh-university/article4031942.ece. Accessed 4 May 2020.

Chapter Thirteen

The Tragedy of Rape Trials: Women, Modesty, and the Law

Priyanka Nupur

Introduction

On May 18, 2015, sixty-six-year-old Aruna Shaunbaug passed away after being in a vegetative state for forty-two years due to a sexual assault in 1973 (Ganesh). In all the ensuing years, the case has been most widely discussed through the lens of euthanasia and other medical aspects (DeSouza); however, there is another dimension to this case that demands attention. The accused in the case, Sohanlal Valmiki, was charged only with robbery and attempted murder, whereas the fact that Shaunbaug had been raped in the hospital where she worked as a nurse by one of the employees was not discussed in this case. The concerns about the reputation of the hospital where Shaun-baug worked and where the crime was perpetrated coupled with concerns about the reputation of the doctor to whom she was engaged and worked with prevented allegations of rape from being registered in the police report. The cultural setting that rejects a rape victim was much to blame for the case of the rape not being charged and the accused winning his freedom after serving a sentence of only seven years. Cultural taboos concerning rape prevented it from even being reported in this case. Unfortunately, in India, even forty-seven years after the gruesome incident, the cultural perceptions regarding rape and rape victims have not changed much.

Rape as a sexual crime continues to be a taboo. It is not just a crime; it is a crime associated with shame and dishonour. Unfortunately, this shame and dishonour become associated not with the accused but with the victim. The raped woman is often dehumanized and equated with a "zinda laash" ("a walking corpse"). The act of sex involved in the crime gives it multiple layers, and, culturally speaking in the Indian context, more attention is given to justifying the rape than punishing the accused. In rape cases, whether the accused is convicted or not, the agony that the rape victim goes through due to the crime, as well as the trial, surpasses what the accused has to face as punishment.

How does rape become a cultural phenomenon? Why, across all cultures, has the functioning of law and the balance of justice been tilted against the rape victims and, more generally, against the female ones? Answers to such questions require examining the cultural context of the society under study to understand how rape is constructed and also how rape itself becomes a culture. As mentioned before, the crime of rape and its associated outcomes form a multilayered phenomenon. One of the major determinants in this dynamic of rape culture is how the female body and female psyche are constructed under a patriarchal lens.

This chapter takes up this particular aspect to look at the construction of so-called moral women, who under Indian cultural norms are the harbinger of both family and community honour. It looks at how the modesty of the victim is judged and manipulated to prove the innocence of the accused by demonstrating the victim's immoral character. The chapter discusses how the idea of a "loose woman" is normalized through the culture and also enters the legal field.

I explore how the victim's modesty (defined through sexual indicators) is used in rape trials to subvert the justice owed to the victim. To begin with, I examine patriarchy and phallocentric ideas through which the modesty and morality of women are constructed. For this, I draw on the arguments of Carol Smart to discuss a phallocentric culture which defines the world and how are women seen through this lens. Further- more, drawing from her analysis, I discuss how rape trials continue to use this phallocentric definition of women. I then look at two cases in India as discussed in the work of Kalpana Kannabiran, to understand how morality is interpreted, understood, and used in giving or holding back justice to the rape victim. I also look at various reforms in Indian laws regarding rape that have entered the legal arena to see how far they conform to or depart from the idea of morality that is defined by phallocentric standards in the Indian society.

Cultural Politics of the Body

Female bodies often act as a terrain in which codes of honour have been written and cultural performances of power have occurred (Mathur 54); they have been historically regarded as the property of the male members of a family (the fathers, husbands, and sons) (Weitz 3). The undefiled female body is a symbol of community honour. The honour, or the "izzat," lies in the female body, more specifically in her sexual purity. General violence may not hurt male honour so much, but an attack on the sexual purity of a female relative can devastate their honour, as the worth of a female, as well the honour of the males associated with her, is defined through her sexual chasteness. The image of a moral woman, hence, is constructed from the societal norms of sexual behaviour and who diligently follows them. A moral woman would rather die rather than let her sexual purity be violated (Baxi 1197). Simultaneously, an immoral woman who does not conform to these norms has no honour and, therefore, cannot be raped. Female modesty becomes the axis of her existence and honour.

Modesty is a part of all cultures across the world. Although modesty is defined through many different dimensions, this chapter focuses upon the sexual dimension of modesty. Female modesty forms the crucial part of this discussion, as codes of sexual conduct are more stringent for females than males. The particular requirements from modest women may vary slightly in form across cultures, but its larger presence as a guide to the development of female personality forms an overarching phenomenon. The ingredients of modesty that have been developed historically and socially are required to be internalized in the female psyche as well as in her social and personal behaviour. Such a development of modesty is facilitated by the process of socialization through family, religion and society (Mathur 55).

These prescriptions and proscriptions for women can influence their dress, demeanor, interaction, and, most importantly, sexual behaviour. Any digression from the norm is met with dire consequences for women; however, for men, expressions of their sexuality are often celebrated as a mark of their masculinity.

This differential treatment of both genders in the sexual dimension should be understood in terms of the social perception that prevails regarding gender. In all societies, females are deemed to be the second sex and are given a lower social position. The whole being of the female is defined through the judgmental eyes of patriarchy. This lens renders them as inferior beings, who must be protected and controlled mentally, physically and sexually. The maintenance of female modesty and the control of her sexuality, thus, become crucial functions of the patriarchal structure.

Tragedies occur when these prevalent ideas of modesty are used to deliver justice in rape trials. Cultural values about sexuality are represented in law (Smart 26), the result of which is that rather than addressing the brutal assault on the women, the trials investigate the modesty of the female who was raped. Misplaced inferences and conclusions about female modesty place the burden of proof on the victim herself. The law of a land is not immune to the cultural setting. But when a culture that disadvantages certain groups combines with laws that further perpetuate modes of female modesty, instead of offering a recourse to justice, the trial becomes the victim's greatest tragedy, which has many more negative social implications for her. The following section looks at how Indian society constructs women and how this construction (both physical and mental) has implications in the legal proceedings.

Phallocentric Culture and Law: Reading the Female Body and Mind

Carol Smart has drawn attention to the overlaps between the law and phallocentric culture. She refers to phallocentric culture as follows: "[It is] a culture which is structured to meet the needs of the masculine imperative. However, the term phallocentric take us beyond the visible surface appearance of male dominance to invoke sexuality, desire, and the subconscious psychic world" (27). Phallocentrism defines various aspects of the sexual dimension. Through it, male or masculine experiences are preferred, and female experiences are understood only in relation to male desires. Any form of female sexual experience or pleasure that does not coincide with the masculine definition is understood as not only unfathomable but also pathological (Smart 29). Phallocentric culture ignores women's agency, even when she says "no" to sexual advances:

In this formulation women's sexuality is constructed as separate from women themselves ... this sexuality of which they have charge is constructed as an essence which can by-pass consciousness or which has a will of its own. This in turn allows for the construction of women's consciousness simply as a one-dimensional prudery, an inappropriate moral standard imposed by mothers and daughters. It is not regarded as an expression of a woman's will but rather the mouthing of a convention which defeats the woman's own potential for sexual satisfaction. In other words if women say "no" they do not really mean it (Smart 30).

Smart's definition of phallocentric culture disqualifies women's experiences and realities, as they are interpreted from a completely patriarchal lens. Courtrooms in India tend to prioritize the phallocentric discourse when adjudicating rape cases. Women who say they have been raped are often not believed, or it is claimed they, in fact, consented to have sex, which calls into question their morality.

An extension of these ideas can be seen in the work of Lynne Henderson, who talks about the myth of male innocence and female guilt which she describes as

...an unexamined belief that men are not morally responsible for their heterosexual conduct, while females are morally responsible both for their conduct and for the conduct of males. Indeed men are entitled to act on their sexual passions, which are viewed as difficult and sometimes impossible to control; this belief also says that women should know this and avoid stimulating them if they do not wish to have sexual intercourse. Also, if men desire, they are entitled to fulfillment of their needs through heterosexual intercourse. The flip side of the belief in men's inability to control themselves is the attribution of uncontrolled sexual passion and lust to women; it is against that lust that men must protect themselves, but if they do not, it is again not their responsibility, but the fault of women. On this view, women's passion and lustfulness mean they are always already consenting to sexual activity (131).

The idea that women are always consenting removes the element of guilt for men in cases of forced sexual relationships. Such an understanding establishes the idea that women are lying when they complain about sexual violence or rape. Henderson quotes St. Albert to highlight the discursive understanding that defines women as liars, who do not admit that they want and enjoy sex: "As I heard in the confessional in Cologne, delicate wooers seduce women with careful touches. The more these women seem to reject them, the more they really long for them and resolve to consent to them. But in order to appear chaste, they act as if they disapprove these things" (St. Albert qtd. in Henderson 135). According to Henderson, this construct is supported by "social institutions and disciplines including religion, philosophy, and law," and, unfortunately, it is this perception that prevails in rape laws in India as well (133).

Rape and Cultural Violence

Problematizing and controlling female sexuality can be found across cultures, and India is no exception. According to Kanchan Mathur, in the "Indian context, the woman's body is the space where culturally coded and socially sanctioned norms of the desirable woman are inscribed" (55). She further states that a "good woman" is "obedient and sacrificing," "upholds the honour of the family," and "maintains the culture of silence" (55). These norms of desirable conduct of women are inculcated in them through different means of socialization.

Sex in India is considered to be an extremely private affair. Talking about and discussing sex in an average Indian family is still considered to be a taboo. Important to note here is that the burden of this privacy and silence on the issues of sex is largely borne by the women. The significance of this silence comes out of the fact that in India, one's sexual behaviour is seen as a major factor in determining one's character and morality. Moreover, whereas men to a large extent enjoy space and opportunities to indulge in sexual explorations, if females show even a hint of any such desire or action, they may face questions over their character and morality.

Another important issue is that in India, family and community honour are often attached to the character of the women within it. Hence, passive sexual behaviour, the noninvolvement in any illicit affair, as well as the non-violation of her body are all deemed crucial to preserve the honour of the family and the community, which are vested in the body of the women. Any sexual violence to the woman's body is, thus, immediately regarded as an attack on the honour of the family and community to which the woman belongs. Radhika Singha argues the following:

It was administrative common sense, the norm of knowing the people that the honour of men, particularly among the respectable orders in India depended upon the chaste reputation of their women. Stories about the 'defiled' woman herself demanding to be killed tended to be accepted as confirmatory 'of the anxiety which the natives of this country feel, on points where female chastity is concerned, to preserve unsullied the reputation of their family (qtd. in Kannabiran 82).

The violence of rape has a cultural element that cannot be ignored. Along with the importance of chastity, the sexual purity of the female must also be protected. This cultural element is most importantly related to the notion of power and the idea that the female should be controlled in all matters, including sexual behaviour. Cultures that deem female honour related to her sexuality and her sexual purity related to family and community honour pave way for rape to be used as an instrument of revenge through bodies of women.

The use of rape as a weapon and strategy of war is well established (Farewell 390; Koo 527-35; Card 7-8; Mookherjee 433-50). Communal riots are another set of events that witness the mass rape of women of one community by men from another community (Chandra 1883; Jaffrelot 14-15,19; Narasimhan-Madhavan 1570). In the case of India, the violence during the partition of the country in 1947, the anti-Sikh riots of 1984, and the communal violence associated with the Gujarat riots of 2002 all involved rape of women (Menon 30), which symbolized patriarchal dominance. Although they are committed on the bodies of women, such acts of violence are actually aimed towards dishonoring and insulting men, who then seek their own vengeance by violating the women of those communities.

Since the female body and female sexuality are seen as mere objects owned by men and in need of their protection, if a woman is physically violated or raped, it is perceived as defilement of her body. Her purity is supposed to be destroyed, and this makes her rehabilitation difficult. Moreover, a commonly held notion prevails that the victim of rape was at fault for such violence that occurred; her faults include the nature of her clothing, her interactions, her being out of the home, and so on. A woman who has been raped is often treated more as a culprit than as a victim of a heinous crime. Stories of her loose morals are often used to justify the crime. Hence, when examining rape trials and judgment in India, the question of modesty offers an important window through which rape trials can be studied, particularly to what extent the victim's modesty is made central to the case and how is it used to turn the case against her, thus eliminating her chances of securing justice.

Rape Trials: Victimizing the Rape Victim in Legal Processes

This section draws on the two case studies discussed in the work of Kannabiran to examine how the morality of a rape victim became a decisive factor in the rape trials in India. The first case is the infamous Mathura rape case that happened in 1972 and the second is the rape case of Rameeza Bee which happened in 1978, which resulted in the creation of the Muktadar Commission.

Tuka Ram and Anr Vs State of Maharashtra, 1978

In 1972, Mathura, a poor tribal girl from Maharashtra, had fallen in love with Ashok (a relative of her employer), and they decided to get married. However, Mathura's brother, Gama, did not approve of this affair, and he lodged a police complain with the neighbouring police station against Mathura's employer, Nunshi, her husband, Laxman, and Ashok for kidnapping Mathura. All of these people, including Mathura, were called to the police station. After recording their statements, Gama was asked to get Mathura's birth certificate while the others, except Mathura, were asked to leave the police station. Mathura, left alone, was raped by one of the constables in the toilet while another one attempted to rape her. When her brother and others found out about the incident, a complaint was lodged; medical examination was conducted on Mathura and the case was taken up by the Sessions Court.

The trial as well as the statements of the judge highlight how the character, morality, and modesty of a girl is defined through patriarchal standards, and if she is found to be deviant according to those standards, it is used against her. The medical examination revealed the past sexual history of Mathura; she had old hymenal tears, and the vagina permitted two fingers easily. The court interpreted these findings as evidence of Mathura's sexual activity as well as her immoral character. Moreover, no traces of semen were found in the pubic hair or in the vaginal smear slides; some traces were, however, found on her clothes. Also, Mathura's body showed no signs of injury.

These findings were used to establish two things: she had an immoral character and she consented to having sex with the policemen. Hence, there was no rape. The Supreme Court judgement in 1978 noted the fact that the district court stated that Mathura was a "shocking liar," whose testimony was "riddled with falsehood and improbabilities"(Para 3). Although the court acknowledged that sex between her and the police officer had occurred, it concluded that sex was not forced. The district court alleged she claimed the sexual encounter was rape because she wanted to sound virtuous. Mathura had surrendered her body to the police officer and did not resist to the act.

Although the accused were acquitted by the district judge, the High Court reversed the order. However, the verdict of the district court was upheld by the Supreme Court in 1978, which accepted that the absence of injury on the body of Mathura reflected the absence of resistance on her part and indicated that the alleged intercourse was a peaceful affair without resistance; her claims of having shouted to raise an alarm and resistance to forceful intercourse were dismissed as lies and fabrications.

Ultimately, the conclusion of the trial went against the victim. The results of the medical report were used to prove that Mathura was of a bad moral character; hence, she lied about being raped. Also, the absence of injuries on her body was proof that she had not resisted to the intercourse, and may be even initiated it, considering her past sexual history. Thus, the basic facts of the case were used against Mathura because she was seen as having an immoral character.

The Rameeza Bee Rape Case and the Muktadar Commission Report, 1978

In 1978, Rameeza Bee, an eighteen-year-old woman, was returning from a movie show late at night with her husband. While they were waiting for a rickshaw, her husband, Ahmed Hussain, went to relieve himself. In the meantime, she was taken into custody by police officers and was raped in the police station by three of them. The police took her back home early in the morning, when she complained to her husband of being raped. When the husband tried to retaliate, he was beaten badly by the police and died that evening. Friends and neighbours of the victimized couple protested at the police station. When an enquiry was set up, the police claimed that Rameeza Bee was a prostitute, who was arrested while soliciting customers and indecently exposing her body; they also claimed her husband was her pimp. The police also produced false medical reports to prove that her husband died due to heart attack and that Rameeza Bee was not raped.

The police, in order to save face, took the strategy of destroying the victim's credibility (Prasad 1497-98). They tried to prove that Rameeza Bee was a prostitute, hence of an immoral character. This strategy was used to disqualify the statement of the victim. The police tried to take several statements from Rameeza Bee, hoping that the differences in her statements may later be used against her (Prasad 1499). The government went out of its way to shield the guilty officers (Kannabiran 83).

The Muktadar Commission was set up to enquire into the case, and it found the officers guilty of the rape of Rameeza Bee, as well as the murder of her husband; it also revealed the close association that the police had with prostitution. However, the case was taken to the Supreme Court. Kannabiran notes that the defence focused on the charges of prostitution against Rameeza Bee rather than her rape. Also, the legality of her marriage with Ahmed Hussain was questioned while Ahmed Hussain himself was charged with being a pimp. The strategy of the defence was to foreground her character, her dishonesty, and her "immoral vocation" (Kannabiran 84). Kannabiran further notes the following:

> Queries about the rape were interspersed with queries about knowledge of the validity of cultural practice, with accusations of theft, with suggestions of a wider community of belonging to the 'immoral' community, and with accusations of mobility associated with that immorality: the bus that took her to a procurer, the rickshaw that was her vehicle for soliciting, and so on. The discursive, and indeed political, strategy achieved a disruption in the statement of the assault against Rameeza and Ahmed Hussain, with the constant back and forth movement blurring the boundaries between Rameeza's alleged immorality and the fact of her rape. (84)

A number of fake witnesses were brought in to prove that Rameeza Bee worked as a prostitute. These false witnesses were either prostitutes or pimps and even fake clients who gave their testimony in favour of the police. Not just Rameeza Bee, but other people in her community, including her mother-in-law, were also accused of being involved in prostitution and the procurement of girls. Pointing to the ordeal of Rameeza Bee whose character assassination was taking place in the court by men unknown to her, Kannabiran says the following:

> Finally, one of the most horrifying events of the Enquiry itself was the sight of the burqa-clad Rameeza standing quietly as one man after another entered the witness box to swear that he had had sex with Rameeza on a certain day at a certain place after paying her Rs 10 or 15. Rameeza would then be asked to lift the burqa, revealing her face for the man (and the packed, tense courtroom) to stare at before he affirmed that she was indeed the same woman. All these men, like Qutubuddin, had been mobilised by the police to testify in favour of the defence. This repeated public unveiling enabled a moral displacement of Rameeza and her reconfiguration as a prostitute: Prostitutes should not veil themselves and must be open at all times to the public gaze. (86)

Through illegitimating her character and marriage, Rameeza Bee's immorality was established, which was used against her. Kannabiran argues that the rape survivors have to constantly deal with the "patriar-chal communitarian discourses" not just in their families and comm-unities but also in the courts (90).

These two cases highlight how discourses of immorality and alleged defects in their character were used against the rape victims. In both these cases, the efforts of the defence concentrated on establishing that the victim was of an immoral character due to her sexual past. India's phallocentric culture, which disqualifies a woman's perspective, was clearly displayed in these two cases.

The Nirbhaya Rape Incidence: Modern Times, Ancient Morality

The gruesome gang rape of a twenty-three-year-old female in Delhi in December, 2012, shook the whole nation. The victim and her male friend were returning from a movie late in the evening when they boarded a private bus, which was where the rape took place. This rape was specifically noted for its gruesome violence and resulted in huge protests demanding justice across the country.

The documentary *India's Daughter*, directed by Leslee Udwin in 2015, records the perspectives of different people (parents and friends of the victim, renowned lawyers, one of the accused, defence lawyers, psychiatrists, and ministers) about the case. This section highlights the statements of one of the accused in the rape case along with the opinions of the defense lawyers. Their arguments illustrate the deeply held prejudices against women in Indian society. The accused who was interviewed said that "decent girls do not roam around late at night, and that a girl is more responsible for rape than the boy who does it ... girls and boys are unequal and girls are supposed to look after households only ... [they] not roam around at night in bars and discos, doing wrong things and wearing wrong clothes." According to the accused, girl who was raped "needed to be taught a lesson as her conduct of being out at night with an unrelated male was wrong ... [the] victim should not have resisted or fought back; then they would have simply let her go after the raping and [would] not [have] inflict[ed] unnecessary violence." Here, rape is justified because the victim went against the established moral norms of the society, which requires females to stay within the household and to associate with only those males who are family members.

The psychiatrist of the rapists suggested that the social environment of the accused normalized violence against women. However, the defense lawyers, who are from the more educated classes, were even more shocking, as one of the lawyers even said, "we have the best culture; in our culture there is no place for women." He reiterated the cultural norms that girls should not go out late at night unaccompanied. He compared women with flowers that needed to be protected from men, who are like thorns. According to him, "women were more precious than gems and if a diamond was let out on streets, certainly dogs will come to get it." The ideas of the lawyers were rooted in the deeply held cultural notions concerning what constituted good women and what constituted bad ones. Women who stayed within the norms were good, whereas the ones who broke them were bad and deserved to be raped. It is ironic that the documentary was banned in India because of the views of these men, even though such ideas define the practical reality of daily lives of women in Indian society and are used to justify violence against them.

Amendments: Past, Present, and the Future

In 1860, the British Government codified crimes and their punishments in the Indian Penal Code (IPC). Sections 375 and 376 of the IPC deal with rape. Whereas section 375 defines rape, section 376 deals with its punishment. According to section 375, rape is defined as sexual intercourse by a man with a woman, under the following circumstances.

First, against her will; secondly, without her consent; thirdly, with her consent, when her consent has been obtained by putting her or any person in whom she is interested in fear of death or of hurt; fourthly, with her consent, when the man knows that he is not her husband, and that her consent is given because she believes that he is another man to whom she is or believes herself to be lawfully married; fifthly, with her consent, when, at the time of giving such consent, by reason of unsoundness of mind or intoxication or the administration by him personally or through another of any stupefying or unwholesome substance, she is unable to understand the nature and consequences of that to which she gives consent; and sixthly, with or without her consent, when she is under sixteen years of age (IPC).

In cases of sexual assault on women, the IPC differentiates between molestation and rape. Whereas molestation refers to an intention to outrage a woman's modesty, an actual violation of modesty constitutes rape; this distinction again is rooted in notion of modesty of women (Mahadevan 45). Cultural prejudices that situate a woman's worth in her sexual purity hierarchize crimes against women on the basis of how far her modesty was outraged.

The rape case of Mathura and the Supreme Court judgment that acquitted the perpetrators was a watershed moment in the history of rape law reforms in India. Public resentment arose from different quarters and the consequent events led to the amendment in criminal law in 1983, including the IPC (1860), the Indian Evidence Act (1872) and the Code of Criminal Procedure (1973).

These amendments most importantly defined the idea of custodial rape and outlined punishment for it. They also provided for in-camera trial (proceedings in private, without public or press attending it) in case of rape trials. The disclosure of the identity of rape victims (without the consent of the victim or the next of kin of the victim, if the victim is minor, is of unsound mind, or is dead) was made a punishable offence. Also, the printing or publication of any matters related to the trial was also prohibited; this was, however, criticized for perpetuating the discourse of shame and honour around rape (Baxi 1197).

One of the most crucial developments of these reforms concerned the notion of consent. In the matter of consent, if the victim records in her statement that she did not consent to the sexual act, then the court was to presume that she did not consent. This amendment shifted the onus of proof from the victim to the accused.

In 2003, an amendment was made to section 146 of Indian Evidence Act, 1872, which prohibited questions regarding the general character of the victim in cross-examinations during rape trials. Given the extent to which the character of victims had been used against them in previous trials, as discussed above, this amendment was an important development. The notion of evidence was also expanded to include circumstantial evidence (Mahadevan 45).

Rukmini Sen argues that reports of the Law Commission of India, which makes recommendations for the formulation of laws in the legal system, are much more progressive than what goes in the amendments themselves (81). She argues that the law constructs gender by promoting certain images of women, which, in turn, "serve to coerce women and make them believe that certain identities are natural and inevitable" (81). These identities and images can be seen to be taken as the basis of judgments, as in the cases of Mathura and Rameeza Bee. Discussing the open letter sent to the chief justice of India concerning the judgment of the Mathura rape case, Sen points out the objections that were raised about the moralistic ideologies used in the case (83). The letter raises two important points concerning morality, as Sen explains: "The judgment had taken a moralistic position on "habitual sexual intercourse"; and consent involves submission, but the reverse is not true. Absence of resistance necessarily does not indicate consent; the colonial and male-dominated notions of what constitutes consent and burden of proof should be done away with" (83). In the backdrop of such events, the 84th Law Commission Report on Rape and Allied Offences (1980) notes that the incident of rape led to the ultimate violation and humiliation of the person, leading to both a sense of fear and powerlessness.

Sen further argues that although the Law Commission reports are more progressive than the amendments, these reports still reinforce old patriarchal ideas about female chastity. The phrasing "ultimate violation of self," for example, encouraged the understanding that if a woman had her chastity and purity violated in rape, she had no reason to live. Such a notion is, again, a reflection of the cultural idea that a woman's worth depends on her chasteness and morality. However, the report did recognize the ordeal faced by a rape victim in trials as well as the traumatic experiences they had searching for justice. Pratiksha Baxi claims that the basis of Indian Evidence Act itself is rooted in the cultural idea of chastity (1197). It assumes that a real victim must be moral and chaste.

The 84th Law Commission Report also distinguished between consent and silence: "Consent may not be vitiated only when a woman is put to fear of death or hurt but also when there is an injury in body, mind, reputation, property, and criminal intimidation." However, Sen argues that this recommendation has not yet been added the section 375 of IPC (83). Another set of recommendations regarding sec. 375 was as follows:

A man is said to have committed "rape"

(1) without her free and voluntary consent,

(2) with her consent when it was obtained by putting her in fear of death or of hurt or of any injury either to herself or to any other person or by criminal intimidation,

(3) with her consent when her consent is given under misconception of fact, when the man knows or has reason to believe that the consent was given in consequence of such misconception,

(4) with her consent, if the consent is given by a woman who, from un-soundness of mind or intoxication or by reason of the consumption or administration of any stupefying or unwholesome substance, is unable to understand the nature and consequences of that to which she gives consent, or is unable to offer effective resistance,

(5) with or without her consent, when she is under eighteen years of age (qtd. in Sen 86)

However, Sen points out that the first three points of this recommendation were not followed (83). These points were important for
how the issue of consent was used to frame the character and morality
of a rape victim. The importance of this idea can be seen in relation to
the fact that in the Mathura rape case, the court held that the absence
of injury marks on the girl's body implied consent.

The December 2012 rape in Delhi marked another crucial point in
the history of rape law reforms in India. Following the rape, the Justice
Verma Committee (JVC) was set up to give its recommendations for
amendments to criminal law. The JVC report is progressive in how it
tries to draw attention to how ideas of modesty and morality were based
on patriarchal notions and how it suggests ways to eliminate these ideas,
including more education to do away with certain negative stereotypes
concerning women and modesty. The report says that India suffers from
a "cult of masculinity and masculine aggression" (390) and argues that
the way boys are taught to silence their emotions and are trained to take
up positions of power and prestige. Similarly, girls are also made to
internalize certain attributes specific to their gender, which arise out of
patriarchal ideologies. The JVC highlights the differences in how female
and male children are socialized by pointing out that "women are made
aware of their sexuality at an early age and at an age when their male
counterparts have relatively more freedom at least physically, while
having their freedom of expression curtailed" (395).

The JVC also discusses notions of honour and states that the gendered
socialization makes girls believe that they are the repositories of the
honour of their family, their community, and their caste. Men wield
power over women, especially in sexual terms. Power and violence reside
in men, whereas girls are brought up to uphold traditional values of
purity, chastity, and virtue which are supposed to lie in a particular part
of their body. The JVC report identifies the roots of such notions as not
only in the family but also in schools, which further encourage such
stereotypes by assigning roles according to gender. The report also
accepts the presence of patriarchal stereotypes in many different prof-
essions, including law. Based on these findings, the JVC suggests
important changes to the Indian Evidence Act, 1872.

After section 53 of the Act, the JVC suggests the insertion of the
following section: "53A. In a prosecution for an offence under Section
354, Section 354A, Section 354B, Section 354C, Section 376(1), Section

376(2), Section 376A, Section 376B(1) or Section 376C of the Indian Penal Code or for attempt to commit any such offence, evidence of the character of the victim or of his or her previous sexual experience with any person shall not be relevant."

For section 114A of the Evidence Act, the JVC suggests the following section to be substituted: "114A. (1) In a prosecution for rape under sub-section (2) of section 376 or for gang rape under Section 376C of the Indian Penal Code, where sexual intercourse by the accused is proved and the question is whether it was without the consent of the other person alleged to have been raped and such other person states in his/her evidence before the court that she or he did not consent, the court shall presume that she or he did not consent."

For section 146 of the Evidence Act, the JVC advises the following provision to be substituted: "Provided that in a prosecution for an offence under Section 376(1), Section 376(2), Section 376A, Section 376 B(1) or Section 376C or for attempt to commit any such offence, it shall not be permissible to adduce evidence or to put questions in the cross-examination of the victim as to his or her general moral character, or as to his or her previous sexual experience with any person."

The above recommendations for amendments were included in the Criminal Amendment Act, 2013. Thus, the JVC report has helped move beyond prevalent ideas of morality and sexual behaviour, and the incorporation of the suggested amendments in the Criminal Amendment Act, 2013 is also a welcomed step. However, its implementation in spirit and in the practice of law has yet to be seen.

Conclusion

The discourse on morality is central not just to rape laws but, more importantly, to the practice of law and the process of imparting justice to the rape victims. In a phallocentric understanding of the world, the obsession with sex and sexual purity becomes concentrated on women's bodies, and in this way, rape and rape trials become influenced by phallocentric attitudes. This culture constructs women as bodies for sexual consumption, protection, and exploitation. As mentioned in the earlier sections, the twisted interplay of culture, legal trials, and social attitudes places a rape victim and her allegations under suspicion, and casts the woman as a liar, which has huge implications for the victim during the rape trials.

Due to the efforts of feminists, legal researchers, and socially concerned lawyers, as well as the aftermath of infamous Delhi rape case of December 2012, changes in the laws concerning judgements about the moral character of the rape victim have been achieved. However, it is common knowledge that there is a difference between laws as they are written and as they are practiced. Changing the words of law does not necessarily change the law in practice. As seen in the documentary *India's Daughter*, the conceptions and beliefs of law practitioners about women continue to be rooted in a cultural system that demeans women. The people who are responsible for imparting justice are themselves very much a product of the same patriarchal structure and ideology against which actions are needed. It is unfortunate that people in positions of power who craft and write laws continue to make insensitive remarks in the public domain.

To see how effective these changes in law have actually been, we will need to closely observe not just future rape trials in India but also the discourses that they use. There are progressive sections of Indian society, including both males and females who have fought for women's rights. Yet this section remains limited, and the majoritarian view concerning women and their proper role in India continues to remain the same.

Works Cited

Baxi, Pratiksha. "Rape, Retribution, State: On Whose Bodies." *Economic and Political Weekly*, vol. 35, no.14, 2000, pp. 1196-1200.

Card, Claudia. "Rape as a Weapon of War." *Hypatia*, vol. 11, no. 4, 1996, pp. 5-18.

Chandra, Sudhir. *"Of Communal Consciousness and Communal Violence: Impressions from Post-Riot Surat."* *Economic and Political Weekly*, vol. 28, no. 36, 1993, pp. 1883-87.

Das, Veena. "Sexual Violence: Discursive Formation and the State." *Economic and Political Weekly*, vol. 31.35, no. 37, 1996, pp. 2411-23.

Desouza, Peter Ronald. "The Incomplete Case of Aruna Shanbaug." *The Hindu*, 10 June 2015, www.thehindu.com/opinion/lead/the-incomplete-case-of-aruna-shanbaug/article7298902.ece. Accessed 5 May 2020.

Farewell, Nancy. "War Rapes: New Conceptualizations and Responses." *Affilia*, vol. 19, no. 4, 2004, pp. 389-403.

Henderson, Lynne. "Rape and Responsibility." *Law and Philosophy*, vol. 11, no. 1/2, 1992, pp. 127-78.

India's Daughter. Directed by Leslee Udwin, BBC, 2015. Documentary.

Jaffrelot, Christophe. "Communal Riots in Gujarat: The State at Risk." Working Paper 17, 2003, archiv.ub.uni-heidelberg.de/volltextserver /4127/1/hpsacp17.pdf. Accessed 5 May. 2020.

Kannabiran, Kalpana. "Sexual Assault and the Law." Challenging the Rule(s) of Law: Colonialism, Criminology and Human Rights in India, edited by Kalpana Kannabiran and Ranbir Singh, Sage, 2008, pp. 78-118.

Koo, Katrina Lee. "Confronting a Disciplinary Blindness: Women, War and Rape in the International Politics of Security." *Australian Journal of Political Science*, vol. 37, no. 3, 2002, pp. 525-36.

Mahadevan, Kanchana. "The Virtuous Woman: Law, Language and Activism." *Economic and Political Weekly*, vol. 43, no. 17, 2008, pp. 44-53.

Mathur, Kanchan. "Body as Space. Body as Site: Bodily Integrity and Women's Empowerment in India." *Economic and Political Weekly*, vol. 43, no. 17, 2008, pp. 54-63.

Menon, Jisha. "Rehearsing the Partition: Gendered Violence in 'Aur Kitne Tukde.'" *Feminist Review*, vol. 84, no. 1, 2006, pp. 29-47.

Mookherjee, Nayanika. "Remembering to Forget: Public Secrecy and Memory of Sexual Violence in the Bangladesh War of 1971." *Journal of the Royal Anthropological Institute*, vol. 12, no. 2, 2006, pp. 433-50.

Ganesh. N. "After Being Raped and in Coma for 42 Years, Aruna Shanbaug Breathes Her Last." *India Today*, 19 May. 2015, www.india today.in/india/story/aruna-shanbaug-dead-rape-mumbai-hospital-coma-euthanasia-253587-2015-05-19. Accessed 5 May 2020.

Narasimhan-Madhavan, Deepa. "Gender, Sexuality and Violence: Permissible Violence against Women during the Partition of India and Pakistan." *Hawwa*, vol. 4, no. 2, 2006, pp. 396-416.

Prasad, P.S.N. "The Police and Rameeza Bee: Muktadar Commission Findings." *Economic and Political Weekly*, vol. 13, no. 35, 1978, pp. 1497-99.

Sen, Rukmini. "Law Commission Reports on Rape." *Economic and Political Weekly*, vol. 45, no. 44, 2010, pp. 81-87.

Smart, Carol. "Rape: Law and the Disqualification of Women's Sexuality." *Feminism and the Power of Law*. Routledge, 1989.

Tharoor, Shashi. "Politicians Talk of Everything Except Rape; That Must Change." *Hindustan Times*, 6 Oct. 2016, https://www.hindustatimes.com/india-news/too-many-politicians-blame-wo men-for- volence-inflicted-on-them-shashi-tharoor/story-7iZ4V2 QausKGAT2 ml8gJML. html. Accessed 23 November 2016.

Verma, Justice J.S., Justice Leila Seth, Gopal Subramanium. *Report to the Committee on Amendments to Criminal Law, 2013.*

Weitz, Rose. "A History of Women's Bodies". *The Politics of Women's Bodies: Sexuality, Appearance and Behaviour*, edited by Rose Weitz, Oxford, 1998, pp. 3-11.

Chapter Fourteen

Changing India's Rape Culture: A Focus on Cultural Values, Bollywood, and Rape Laws

Sona Kaur and Eileen L. Zurbriggen

India has a long history of respecting traditional values and cultural norms (Kallivayalil), many of which involve conservative gender roles that place men and boys in positions of status and power but subjugate girls and women (Derne and Jadwin 259). These gender inequities contribute to rape culture but also provide an avenue towards rape prevention. Although Bollywood, India's iconic film industry, has been criticized for its stereotypical portrayals of violence against women (e.g., Manohar and Kline 242), it also offers a medium through which social change can be achieved.

In this chapter, we analyze the interplay between traditional Indian cultural values, messages about gender, sexuality, and sexual violence presented in Bollywood films, and rape prevention and intervention in India. We begin by examining how sexual violence within marriage may bring unique challenges to Indian women due to the inherent nature of these relationships. We continue by presenting research on how rape and other forms of sexual violence are presented in Bollywood films. We also contemplate the influence of the industry's "item" songs[1] on viewers' attitudes about women, their bodies, and their sexuality. We provide recommendations to change India's rape laws, which ought to redefine sexual violence against women by acknowledging marital rape as a true crime. Then, we return to Bollywood to explore how viewers may be presented with more liberal ideas about women, which could have the potential to reduce support for rape myths. We close by applauding the work of Indian organizations who aim to reduce rape and other forms of violence against women.

Indian Cultural Values and Attitudes Regarding Gender, Marriage, and Sex

In traditional Indian culture, men and women are accorded different statuses and subjected to differential treatment. For instance, although both daughters and sons hold a special place in the larger familial structure, daughters are more likely to be subjected to severe punishment if they fall outside of their prescribed gender role expectations (Das and Kemp 26-27). Indian culture's emphasis on family honour, or "izzat," is maintained through women (Kallivayalil). Combined with practices such as arranged marriages, which centre more on the compatibility of the two families rather than on the bride and groom themselves, these traditions and values about honour may especially make women's experiences with dating and sex more limited (Das and Kemp 31). They also stress the responsibility that falls on women to be chaste in order to embody the image of the traditional Indian woman. Such a woman is one who is more committed to her family than her own individual aspirations (Derne and Jadwin 257-58).

As mentioned, it is not uncommon for young Indian female adolescents and women to be restricted from dating and sex. Rather, sexual relations between two individuals are understood to be acceptable only within the marital context, and as such, premarital virginity is highly valued. These sexual values are considered especially important for young Indian women (Ghule, Balaiah, and Joshi 6), who must monitor their behaviours to ensure they do not reduce their value as future wives and daughters-in-law. Indeed, female Indian American participants in Diya Kallivayalil's study shared their experiences of being reminded, usually by their mothers, that their actions will affect their likelihood of obtaining a marriage partner (548). These same restrictions are often not imposed on Indian male adolescents and young men—a discrepancy that is not lost on young Indian girls and women, who clearly perceive these sexual double standards and must navigate through them. For instance, one participant in Kallivayalil's study noted: "I know the rules would be different if I wasn't a girl because they [her parents] don't have to uphold their [boys'] purity till they're married" (547). Indian women, then, learn early on the value of marriage to their status and reputation in society. This kind of socialization can often promote marital rape by encouraging a woman not to speak out against the sexual violence perpetrated by her husband.

Evidence suggests that women commonly experience unwanted sexual advances from their husbands, despite informing their husbands that sex is unwanted. For instance, in a multimethod study conducted with 1,664 married women in Gujarat and West Bengal, 44 per cent said they had experienced unwanted sex (Santhya et al. 128). In another study from Bangladesh, 59 per cent of the sample experienced sexual violence regularly or sometimes (Khan, Townsend, and D'Costa 251). In another mixed-methods study, which included interviews with twenty-six women and nineteen men in Mumbai, 54 per cent of the women said they had experienced sexual violence at least once in their marriage (Maitra and Schensul 145). Husbands' responses in this study further indicated how common these events were, with about 74 per cent of men reporting they had forced their wives to have sex with them (146). The prevalence of marital sexual violence has also been noted in additional largescale studies with husbands as well. Research examining factors contributing to domestic violence has revealed that among a sample of 4,520 married men living in Uttar Pradesh, 45 per cent used physical force (e.g., slapping and kicking) to get their wives to have sex with them in the past year (Koenig et al. 135). These statistics clearly indicate that marital sexual violence is widespread in India.

Studies suggest that young female adolescents and women may experience violent sex during their very first sexual encounter, which often occurs on their wedding night with their new husbands (Maitra and Schensul 139). Researchers have noted that much of the sexual coercion in India takes place within marital relationships, given the traditional practice of arranged marriages, which discourages male-female interactions beyond the family (Waldner, Vaden-Goad, and Sikka 534). Therefore, it is likely that until marriage, women's interactions with men and experiences of sex are limited and, perhaps, their experiences of sexual violence as well. For those who do experience unwanted sex, the anguish from this violence may be further exacerbated by the fact that these young girls and women often enter into a marriage with no prior sexual knowledge. M. E. Khan, John Townsend, and Shampa D'Costa report this to be the case for 44 per cent of the women in their sample from Bangladesh (242). In these cases, newly married women were informed about sex to varying degrees from family sources, such as their sisters-in-law (242-43).

Married women soon begin to learn about sex from their new husbands as well; specifically, they come to understand their husbands' expectations around sex. For instance, interviews conducted in Mumbai about how married couples negotiate sex indicate that it was common for husbands to speak of their right to sex and to believe that physical force was an acceptable means to obtain sexual access when necessary (George 91). Interestingly, the belief that sex is a male right tended to be held by wives as well. Almost all of the twenty-six women who were interviewed in a study on marital sexual relationships expressed a similar belief that men were entitled to sex with their wives, as illustrated in the following quote: "I can't say no; after all he is my husband. If he won't do it with me who will he do it with? A woman is made for a man only" (qtd. in Maitra and Schensul 143-44). For these couples, then, consent to sex is not part of the conversation. Rather, women's sexual roles are understood early on in the marriage, and they involve permanent and "free sexual access" to husbands (Lazar 336). Although some wives willingly adhere to their husbands' demands for sex, other women find it difficult to make themselves sexually available to them at all times, especially when they feel that such interactions are devoid of all emotions. The following quote illustrates this type of internal struggle faced by wives: "...whenever sex happens, it happens with force, not with love, not from the heart.... I have no peace when he does it with me, only grief in my heart..." (qtd. in George 90). Thus, wives' experiences of sexual violence often involve feeling disrespected and hurt, both emotionally and physically from the sexual trauma.

To fully appreciate women's experiences of marital rape requires an understanding of additional factors that give rise to this type of violence. For instance, a mismatch between the sexual expression of a husband and wife may bring about conflict in a marriage. Khan, Townsend, and D'Costa note that of the fifty married women who sexually desired their husbands, twenty-four refrained from initiating sex (246). Women in this study believed it would be shameful for them to talk about these matters openly. Similar worries were voiced in other studies as well, as women feared being perceived as lacking modesty by their husbands (George 91). These women might have internalized cultural expectations implicated in sexual violence—namely, the sexual double standard, which encourages women to be sexually submissive.

The sexual double standard may play a role in men's sexually violent behaviour against women, as it also states that women who are sexually expressive are promiscuous (George 91) but not men who practice the same behaviour—promiscuity is reflective of their masculinity. Dinesh Bhugra et al. conducted a qualitative study in Delhi concerning individuals' attitudes about sex and found that whereas male respondents felt more comfortable in expressing their sexual needs (85) and engaging in more varied sexual practices (e.g., masturbation and extramarital affairs) (86), female respondents were more traditional in their sexual attitudes and behaviours. Although some women considered it acceptable to have premarital sex within the context of a committed relationship (85), they endorsed a sexual double standard that allowed men to be more sexually promiscuous. For instance, although male participants understood the need for a man to have sex with other women if his needs were not being met by his wife, this was not an option for wives (86).

The double standard further claims that women must avoid sexual situations in order to uphold their reputation (Muehlenhard 97). Concerned about being perceived as indecent if they are too open with their sexuality, women become passive and disinterested in sex, which may lead to situations where "men ... resort to persuasion, negotiation, manipulation and finally coercion to get sexual access" (qtd. in George 91). Due to these cultural expectations, men tend to be aware of women's inclination to refuse sex, but they still feel it is their responsibility to engage their wives in it anyways (Maitra and Schensul 146). Men who are aware of this double standard and who mistakenly assume that women's "no" actually means "yes" may continue their (unwanted) sexual advances towards them, thinking that a woman wants sex but is hesitating or refusing on purpose (Muehlenhard, 104-5). Men and women are then put in a bind—whereas men are encouraged to be sexually dominant, women are expected to be submissive (Muehlenhard). This conflict may then play out in a sexual situation marred with miscommunication, coercion, and, ultimately, force in the form of rape.

As discussed, Indian women are encouraged to embody the stereotypical image of a sexually passive wife. One issue that plays a role in this passivity is the commonplace belief held by both husbands and wives that men's sexual urges are uncontrollable, which is why women should submit to their husbands. The following quote illustrates this misconception about men's sexuality: "Sometimes if I want it and she doesn't agree then there is a fight. If a man doesn't get it [sex] he gets very tense. He loses control, as if he is drunk. He just wants to do it" (qtd. in Maitra and Schensul 143). The view that men cannot control their sexual desires—and therefore must quench them at all costs—may justify the idea of marital sexual violence. By suggesting that men have no choice in the matter deflects any responsibility away from them, which further trivializes the violence they perpetrate against women. Positioning men as sex-driven in this way suggests that husbands and wives engage in opposite, but complementary roles in the sexual realm: Women are expected "to be the gatekeepers of 'uncontrollable' male sexuality" (qtd. in Murnen, Wright and Kaluzny 372), whereas men are expected to break down these gates in order to fulfill their sexual appetites. Indeed, many of today's rape myths suggest that rape is a result of these uncontrollable sexual urges (Payne, Lonsway, and Fitzgerald 49). These beliefs are further supported by political figures who have commented on rape. For instance, Ramsevak Paikra, a senior minister of Chhattisgarh (an Indian state), has stated the following: "Such incidents [rapes] do not happen deliberately. These kind of incidents happen accidentally" (qtd. in Payne).

Along with cultural expectations that women be sexually submissive, wives also express several other reasons as to why they continue to endure sexual violence from their husbands. For instance, one woman mentioned that her husband would beat her, threaten to leave her, and engage in extramarital affairs when she refused sex (Khan, Townsend, and D'Costa 252). Another feature of these sexually violent relationships relates to a wife's familiarity with her husband at the time of marriage as well as the type of family arrangement they live in. Specifically, women are at higher risk of experiencing sex against their will when they are less familiar with their husbands (Santhya et al. 129). They are also less likely to say no to unwanted sex with their husbands when they live in joint versus nuclear families (Santhya et al. 127). These features are oftentimes inherent in arranged marriages, where it is not uncommon for the bride and groom to know little about each other, as they may leave it to their parents or other elders in the family to choose their life partner for them. Based on tradition, women are expected to live with their husbands alongside his family members (e.g., parents, grandparents, unmarried sisters, and brothers, who may also be married and have children of their own) (Das and Kemp 25).

Women's experiences of sexual violence may be further exacerbated by the arranged nature of their marriage. They are victimized by husbands who they do not know well, and this violation occurs in a home and among family members they are unfamiliar with. However, a woman must continue to fulfill her roles and responsibilities as a wife and daughter-in-law to maintain harmony among both households (i.e., her native family and in-laws) and uphold the honour of her native family, which may make it less likely for her to speak out against marital rape. Furthermore, Indian parents may internalize the belief that their daughters' true home is with their in-laws (Das and Kemp 27). As previously alluded to, women's roles in the family and society at large are solidified through their marital status (George 94). Given the centrality of the marriage institution to women's lives, wives may feel immense pressure to make their marriage work no matter the extent of their suffering. Annie George notes that parents do not approve of their daughters separating from or leaving their married home (94). Thus, women may be well aware that they would be ostracized if they left their husbands— even if it is due to violence. To make the abuse more endurable, they may internalize cultural norms that make sexual violence within marriage acceptable (Khan, Townsend, and D'Costa 252).

Other research has found that conforming to gender norms can result in a loss of autonomy in sexual relationships, leading to a diminishing sense of choice as well as engaging in behaviours that feel unsatisfying (Sanchez, Crocker, and Boike 1449). For Indian women, these gender norms include the sexual double standard and sexual subservience. These circumstances may make negotiating consent and safe sex practices much more difficult for married women, heightening their experiences of sexual violence. Unfortunately, wives may be left with no choice but to endure this violence due to rape myths surrounding men's uncontrollable sexual urges, the belief that sex is a husband's right, and the perception that one of the most crucial roles for Indian women is that of a wife and daughter-in-law. Considering these challenges, marital sexual violence continues to remain unrecognized and unchallenged by much of Indian society and law. As discussed, notions of honour that are commonly attributed to women may limit their sexual experiences. Lacking sexual knowledge, many women are expected to embody the image of the traditional, sexually servient woman when they marry. They internalize sexual double standards, which for many makes their sexual and marital relationships unsatisfying. On the other hand, nontraditional women who reject these expectations are considered fair game for men's objectifying gaze (Derne and Jadwin 258), which can play a role in men's sexually violent tendencies. In this next section, we examine how Indians may be socialized about these issues through Bollywood, India's leading film industry. Here, we explore the stereotypical nature of sexually violent scenes on screen (which, noticeably, do not focus on marital rape) and discuss the implications for viewers' attitudes towards this violence.

Bollywood and Sexual Violence

The media play an important role in influencing individuals' gender and sexual attitudes (Kahlor and Morrison; Zurbriggen and Morgan). Furthermore, research finds that consuming media containing sexualized content is related to negative attitudes towards women (Kistler and Lee 82), which may be implicated in sexual violence towards them. Although such findings are well supported in the Western psychological literature, it is unclear whether similar results would hold in a more traditional and sexually conservative culture, such as in India. Given the increasing attention being paid to women's status and safety in India, it is crucial to consider the potential role Indian media has on viewers' attitudes about gender roles and sex and whether these attitudes may play a part in the sex crimes often perpetrated against Indian women.

Bollywood is a "film and music industry rolled into one" (qtd. in Nijhawan 102) and is considered to be especially central to Indian culture. Bollywood has amassed great success over past generations, and its influence has spread across many countries beyond India (Malik, Trimzi, and Galluci 176). India's Central Board of Film Certification notes that the country produces the greatest number of films worldwide (5). Despite this and its worldwide reach, research on Bollywood and its impact on viewers is limited. Although some published work has examined such topics as the portrayal of mental illness in Bollywood films (Bhugra) and the globalization of Bollywood films (Rao), few empirical studies exist specifically examining how gender and sexuality are portrayed in the industry; to our knowledge, no research directly links exposure to this media with viewers' attitudes towards women and rape.

Bollywood has been criticized for its objectifying depictions of women (e.g., We the People). Researchers conducting qualitative analyses (Derne; Manohar, and Kline; Ramasubramanian and Oliver) have noted that the films may socialize young Indian viewers regarding their sexuality and their attitudes about gender and violence. Bollywood has traditionally been mindful of its portrayals of on-screen sex, either presenting such scenes in a conservative manner or avoiding them altogether, although this has shifted in recent years (Deakin and Bhugra 169). For instance, the previously pure and traditional women in Bollywood films are now more likely to be depicted as Westernized and engaging in a variety of relationships—both romantic and sexual (Deakin and Bhugra 169). These modern portrayals of female sexuality are sure to trouble traditional viewers' preexisting attitudes about women.

Interestingly, some research has noted various problematic content regarding gender and sex in Bollywood films. Sexual violence against women has been identified as a common theme in several films. Uttara Manohar and Susan Kline conducted a content analysis of twenty-four Bollywood films released between 2000 and 2012, and they find that the films presented viewers with a recurring sexual assault narrative about the preconditions, actions during the assault, and consequences of the assault for both victims and perpetrators. Their analysis found that about 90 per cent of the victims in the sexual assault scenes were young women perceived to be between eighteen and thirty-five years of age (238, 240). They also found that victims were not differentiated by their marital status, social class, or caste (240). The authors argue that these results suggest women (in general) are at risk for sexual violence (241-2), despite having background characteristics that could be considered protective against such violence (e.g., being married). Furthermore, in about 45 per cent of the films, responsibility for the violence was attributed to the victims (240)—it was their actions that somehow triggered the attack (238). During the assault, women were shown to actively resist the attack in approximately 65 per cent of the films (241), using such strategies as physical resistance or escaping the scene of the attack entirely (238). After the sexual assault, it was common for the victim's reputation to be negatively affected or for her to die following the attack (through committing suicide or being murdered by the perpetrator), although about 42 per cent of the films do depict the victims as later marrying a man (241), suggesting that she was ultimately not shunned by society following her rape.

These findings suggest that Bollywood films may propagate a one-sided, narrow picture of sexual violence—for the violence to be considered rape, a woman must actively resist the attack (Manohar and Kline 243). They also confirm several other rape myths and cultural beliefs about women and their honour. That several of the assault victims in the films analyzed by Manohar and Kline were married in the end implies that one of the only ways to restore a woman's honour and reputation after she has been raped is through a man (242). Interestingly, some of the films' portrayals of sexual violence go against rape myths widely held by Indians. For instance, those who endorse rape myths believe that women who stray from traditional gender norms deserve violence perpetrated against them (Kohli 15). However, Manohar and Kline found that in the analyzed films, about 61 per cent of the female victims of sexual violence acted traditional in their gender role performance (240), such as by dressing conservatively or limiting opposite-sex interactions (238).

The consequences of being exposed to filmed sexual violence has been well examined in Western research and may provide a clearer picture of the potential outcomes viewers of Bollywood films that depict such scenes may face. For instance, Monica Weisz and Christopher Earls found that compared to those who watched films containing physical violence or neutral content, men exposed to films with sexual violence were more likely to endorse favourable attitudes about relationship violence and sexual aggression. Moreover, men viewing sexually violent films tended to endorse beliefs justifying rape at higher levels (Weisz and Earls 79). Especially informative here is the finding regarding attitudes about interpersonal violence, as this has been shown to be a strong predictor of beliefs excusing rape (Burt 229). Extrapolating these findings to Bollywood films may indicate that viewing on-screen sexual violence could also influence various off-screen attitudes about rape and other forms of violence.

On the surface, it appears that the main sexual assault narrative in Bollywood includes such elements as extreme violence as well as the victim's incessant resistance to the perpetrator's advances. However, other scholars have argued that Bollywood films also contain milder forms of sexual violence that often go unnoticed. Srividya Ramasubramanian and Mary Beth Oliver analyzed nine films released between 1997 and 1999 and noted the extent to which sexual violence was present in the films, focusing specifically on sexual scenes. The researchers also examined the scenes to determine how the violence was portrayed to viewers (i.e., as fun or serious) and what type of character perpetrated the violence (e.g., a hero or a villain). The results reveal that about 41 per cent of the scenes showed sexual violence that differed in severity. Specifically, the manner in which moderate sexual violence (e.g., domestic violence and sexual harassment) was depicted contrasted sharply with portrayals of severe sexual violence (i.e., eroticized murder and rape). Their analysis shows that severe sexual violence was portrayed as being more criminal, serious, and often perpetrated by the antagonist in the film plot, whereas moderate sexual violence was presented as fun, romantic, and perpetrated by the male protagonist of the film (330-33).

Ramasubramanian and Oliver note that the findings regarding moderate sexual violence are particularly concerning. First, they may suggest to viewers that only certain types of violence—what is considered more extreme and perpetrated by the villain—is problematic and deserving of punishment, whereas other forms of violence should be taken more lightly (334). The authors argue that because the perpetrators of moderate sexual violence are often a film's protagonist, who can serve as a masculine role model to male viewers, those who identify with such a character may adopt similarly aggressive behaviours (334). Furthermore, when women are shown not resisting any form of violence or harassment by male actors in the films, these portrayals may encourage viewers to think that women enjoy being mistreated (Derne 562-63). Such a perspective would be supported by Albert Bandura's social learning theory, which argues that individuals learn by observing others and are more likely to model their behaviour after those who receive positive reinforcements (Ramasubramanian and Oliver 334). Thus, it is possible that Bollywood's portrayal of moderate sexual violence may contribute to a culture that normalizes sexual violence against women.

An additional criticism of these sexually violent images reflects the concern that such mistreatment of women may even be romanticized. Ramasubramanian and Oliver assert that since much of the violence between the male protagonists and female victims take place against the backdrop of a fun song-and-dance scene, these portrayals further normalize problematic relationship behaviours (333-34). Other researchers have also noted that men's use of sexual violence can be seen as an appropriate strategy in their romantic pursuits. Indeed, in another content analysis of films released in between the mid-1980s and early 1990s, Steve Derne found a common theme of conflating love and sex with force. That much of this force was perpetrated by male protagonists against their future female partners suggests that such force is legitimized when used to court women (552). Even when the female protagonist's affections are not won on screen, sexual violence is still used by male perpetrators when "pursuing their one-sided love" (qtd. in Manohar and Kline 240-41).

Considering these findings, which provide a qualitatively rich picture of the nature of sexual violence in Indian media, it is clear that the potential for Bollywood films to serve as an educational resource regarding gender, sexuality, and violence against women is great. Due to conservative Indian values, though, sex and sexuality are not openly discussed, making it difficult for individuals to have access to reliable information regarding these topics (Derne 555). Thus, some may turn to Bollywood films to learn about sex. (Derne notes how some film plots focus on this lack of knowledge about sexuality and how characters struggle in navigating their initial sexual experiences as a result.)

However, these findings are only suggestive, as these qualitative findings cannot be generalized to any large extent. Moreover, correlational studies linking Bollywood movies and attitudes regarding rape and women, or experimental research directly testing a causal relationship between film exposure and attitudes, have not been published. Indeed, there is a need for studies that would allow for more of these conclusive relationships (Manohar and Kline 243; Ramasubramanian and Oliver 335).

Although some available research on Bollywood films has focused primarily on identifying themes surrounding sexual assault portrayals, these films present countless other messages about gender and sexuality that may also encourage sexual violence against women. One of the most distinguishing factors of Bollywood films is that the majority are musicals. Any given film may contain eight to ten songs in its soundtrack (Malik, Trimzi, and Galluci 176), with one usually being the "item number"—a commercially successful song-and-dance number that may play little to no role in furthering the plot (Rao 70-71). These songs rely heavily on the "item girl," who is a young, attractive woman wearing revealing clothes and who dances suggestively for the entertainment and pleasure of a mostly male audience. Although previously item girls were played by women who had few (if any) acting roles to their name (e.g., Malaika Arora and Rakhi Sawant), in today's films, even well-established actresses play this part in these songs. Regardless of whether the item girl is well known or not, the emphasis remains on her sexuality. For instance, in the item song "Lovely," from the film *Happy New Year*, the viewer sees a large crowd of cheering men, alcohol in hand, throwing money around. The item girl, played by successful actress Deepika Padukone, wears a belly shirt and a long skirt with high slits, which exposes much skin. The camera often emphasizes Padukone's toned abdomen and legs, hip movements, and other sexually suggestive dance moves. Such an image is representative of today's item songs.

Although Bollywood songs are quite eroticized and speak much to the taboo of female sexuality (Malik, Trimzi and Galluci 176), this is especially true for these item songs. Such portrayals of women's sexuality may be considered empowering and a welcome divergence from the more conservative and traditional representations of women in Indian cinema, yet feminists tend to argue that these item songs are sexually objectifying and contribute to a culture of rape and violence against women (We the People). Indeed, much research in Western psychology supports this latter view. For instance, an experimental study in which participants were assigned to view music videos with either high or low sexualized content found that men in the highly sexualized video condition scored higher on measures examining sexual objectification of women, stereotypical attitudes about gender, and rape myth acceptance (Kistler and Lee 79, 81). The video stimuli used in this study depicted female performers dancing suggestively for a male audience, with little clothing (74), which closely resembles the imagery in Bollywood's item songs.

It is important to note why and how sexualized media portrayals of women may lead to the problematic outcomes found by Michelle Kistler and Moon Lee. According to objectification theory, the media's focus on women's sexuality and their bodies reduces them to just their body parts; meanwhile, their internal qualities and capabilities are ignored (Fredrickson and Roberts 176-77). When women are portrayed in this way, their personhood is not emphasized, and, as such, they are viewed as sex objects for the pleasure and use of others (Frederickson and Roberts 175). Jennifer Aubrey and Cynthia Frisby assert that object-ification involves a sense of decreased agency, in which one's decision-making capacity can be affected (479). Thus, men who view women in this manner may believe they have power over them and can control and sexually dominate them. A key facet of the sexually explicit item songs in Bollywood is that women are providing sexual entertainment to a primarily male audience. If women are shown solely to fulfill men's sexual desires and fantasies in this way, viewers may believe that women exist only for men's pleasure and that they are not thinking and feeling individuals—viewpoints that have potential to perpetuate sexual violence and rape culture. In fact, thinking of women as sexual objects can influence the relationship between viewing sexually objectifying media and endorsing attitudes excusing sexual violence. Researchers have found that men who viewed objectifying media more often were more likely to hold objectifying attitudes towards women. In turn, sexual objectification also predicted greater acceptance of rape myths (Wright and Tokunaga 960). Paul Wright and Robert Tokunaga posit that media does not have to depict actual sexual violence for it to inform viewers' attitudes. Rather, objectifying media by itself should be a cause for concern.

For these reasons, it is likely that the effect of sexually explicit item songs on the way viewers conceptualize attitudes about Indian women and sex is strong. Given that the use of item songs in films is so common—as it is a widely used strategy by filmmakers to ensure that films are successful and appeal to a wider audience (Rao 71)—one can safely assume that viewers will continue to be exposed to this type of sexualized media. Thus, as opined by other scholars (e.g., Manohar and Kline 243), the socializing influence of Bollywood's iconic item songs must be analyzed to have a better understanding of the gendered and sexual messages viewers may be receiving from Indian media.

Programming Change

Thus far, we have examined how traditional attitudes about Indian women's honour and sexuality, socialization regarding the importance of marriage for Indian women, and controversial depictions in Bollywood of sexual assault and women's bodies may be implicated in rape and other forms of sexual violence. In order to address India's rape culture, it is crucial to tackle rape myths and stereotypical gender norms that encourage male dominance and female submission. Because these myths and norms permeate various aspects of Indian society, interventions must be targeted towards these different realms. In this final section, we discuss the need to amend rape laws so that marital rape is recognized by those in power (e.g., judges and politicians who influence public opinion and policies). We also examine interventions that serve to reduce gender inequalities to understand how more liberal notions of gender roles and sexuality may reduce support for rape myths. Indian media is presented as a possible source of intervention. By portraying gender and sex in more liberal terms, we discuss how Bollywood may be a positive socializing force for Indian audiences. We end by acknowledging the work of initiatives that strive to address rape culture among Indians.

Rape Laws and India's Justice and Political System

Saptarshi Mandal states that marital rape, as well as the need for it to be criminalized, has been extensively debated in India (257). Whereas women's rights activists and feminists argue for criminalizing marital rape (257), some political and judicial officials claim that the institution of marriage is beyond the scope of law because of the religious significance of Indian marriages (259). Moreover, beliefs about the nature of sexual relations within a lawful marriage further explain why some argue against criminalizing marital rape. The notion of presumed consent claims that consent is considered continuous in a marriage based on previous sexual interactions between a husband and wife. If wives tend to consent to sex with their husbands under one condition, it is reasonable for husbands to expect this consent during later sexual interactions as well (Lazar 358).

The need to repeal the marital rape exemption in India was especially expressed among the three-member Verma Committee, which was established in response to the 2012 Delhi gang rape of medical student

Jyoti Singh—a case which brought intense national and international scrutiny to India's treatment of rape cases and women's safety and status in Indian society ("Delhi Gangrape"; Lodhia 97-98). The more than six-hundred-page Verma Report made a number of suggestions to make the criminal justice system more supportive of survivors and harsher for rapists. For instance, it called for life imprisonment for perpetrators when a gang rape resulted in the victim's death or led them to be in a vegetative state (Verma, Seth, and Subramanium 444). This sentence was also recommended for those with prior rape convictions (445). Regarding marital rape in particular, the Verma Committee recommended that husbands be held accountable for sexual crimes committed against their spouse, citing, among others, the principle that rape is a crime no matter who it is perpetrated against (Verma, Seth, and Subramanium 114, 117). Furthermore, the couples' relationship status ought not to be used as a means of reducing sentences for rapists in a court of law (117). Additionally, the Verma Committee claimed that the notion of presumed consent between married couples is not a valid justification for marital sexual violence (440). Clearly, these recommendations marked a sharp contrast to how rape, and particularly marital rape, was previously conceptualized in India.

Although the efforts of the Verma Committee were commendable, there was also opposition to these suggested changes. Several explanations have been offered as to why it has been difficult to label unwanted sexual relations between a husband and wife as actual rape. As noted, some consider the sanctity of marriage to be so great that intervention by the state and judicial system would not be preferred, even in cases where it is clear that rape has occurred. Rather, the family itself should address the situation directly, rather than a court of criminal law (Parliament of India Rajya Sabha 47). Madhu Kishwar, founder of Manushi—an organization addressing various economic, political, and social issues facing India—argues that although wives ought to be sexually assertive and should be able to refuse sex, making marital rape a punishable crime may be difficult: "How does a man prove that the sexual relation on a particular day or night with his wife was with her consent? Have her sign an affidavit every time they go to bed together?" (qtd. in "Police & Judicial Reforms First Priority"). Such perspectives suggest that where consent begins and ends is a blurry line and complicated by marital status—a view the Verma Committee took a stand against.

Despite efforts by the Verma Committee, marital rape continues to be unrecognized by the law (Parliament of India Rajya Sabha 81). However, women's activist groups and lawmakers must continue to fight for the provisions recommended by the Verma Committee in order to have a more exhaustive antirape law, one that includes recognition of marital rape.

Bollywood's Role in Tackling Rape Culture

As previously discussed, Bollywood has been criticized for its stereotypical portrayals of women as well as its romanticization of violence against women (e.g., Manohar and Kline 242; Ramasubra-manian and Oliver 334). Item songs in particular have been called out for objectifying women's bodies and, thus, playing a role in rape culture (We the People). However, the film industry has also been lauded for presenting viewers with more liberal ideas regarding gender roles and women's sexuality, which may combat rape myths and other limiting beliefs about women's rights.

Sukanya Gupta's analysis of Bollywood films shows that attention is moving away from male characters and is instead being focused on women's empowerment, offering evidence of the shifting gender roles being permeated through films. She argues that traditionally, "female characters generally do not have much meaning without their male counterparts.... Even when these women are assertive and capable ... they are primarily seen as symbols of family, patriarchy and nation" (107). Women's lives are often understood in relation to others. Indeed, this was the sentiment after the 2012 Delhi gang rape case where the victim, Jyoti Singh, was regarded as "India's daughter," and her rape translated into India, as a country, being raped (Lodhia 91). Indian women are often portrayed as passive characters in the media, serving primarily as an accessory to the more important and celebrated male characters (Gupta 107), which is similar to how women's roles have traditionally been defined in reality. For instance, older Bollywood films tended to discredit strong, assertive women, painting them as immature and unfeminine, whereas traditional women who were domestic and submissive were presented more positively (Gupta 109). However, in contemporary Bollywood films, Indian women have more individualistic, agentic, and substantive roles (Gupta).

Increasing depictions of sex on screen have also changed perceptions of women and their sexuality. Films show women engaging in sexual practices outside of the traditional realm of marriage and encourage the view that they are sexual beings. These liberal portrayals may help change cultural expectations of the sexually dominant man versus the sexually submissive woman dichotomy, which are implicated in marital rape. However, these same films also show women experiencing negative consequences as a result of being sexually active, such as by becoming pregnant (when this is not desired) or having to forsake their career (Gupta 110). Such messages may socialize viewers into thinking that these negative outcomes can be expected if a woman engages in premarital sexual activity. Based on this interpretation, Bollywood films may serve as a deterrent for women who are sexually active. However, it is crucial that when films do focus on women's sexuality, they present it in more positive and satisfying terms (e.g., by presenting sexually active women who also have successful careers).

Bollywood films may also positively influence viewers' attitudes about women by dissociating them from sex entirely. As noted, item songs tend to present women in completely sexual terms, whereby their bodies are objectified and used primarily as a site for male pleasure and entertainment (We the People). Films that instead focus on a female character's individual character development, and not her sexuality, may discourage audiences in perceiving women primarily as sex objects. In fact, Gupta's analysis of three contemporary films showcasing strong female leads found that these films did not include any item songs whatsoever and instead contained songs that highlighted the women's journey to self-discovery (114). Films with these messages present viewers with an image of a woman whose value is not tied to the sexual pleasure she can offer audiences. She is not a sexual being for the use of others—something that is commonly understood among both men and women who believe sex to be a husband's right (George 91; Maitra and Schensul 143). Rather, she is her own woman, and she does not owe anyone any part of her.

Organizational Efforts to Reduce Rape Myths among Indians

The reality of rape and other forms of violence against Indian women have encouraged many to challenge injustice and work to reduce the prevalence of these gendered crimes. Part of this commitment to social justice is an attempt to identify some of the root causes of violence against women and to target those causes in prevention and intervention efforts. Here, we commend the work of two such initiatives: Breakthrough India and Priya's Shakti.

Breakthrough India is a nongovernmental human rights organization dedicated to reducing violence and discrimination against girls and women. Through diverse methods—such as media campaigns, leadership trainings and workshops, and mobilizing members of the community to work from the ground up—Breakthrough recognizes that specific cultural and gender norms and practices set up the conditions for violence. In India specifically, Breakthrough has developed projects focusing on key issues that women and young girls continue to face, including domestic violence, sexual harassment, gender-biased sex selection, and early marriage.

As men are often perpetrators of violence against women, Breakthrough understands the need to especially involve them in their endeavours. Changing traditional male gender norms and notions of masculinity that are implicated in gender-based violence are at the heart of many of Breakthrough's campaigns. These campaigns use the concept of entertainment education to both entertain and educate audiences about women's rights (Lapsansky and Chatterjee 38). In their analysis, Charlotte Lapsansky and Joyee Chatterjee examine the different roles attributed to Indian men in four of Breakthrough's media campaigns that aim to bring awareness to women's experiences of violence (43-44). One of these campaigns, titled Bell Bajao (or Ring the Bell), consists of a number of ads depicting men intervening in cases of domestic violence. In one ad, a man—played by well-known Bollywood actor Boman Irani—overhears his neighbour beating his wife. The neighbour is heard yelling aggressively, and his wife is heard shrieking and sobbing. Irani enters his building, walks up the stairs and heads toward the neighbour's apartment. When the man answers the door, Irani asks if he can make a phone call. Before the man can answer, Irani's own phone rings in his pocket. Irani picks it up with a knowing look, and it is clear to the perpetrator and the viewer that Irani's intent was to intervene

(Breakthrough India, "Bell Bajao—Ring Ring"). Another ad similarly depicts adolescent boys "ringing the bell" of a perpetrator's door when they overhear him abusing a woman inside an apartment, indicating that all boys and men, regardless of their age, can help bring domestic violence to an end (Breakthrough India, "Bell Bajao—Knock Knock. Who's There?"). Though not specifically focused on rape and other forms of sexual violence, this ad shows the necessity of involving men and boys in the movement for women's rights. These ads model a more progressive masculinity that challenge inequitable gender norms that give rise to all forms of violence against women (Lapsansky and Chatterjee 50). Such positive masculinities were also observed in response to the 2012 Delhi gang rape, where male protestors mobilized to demonstrate their support for women's rights and safety and the victim of the attack, Jyoti Singh, in particular (Lodhia 92).

Priya's Shakti (translated to Priya's Power) is an initiative that examines the issue of sexual violence specifically through a comic book. Inspired by Jyoti Singh, the main character of this comic book is Priya, a survivor of a gang rape who experiences multiple gender inequities and confronts several rape myths endorsed by members of her family and larger community. The story, as illustrated through the comic book, depicts Priya as being subjected to various patriarchal norms, such as being ordered by her father to stop attending school in order to tend to the house. When older, Priya is raped, and her family responds by throwing her out of the home due to the resulting shame and stigma. The story follows Priya, who through intervention by Hindu gods and goddesses transforms into a superhero and becomes empowered to fight against rape in her community (Priya's Shakti).

Many of the efforts involved in this initiative revolve around combatting India's rape culture by acknowledging core rape myths (e.g., women provoke men who assault them or women should not go outside by themselves) (Priya's Shakti). The comic book can also be enjoyed in its animated form through its interactive component, which includes snippets of real interviews conducted with a rape survivor as well as with men residing in Delhi. These interviews reveal the prevalence of other rape myths, such as the idea that certain types of women get raped, including so-called loose women or provocative women who dress in enticing ways. Similar rape myths about women's dress and mobility have been studied by scholars as well (Burt 223; Payne, Lonsway, and

Fitzgerald 49). Indeed, women's movements outside of the home are especially monitored compared to their male counterparts. The need for women to be restricted in public spaces has been voiced by male participants in Steve Derne and Lisa Jadwin's research. They note how men who believe modest and cultured Indian women ought to be protected from other men's gaze may restrict these women's movements outside the home. Ultimately, these restrictions can have implications for women's career, educational, and other public opportunities (259). However, imposing these beliefs on women and limiting their movements to prevent violence outside the home also directly contradict findings that much sexual violence occurs within the home itself and is perpetrated by known partners or acquaintances, such as husbands (e.g., Maitra and Schensul; Santhya et al.).

Conclusion

India's rape culture is complex. Old traditions and values, though a hallmark of Indian culture, also have the potential to negatively affect women's lived experiences. Although marriages are celebrated in India, the centrality of the marital relationship to women's lives may make it difficult for victims of marital rape to speak out. India's judicial system and women's activist groups must continue to fight to remove the marital rape exemption. Even though Bollywood has been criticized for its problematic representations of gender, relationships, and sex, this revered cultural institution also has the power to shift audience perceptions in India regarding these issues. Indeed, media campaigns by organizations committed to women's rights have proven this potential—and must continue to do so.

Endnotes

1. An item song is a commercially successful song that can either be part of a film or be disassociated with a film entirely. An item song is highly sensationalized and includes such features as lead actresses and female dancers wearing revealing clothes, sexually suggestive dance moves, alcohol, and crowds of men as onlookers.

Works Cited

Aubrey, Jennifer Stevens, and Cynthia M. Frisby. "Sexual Objectification in Music Videos: A Content Analysis Comparing Gender and Genre." *Mass Communication and Society*, vol. 14, no. 4, 2011, pp. 475-501.

Bandura, Albert. *Social Learning Theory*. 2nd ed. Prentice-Hall, 1977. Print.

Breakthrough India. "Bell Bajao—Knock Knock. Who's There? (English) (Subtitled)." *YouTube*, 5 Dec. 2008, www.youtube.com/watch?v=-9dKXXriVmo. Accessed 6 May 2020.

Breakthrough India. "Bell Bajao—Ring Ring (English) (Subtitled)." *YouTube*, 1 July 2010, https://www.youtube.com/watch?v=zmNz0c TcxFU&list=PL17CE7B962F802F82&index=7. Accessed 6 May 2020.

Bhugra, Dinesh. "Mad Tales from Bollywood: The Impact of Social, Political, and Economic Climate on the Portrayal of Mental Illness in Hindi Films." *Acta Psychiatrica Scandinavica*, vol. 112, no. 4, 2005, pp. 250-56.

Bhugra, Dinesh, et al. "Sexual Attitudes and Practices in North India: A Qualitative Study." *Sexual and Relationship Therapy*, vol. 22, no. 1, 2007, pp. 83-90.

Burt, Martha R. "Cultural Myths and Supports for Rape." *Journal of Personality and Social Psychology*, vol. 38, no. 2, 1980, pp. 217-30.

Das, Ajit K., and Sharon F. Kemp. "Between Two Worlds: Counseling South Asian Americans." *Journal of Multicultural Counseling and Development*, vol. 25, no. 1, 1997, pp. 23-33.

Deakin, Nicholas, and Dinesh Bhugra. "Families in Bollywood Cinema: Changes and Context." *International Review of Psychiatry*, vol. 24, no. 2, 2012, pp. 166-72.

"Delhi Gangrape Victim's Friend Relives the Horrifying 84 Minutes of December 16 Night." *India Today Online*, 13 Sept. 2013, www.indiatoday.in/india/north/story/delhi-gangrape-victims-friend-relives-the-horrifying-84-minutes-of-december-16-night-210874-2013-09-13. Accessed 6 May 2020.

Derne, Steve. "Making Sex Violent: Love as Force in Recent Hindi Films." *Violence against Women*, vol. 5, no. 5, 1999, pp. 548-75.

Derne, Steve, and Lisa Jadwin. "Male Hindi Filmgoers' Gaze: An Eth-nographic Interpretation." *Contributions to Indian Sociology*, vol. 34, no. 2, 2000, pp. 243-69.

Fredrickson, Barbara L., and Tomi-Ann Roberts. "Objectification Theory: Toward Understanding Women's Lived Experiences and Mental Health Risks." *Psychology of Women Quarterly*, vol. 21, no. 2, 1997, pp. 173-206.

George, Annie. "Differential Perspectives of Men and Women in Mumbai, India on Sexual Relations and Negotiations within Mar-riage." *Reproductive Health Matters*, vol. 6, no. 12 1998, pp. 87-96.

Ghule, Mohan, Donta Balaiah, and Beena Joshi. "Attitude towards Premarital Sex among Rural College Youth in Maharashtra, India." *Sexuality & Culture*, vol. 11, no. 4, 2007, pp. 1-17.

Gupta, Sukanya. "Kahaani, Gulaab Gang and Queen: Remaking the Queens of Bollywood." *South Asian Popular Culture*, vol. 13, no. 2, 2015, pp. 107-23.

Happy New Year. Directed by Farah Khan, performances by Deepika Padukone and Shahrukh Khan, Red Chillies Entertainment, 2014.

India. Ministry of Information and Broadcasting Government of India. Central Board of Film Certification. "Annual Report from April 2015 to March 2016." *Central Board of Film Certification*, 2015, https://www.cbfcindia.gov.in/main/CBFC_English/Attachments/ AR 2015-2016 English.pdf. Accessed 11 May 2020.

India. Parliament of India Rajya Sabha. Department-Related Parlia-mentary Standing Committee on Home Affairs. "One Hundred and Sixty Seventh Report on The Criminal Law (Amendment) Bill, 2012." *Parliament of India Rajya Sabha*, 1 Mar. 2013, https://www. prsindia.org/uploads/media/Criminal%20Law/SCR%20Crimi-nal%20Law%20Bill.pdf. Accessed 11 May 2020.

Kahlor, LeeAnn, and Dan Morrison. "Television Viewing and Rape Myth Acceptance among College Women." *Sex Roles*, vol. 56, no. 11-12, 2007, pp. 729-39.

Kallivayalil, Diya. "Gender and Cultural Socialization in Indian Imm-igrant Families in the United States." *Feminism & Psychology*, vol. 14, no. 4, 2004, pp. 535-59.

Khan, M. E., John W. Townsend, and Shampa D'Costa. "Behind Closed Doors: A Qualitative Study of Sexual Behaviour of Married

Women in Bangladesh." *Culture, Health & Sexuality*, vol. 4, no. 2, 2002, pp. 237-56.

Kistler, Michelle E., and Moon J. Lee. "Does Exposure to Sexual Hip-Hop Music Videos Influence the Sexual Attitudes of College Students?" *Mass Communication and Society*, vol. 13, no. 1, 2009, pp. 67-86.

Koenig, Michael A., et al. "Individual and Contextual Determinants of Domestic Violence in North India." *American Journal of Public Health*, vol. 96, no. 1, 2006, pp. 132-38.

Kohli, Ambika. "Gang Rapes and Molestation Cases in India: Creating Mores for Eve-Teasing." *Te Awatea Review*, vol. 10, no. 1-2, 2012, pp. 13-17.

Lapsansky, Charlotte, and Joyee S. Chatterjee. "Masculinity Matters: Using Entertainment Education to Engage Men in Ending Violence against Women in India." *Critical Arts*, vol. 27, no. 1, 2013, pp. 36-55.

Lazar, Ruthy. "Negotiating Sex: The Legal Construct of Consent in Cases of Wife Rape in Ontario, Canada." *Canadian Journal of Women & the Law*, vol. 22, no. 2, 2010, pp. 329-63.

Lodhia, Sharmila. "From 'Living Corpse' to India's Daughter: Exploring the Social, Political and Legal Landscape of the 2012 Delhi Gang Rape." *Women's Studies International Forum*, vol. 50 2015, pp. 89-101.

Maitra, Shubhada, and Stephen L. Schensul. "Reflecting Diversity and Complexity in Marital Sexual Relationships in a Low-Income Community in Mumbai." *Culture, Health & Sexuality*, vol. 4, no. 2, 2002, pp. 133-51.

Malik, Mansoor, Imran Trimzi, and Gerard Galluci. "Bollywood as Witness: Changing Perceptions of Mental Illness in India (1913–2010)." *International Journal of Applied Psychoanalytic Studies*, vol. 8, no. 2, 2011, pp. 175-84.

Mandal, Saptarshi. "The Impossibility of Marital Rape: Contestations around Marriage, Sex, Violence and the Law in Contemporary India." *Australian Feminist Studies*, vol. 29, no. 81, 2014, pp. 255-72.

Manohar, Uttara, and Susan L. Kline. "Sexual Assault Portrayals in Hindi Cinema." *Sex Roles*, vol. 71, no. 5-8, 2014, pp. 233-45.

Muehlenhard, Charlene L. "'Nice Women' Don't Say Yes and 'Real Men' Don't Say No: How Miscommunication and the Double Standard Can Cause Sexual Problems." *Women & Therapy*, vol. 7, no. 2-3, 1988, pp. 95-108.

Murnen, Sarah K., Carrie Wright, and Gretchen Kaluzny. "If 'Boys Will Be Boys,' Then Girls Will Be Victims? A Meta-Analytic Review of the Research that Relates Masculine Ideology to Sexual Aggression." *Sex Roles*, vol. 46, no. 11-12, 2002, pp. 359-75.

Nijhawan, Amita. "Excusing the Female Dancer: Tradition and Transgression in Bollywood Dancing." *South Asian Popular Culture*, vol. 7, no. 2, 2009, pp. 99-112.

Payne, Tom. "Indian State Minister Ramsevak Paikra Says Rapes Happen 'Accidentally.'" *Independent*, 8 June 2014, www.independent. co.uk/news/world/asia/indian-state-minister-ramsevak-paikra-says-rapes-happen-accidentally-9508427.html. Accessed 6 May 2020.

Payne, Diana L., Kimberly A. Lonsway, and Louise F. Fitzgerald. "Rape Myth Acceptance: Exploration of its Structure and its Measurement Using the Illinois Rape Myth Acceptance Scale." *Journal of Research in Personality*, vol. 33, no. 1, 1999, pp. 27-68.

"Police & Judicial Reforms First Priority." *Manushi–Working Towards Solutions: Forum for Women's Rights and Democratic Reforms*. 24 Jan. 2013, yourmanushi.wordpress.com/2013/04/30/police-judicial-reforms-first-priority/. Accessed 6 May 2020.

Ramasubramanian, Srividya, and Mary Beth Oliver. "Portrayals of Sexual Violence in Popular Hindi Films, 1997-99." *Sex Roles*, vol. 48, no. 7-8, 2003, pp. 327-36.

Rao, Shakuntala. "The Globalization of Bollywood: An Ethnography of Non-Elite Audiences in India." *The Communication Review*, vol. 10, no. 1, 2007, pp. 57-76.

Sanchez, Diana T., Jennifer Crocker, and Karlee R. Boike. "Doing Gender in the Bedroom: Investing in Gender Norms and the Sexual Experience." *Personality and Social Psychology Bulletin*, vol. 31, no. 10, 2005, pp. 1445-55.

Santhya, K.G., et al. "Consent and Coercion: Examining Unwanted Sex among Married Young Women in India." *International Family Planning Perspectives*, vol. 33, no. 3, 2007, pp. 124-32.

Verma, J.S., Leila Seth, and Gopal Subramanium. *Report of the Committee on Amendments to Criminal Law.* 23 Jan. 2013, https://www.prsindia.org/uploads/media/Justice%20verma%20committee/Js%20verma%20committe%20report.pdf. Accessed 11 May 2020.

Waldner, Lisa K., Linda Vaden-Goad, and Anjoo Sikka. "Sexual Coercion in India: An Exploratory Analysis Using Demographic Variables." *Archives of Sexual Behavior*, vol. 28, no. 6, 1999, pp. 523-38.

Weisz, Monica G., and Christopher M. Earls. "The Effects of Exposure to Filmed Sexual Violence on Attitudes toward Rape." *Journal of Interpersonal Violence*, vol. 10, no. 1, 1995, pp. 71-84.

We the People. "Do Films Celebrate Women or 'Item'-ise Them?" *NDTV*, 13 Jan. 2013, https://www.ndtv.com/video/news/we-the-people/do-films-celebrate-women-or-item-ise-them-261719. Accessed 11 May 2020.

Wright, Paul J., and Robert S. Tokunaga. "Men's Objectifying Media Consumption, Objectification of Women, and Attitudes Supportive of Violence against Women." *Archives of Sexual Behavior*, vol. 45, no. 4, 2016, pp. 955-64.

Zurbriggen, Eileen L., and Elizabeth M. Morgan. "Who Wants to Marry a Millionaire? Reality Dating Television Programs, Attitudes toward Sex, and Sexual Behaviors." *Sex Roles*, vol. 54, no. 1-2, 2006, pp. 1-17.

Chapter Fifteen

Disrupting Ideological Comfortabilty about Rape: Strategies for the Classroom

Carole Sheffield

After four decades (and counting) of rape-related activism and reform in the United States (U.S.) and around the globe, rape endures. Scholarship on rape (and all forms of violence against girls and women) is vast, multidisciplinary, and transformative. We have witnessed considerable success in legal reform—as well as progress in retraining the judiciary, the police, medical personnel—and have implemented creative and vital curricula in schools. Maria Bevacqua argues persuasively that a "major achievement of the anti-rape movement has been to move the issue from the strictly feminist agenda to the national policy agenda" (112). And Martha McCaughey points out: "Since 1990 the problem of men's violence has been a topic of national discussion" (18). Discussion, however, does not necessarily lead to understanding, as a highly visible regressive discourse has emerged over the last several years.

In a blog piece entitled "Rape and Women's Voice," published in the *Huffington Post*, Michael Kimmel writes: "You have to pinch yourself sometimes to remind yourself that it's 2012 and we still don't know how to talk about rape in this country (U.S.). Who would have thought that after half a century of feminist activism—and millennia of trying to understand the horrifying personal trauma of rape—we'd be discussing it as if we hadn't a clue." Kimmel references examples of ignorance of rape by men and boys—former Missouri Congressman Todd Akin's infamous remark that victims of "legitimate rape" rarely get pregnant because their bodies shut down; comedian Daniel Tosh's response to a woman in his audience, "Wouldn't it be funny if that girl got raped by, like, five guys right now? Like right now?"; and Kimmel's adolescent son telling him that the word "rape" is being used as a metaphor for a wide variety of circumstances.

In September 2016, CNN reported on the Canadian Federal Court Judge Robin Camp who asked a rape victim (in a 2014 trial) why she could not "just keep [her] knees together." In a hearing about his fitness to serve as a judge, CNN reported:

> The 19-year-old woman said she was raped over a bathroom sink during a house party. According to the trial records, Camp asked her why she didn't "skew her pelvis" or push her bottom into the sink to avoid penetration. He openly wondered, "Why couldn't you just keep your knees together?" Further, "On the subject of sex in general, and sex with young women in particular," he said, "Young wom[e]n want to have sex, particularly if they're drunk." In a different part of the trial, he said 'Some sex and pain sometimes go together ... that's not necessarily a bad thing." (qtd. in Willingham and Hassan)

Rape endures. Ignorance about rape endures. Why? There are no easy answers, of course. These questions vex everyone whose work intersects with the reality of rape. For educators, the interrogation of these questions is essential to moving students beyond thinking of rape as a random, tragic, but disconnected event with no political meaning.

Evolutionary theorists have argued that rape endures because male sexuality needs to be understood as "acultural, primal" (McCaughey 3). The essentializing of male sexual aggression is not new, although it achieved prominence with the publication of Randy Thornhill and Craig Palmer's *A Natural History of Rape: Biological Bases of Sexual Coercion* in 2000. The early twentieth-century work of sexologists, such as Havelock Ellis, provided the building blocks of this discourse. "Rooted in the sexual instinct" of women, according to Ellis, "we find a delight in roughness, violence, pain and danger." Naturally, "the masculine tendency" is to delight in domination (qtd. in Gavey 19). In *Ideal Marriage* (1930), a highly influential text until the 1970s, T. H. van de Velde writes:

What both man and woman, driven by obscure primitive urges, whish [sic] to feel in the sexual act, is the essential force of maleness, which expresses itself in a sort of violent and absolute possession of the woman. And so both of them can and do exult in a certain degree of male aggression and dominance—whether actual or apparent—which proclaims this essential force. (qtd. in Gavey 20)

Unsurprisingly, feminists have rejected the naturalist explanations for male sexual aggression from the sexologists as well as the human behavior evolutionists. Both early second-wave feminist theorists and recent scholarly forays into the mystery of rape endurance suggest a common denominator—variously called ideology, discourse, or narrative. In 1971, Susan Griffin, in her groundbreaking article "Rape: The All-American Crime," identified the role of ideology in supporting rape. She argued that it is "male mythology which defines and perpetuates rape" (30). In particular, this mythology is rooted in dichotomous constructs of violent masculinity and passive femininity. Martha Burt's empirical research has demonstrated that "rape attitudes are strongly connected to other deeply held and pervasive attitudes such as sex role stereotyping, distrust of the opposite sex (adversarial sexual beliefs), and acceptance of interpersonal violence" (229). She uses the term "rape myths" to refer to "prejudicial, stereotyped, or false beliefs about rape, rape victims, and rapists" (217).

Lynn Phillips superbly unpacks the meanings of discourses and the roles they play in understanding ourselves, our lives and experiences, and our culture:

Discourses represent sets of prevailing ideas or cultural messages about the way things are and the way things should be. They promote certain values and perspectives (and marginalize others) that tell us what is natural, inevitable, desirable, and appropriate in human behavior and social phenomena. Discourses both reflect and give shape to the ways we conceptualize, question, and talk about things. Both produced and reproduced by the institutions and social practices with which we live, discourses subtly instruct us how to think, speak and act in ways that identify us a part of some socially meaningful group (e.g., a "woman," a "student," a "good citizen"). We do not simply live inside our cultures. In many ways, our cultures live inside us.... Our relationships to those discourses shape not only what we see, but how we see—what we imagine is possible and what we take for granted. (16-17)

Most importantly, Phillips also argues: "We are never without context, for our lives do not exist in a social vacuum....Whether or not we are consciously aware of their influence, social messages, practices, and power relations impact on who we are and how we move through our lives" (16). Significantly, she notes that discourses are multiple and competing (17).

Patricia Yancey Martin provides a useful table in *Rape Work: Victims, Gender, and Emotions in Organization and Community Context* that illustrates Phillips's point. She poses eight specific questions about rape— "Is rape theorized as a gender issue? Why does rape occur? Who rapes? Can rape be eliminated from society (Why and, if yes, how?)? Can rape be prevented and, if yes, by whom and how? In this view, can a person cause herself (or himself) to be raped? How much responsibility do rapists vs. victims have as precipitators of rape? Are those who use this discourse to inform outsiders about rape trying to change society?" (123-24)—and offers both feminist and dominant responses to the each of the questions.

Martin's table is an excellent pedagogical tool. It reveals the tensions between the two competing discourses as well as the contradictory responses within the dominant discourse itself. It demonstrates the purpose of ideology (discourse and/or narrative) itself: to provide a framework for making meaning in order to process and evaluate social phenomenon.

In writing about oppressive social systems, Allan Johnson argues that "All of us are part of the problem. There is no way to avoid that as long as we live in the world" (vii). In *Privilege, Power, and Difference*, he encourages readers to see not only "where the trouble comes from but also how we as individuals are connected to it, which is the only thing that gives us the potential to make a difference" (vii). "If we can change how we think", he argues, "we can change how we act" (viii). To change how we think is, I believe, precisely the approach needed to address the complex issues of rape and rape culture. From four decades of teaching about violence against girls and women, I know that (many) women as well as (many) men do not know how to talk about rape and do not know how to begin to understand the horror of rape and sexual assault or to see how they are connected to it.

Rape persists because the stories we tell about rape make us comfortable with the reality of rape at the same time we deplore the act of rape. I refer to this form of cognitive dissonance as "ideological comfortability." I routinely witness ideological comfortability in the responses of students every time we discuss rape. It is the implicit, and more often explicit, "but" that is inevitably voiced by some of my students after viewing the documentary *Rape Is*. Although the students are clearly moved and appalled by the survivors' narratives of rape in the film, they claim that although one of the victims "shouldn't have been raped, [but] she [also] shouldn't have gone to the rapist's apartment." And so it goes: "But she shouldn't have been jogging in Central Park"; "But she shouldn't have gone to [insert name of celebrity's or athlete's or friend's] room"; "But she should not have ..." What follows the "but" is always a manifestation of ideological comfortability that rests on a desired result of patriarchal ideology—blame the victim. Blaming the victim is complex and takes many forms. Its impact in maintaining rape-supportive reasoning, however, is stunning.

In *Accounting for Rape: Psychology, Feminism, and Discourse Analysis in the Study of Sexual Violence*, Irina Anderson and Kathy Doherty argue that rape "is both socially produced and socially legitimated" (4). In affirming that blaming the victim is a social product they cite the following statistics:

[The] 2005 Amnesty International Survey ... showed that of the 1096 adults interviewed, 22% of the respondents thought that the woman is at least partially or totally responsible for the rape if she were alone in a deserted spot at the time of the attack. The same number of respondents thought that she is partially or totally responsible if she has had many sexual partners. Thirty percent of respondents thought that the woman is partially or totally responsible if she was drunk at the time of the rape, 37% thought the same if she failed to say 'no' clearly enough and 26% thought that she is partially or totally responsible if she was wearing revealing clothing at the time of the rape (3).

Rape-supportive reasoning leads us to condemn rape but rarely the rapist. We make ideological sense of rape by navigating through a maze of intersecting and reinforcing myths until we are comfortable with the narratives we live with. These myths code for us the myriad ways we learn to assign culpability to the victim and normalize the behavior of the rapist. A rape culture requires that rape supportive myths are produced and reproduced so that rape remains ideologically comfortable and rape culture remains essentially unchanged.

Strategies to Disrupt Ideological Comfortability

In addition to the table in Martin's book, I use two other pedagogical strategies to expose the structural supports of rape culture and to unsettle and disrupt students' ideological comfortability about rape. In *Just Sex: The Cultural Scaffolding of Rape*, Nicola Gavey uses the metaphor of scaffolding to argue that the commonly held "discourses of sex and gender produce ... forms of heterosex that set up the preconditions for rape" (3). That is, "cultural norms and practices" (3) support rape and a rape culture. Moreover, Gavey argues that rape-supportive myths and rape-supportive reasoning provide a "vocabulary of justification" (22) for rape. Exposing this vocabulary is at the core of the disrupting ideological comfortability.

The first pedagogical strategy is drawn from Timothy Beneke's groundbreaking book M*en on Rape*, in which he defines the concept of a "rape sign"—"a way of expressing ideas and feelings about rape without acknowledging them to ourselves" (7). Using the common image of a caveman carrying a club and dragging a cavewoman by her hair towards a cave, Beneke illustrates how rape signs work and how ideas about rape are deeply embedded in the culture: "The caveman scene expresses many ideas and feelings related to rape, yet we ordinarily fail to notice that the scene is about rape. Rape signs are manifest in jokes, images, verbal expressions, songs, stories, etc. Rape can be humorized, eroticized, aestheticized, athleticized, and (usually) trivialized, without anyone realizing that rape has been referred to" (7). Key to understanding how rape is made ideologically comfortable is Beneke's claim that as a consequence of rape signs, "rape is made safe because we are allowed to express possibly dangerous feelings and thoughts while simultaneously discounting them. Rape signs mask a tenuous, anxiety-ridden relationship to rape" (7). Rape signs are functional, Beneke argues, because "they stand between us and the reality of rape, obfuscating and numbing our vision and sensitivity" (7). And he concludes, "they paralyze thought" (7). Recently marketed t-shirts exemplify Beneke's point: At a music festival in 2015, a male proudly wore a t-shirt that read "Eat Sleep Rape Repeat" (Lhooq). Michael Fowler's now defunct company sold "Keep Calm and ..." tee-shirts. "Keep Calm and Rape Me" for women as well as "Keep Calm and Rape a Lot" and "Keep Calm and Rape Them" for men. (Taibi).

Beneke's caveman analogy provides a multidimensional approach to understanding the endurance of rape acceptance mythology and the persistence of rape. Beneke articulates seven enduring messages about rape contained within that iconic cartoon image: "1) Rape is natural; 2) Since rape is natural, men are not ultimately responsible; 3) Rape isn't rape; 4) Physical strength is a legitimate source of power in man/woman interactions; 5) Women don't really suffer when they are attacked and raped; 6) Women are attracted to brute strength; and, ultimately, message 7—The caveman's experience is legitimized" (8-9).

For years, I used this framework to introduce the concept of deeply embedded nonconscious ideology in rape-supportive reasoning. Taken one at a time, each message is analyzed with a wide range of supportive evidence from popular culture to illustrate the viability of that particular rape-supportive message. Early on in my using Beneke's caveman analogy as a pedagogical device, a male student thoughtfully noted that "Mr. Beneke left out the most important message: "Rape is funny." After all, he pointed out, "it is a cartoon." Ironically, in presenting the caveman analogy, Beneke asks, "How is it that many of us have been laughing at rape for years without knowing it?" (7), yet he did not articulate the message that "rape is funny" in his typology. As a result of the student's keen observation, I added "rape is funny" as an eighth message about rape that reinforces ideological comfortability.

The value of Beneke's framework in effectively teaching about rape endurance cannot be overstated. I have used it every semester for thirty-five years. The examples used to illustrate and elaborate on each message change frequently to reflect contemporary culture, but the framework offered in the caveman analogy remains profoundly useful. Every semester, my students are able to provide examples from their own lives and their own consumption of popular culture, and they are often amazed at how accessible and plentiful such examples are, especially the "rape is funny" message. The first message (rape is natural) opens up an examination of the ideological construct of masculinity and of the psychological and evolutionary theories that argue that rape is natural and biologically based. There is no shortage of evidence that the second message (since rape is natural, men are not responsible) is manifested widely in the culture. Examples range from professional, college, and high school athletes to politicians, celebrities, clergy, husbands, and soldiers. The messages often overlap in the maintenance of rape-supportive reasoning. For example, both messages three and seven (rape is not rape; the caveman's experience is legitimized) demonstrate the many ways that rape denial, rape redefinition, and rape trivialization take place. Messages five and six (women do not really suffer when attacked and raped; women are attracted to brute strength) provide an opportunity to critique the construct of femininity as well as the psychological theories that women fantasize about being raped and secretly desire rape. Messages three and eight (rape is not rape and rape is funny) are mutually reinforcing.

The analysis that results from applying the caveman analogy is foundational to changing rape culture. Understanding how and where rape-supportive ideas are reproduced in the culture can help transform how we think about rape and can help in recognizing the cultural, as well as our own, ambivalence about rape and sexual assault. Unpacking these messages is essential to understanding and disrupting rape-supportive reasoning and ideological comfortability. Importantly, the analysis of these messages provides a way to engage students in a conversation about how these constructs may be reframed as non-rape-supportive.

Another useful pedagogic framework comes from the cover art of an album released in 1986 on the Enigma label by a heavy metal band called Predator and the lyrics to the title song, "Easy Prey." The album cover depicts a man, his face covered with a stocking, reaching out menacingly behind a shoreline piling towards a woman walking on the beach. The back cover shows the woman slung over his shoulder in a dead-weight pose and he is holding a large blade in one hand. I use "Easy Prey" as the introduction to the study of sexual terrorism. The system of male violence against women constitutes a system of terrorism, and I define it as "the system by which males frighten and by frightening, dominate and control females" (Sheffield 1). The core component of sexual terrorism (as in every system of terrorism) is indiscriminate and amoral violence.

Furthermore, I maintain that sexual terrorism operates through a trilogy of strategies: the threat of violence, actual violence, and the propaganda of fear.

The album photos alone embody the essence of sexual terrorism and the lyrics to the title song "Easy Prey" vividly demonstrate the ideological comfortability with rape:

Easy Prey
I'm out on the loose and I'm looking for a woman to take
On big city streets in the dark gloomy shadows I wait
Then I see her a fine looking bitch with her pants oh so tight
I've just got to grab her and have her and taste her tonight
Easy Prey
They're out all around just waiting to be laid
I sample a different young woman most every night
They strut all around so enticing it serves them right
Follow her home until she's all alone, then I strike
I'll have my way then run off in the dead of the night
Easy Prey
They're out all around just waiting to be laid
Now comes the moment of truth I am half-crazed with lust
Oh when they bite and fight back it excites me so much
Whimpering and crying, it's so satisfying for me
But I can tell that she wants it, as I ravage her body completely.

To begin the exercise, I project the front of the album on the screen and invite students to deconstruct the image. Next, I project the back of the album cover and again ask students to think critically about the image and its meanings. Lastly, I project the lyrics and leave them on the screen. Students are asked to translate the lyrics into specific, well-known and routinely articulated rape-supportive myths. Initially, students are unable to do more than just repeat a particular lyric. The lyric they select is indeed rape supportive, but I encourage them to reach into their culturally acquired rape-supportive reasoning data bank and excavate the specific rape-supportive myth that a particular lyric has encoded. After a few attempts, they get it, and then they easily identify several widely held rape-supportive myths. I write their responses on the board in a particular way, and rather quickly, they see—vividly and clearly—the three categories of rape-supportive myths that this song celebrates: myths about the victims of rape, myths about the rapists, and myths about rape itself. Typically, students connect specific lyrics to several commonly held victim-blaming myths: she asked for it, she deserved it, she enjoyed it, she wanted it, "no" means "yes," and she was not in her proper place. Students see that these myths are consistent in placing responsibility for the rape on the victim; they also see the redundancy in the expression of the myths. They realize then that what matters most to patriarchal ideology is that the core message—blame the victim—is inescapable, whether the blame is assigned for wearing "pants oh so tight" or because "they strut all around so enticing it serves them right" or because "they're out all around just waiting to be laid." Most significantly, the rape-supportive myth that "no" means "yes" is affirmed by translating her non-consent into wanting sex—"Whimpering and crying, it's so satisfying for me. But I can tell that she wants it, as I ravage her body completely."

The easily recognizable myths about the rapists illustrate Phillips's and Martin's contention that discourses are multiple and competing: rapists are sick ("half-crazed") and that rapists are driven by natural lust. Students immediately notice the contradictory nature of the myths about the rapists. Students also note that the myths about the rapists are considerably fewer in number than the myths about the victims of rape and that the myths function to render male sexual predation both understandable and excusable.

The singular myth about rape itself—the enduring myth that rape is committed by a stranger in the middle of the night—is instantly recognized by my students. The rape-supportive lyrics in Easy Prey demonstrate the "scaffolding" concept of Nicola Gavey; there is a range and a plentitude of deeply ingrained sense-making frameworks that result in victim blaming as the cultural and individual default position. Through this exercise, students come to realize that they did already know the rape-supportive myths and that the myths are present in their knowledge systems—even when they would consciously reject an assertion of an explicitly stated rape-supportive myth, such as "she asked for it." They understand how easy it is not to recognize or question the myth when it is stated less explicitly or when it is consumed in a format that is familiar and comfortable. These realizations prompt them to start sharing lyrics from their favorite songs and lamenting that although they sang along perhaps hundreds of times, they never noticed the rape-supportive reasoning until after doing this exercise.

Furthermore, the discussion of the Predator album photographs and the Easy Prey lyrics provides an opportunity to discuss the principle of intention versus effect. In every class, some students want to argue that the ways the class analyzed the photos/lyrics may not reflect what the songwriter intended. This argument most often comes from a desire to deny the rape-supportive reasoning that we identified. In every system of unequal power and privilege, negating intention is employed to excuse the behavior of the person or group with greater power. How the band intended their song to be received and what they intended their message to be may be far from its actual effect. In his essay, "The Lie of Entitlement," Terrence Crowley, an activist in the men's movement against sexual violence, writes: "My intentions are not necessarily what gives my actions their moral value but rather their effects on others—specifically, those people who are disenfranchised by my privilege, those marginalized by my sense of entitlement" (304).

Students are asked to consider whose power, authority, or freedom is represented or celebrated, whose inequality and vulnerability are reinforced, and how we may extend this analysis to other areas of rape culture.

Conclusion

Renee Heberle says the following about patriarchy: "[It] is never final-ly successful in its project of dominance. It is constantly reinventing itself and reconstituting the terms of its legitimacy" (65). Despite fem-inist-inspired cultural shifts in understanding the manifestation of the many forms of sexual violence and of rape in particular, the denial of rape and the production and reproduction of rape-supportive reasoning undergird rape culture. In other words, rape culture cannot survive without its explanatory frameworks. Therefore, as long as rape culture exists, educational strategies—such as comparing dominant and fem-inist discourses about rape, deconstructing and applying the caveman analogy, and analyzing the Easy Prey lyrics—must be employed to dis-rupt and unsettle ideological comfortability. These strategies inform students about how deeply and broadly rape-supportive reasoning per-sists in the culture. They also provide students with the critical skills they need to recognize rape-supportive reasoning, as it manifests itself in their everyday lives. I challenge my students to imagine an answer to this question: If we expose and remove rape-supportive reasoning from our framework of meaning about rape, what truths are we left with? Social change demands an answer to that question. Real, lasting change can only take place when we become uncomfortable with rape-supportive reasoning.

Works Cited

Anderson, Irina, and Kathy Doherty. *Accounting for Rape: Psychology, Feminism and Discourse Analysis in the Study of Sexual Violence.* Routledge, 2008.

Beneke, Timothy. *Men On Rape: What They Have to Say about Sexual Violence.* St. Martin's Press, 1982.

Burt, Martha R. "Cultural Myths and Supports for Rape." *Journal of Personality and Social Psychology*, vol. 38, no. 2, 1980, pp. 217-30.

Crowley, Terrance. "The Lie of Entitlement." *Transforming a Rape Culture*, edited by Emilie Buchwald, Pamela Fletcher, and Martha Roth, Milkweed Editions, 1993, pp. 301-309.

Gavey, Nicola. *Just Sex? The Cultural Scaffolding of Rape.* Routledge, 2005.

Griffin, Susan. "Rape: The All-American Crime," *Ramparts Magazine*, Sept. 1971, www.unz.org/pub/ramparts-1971sep-00026. Accessed 7 May 2020.

Herble, Renee. "Deconstructive Strategies and the Movement against Sexual Violence." *Hypatia*, vol. 11, no. 4, 1996, pp. 63-77.

Johnson, Allan G. *Privilege, Power, and Difference.* McGraw Hill, 2006.

Kimmel, Michael. "Rape and Women's Voice." *Huffington Post*, 23 Aug. 2012, www.huffingtonpost.com/michael-kimmel/rape-and-womens-voice_b_1820021.html. Accessed 7 May 2020.

Lhooq, Michelle. "What the 'Eat Sleep Rape Repeat' Shirt at Coachella Says About Rape Culture at Music Festivals." *Thump*, 13 Apr. 2013, www.thump.vice.com/en_us/article/what-the-eat-sleep-rape-repeat-shirt-at-coachella-says-about- rape-culture-at-music-festival. Accessed 7 May 2020.

Martin, Patricia Yancey. *Rape Work: Victims, Gender, and Emotions in Organization and Community Context.* Routledge, 2005.

McCaughey, Martha. *The Caveman Mystique: Pop-Darwinism and the Debates over Sex, Violence, and Science.* Routledge, 2008.

Phillips, Lynn M. *Flirting with Danger: Young Women's Reflections on Sexuality and Domination.* New York University Press, 2000.

Predator. "Lyrics to 'Easy Prey.'" *Metallyrica,* metallyrica.com/lyrica/predator_us/easy_prey.html. Accessed 7 May 2020.

Sheffield, Carole J. "Sexual Terrorism." *Women: A Feminist Perspective,* edited by Jo Freeman, Mayfield Publishing Co., 1994, pp 1-21.

Taibi, Catherine. "'Keep Calm and Rape' T-Shirt Maker Shutters after Harsh Backlash." *Huffington Post,* 25 June 2013, www.huffington-post.com/2013/06/25/keep-calm-and-rape- shirt_n_3492411.html. Accessed 7 May 2020.

Thornhill, Randy, and Craig Palmer. *A Natural History of Rape: Biological Bases of Sexual Coercion.* MIT Press, 2000.

Willingham, AJ, and Carma Hassan. "Judge to Woman in Rape Case: 'Why Couldn't You Just Keep Your Knees Together?'" *CNN,* 13 Sept. 2016, www.cnn.com/2016/09/12/world/robin-camp-rape-comments-trnd/. Accessed 7 May 2020.

Notes on Contributors

Geraldine Cannon Becker is Professor of English and Creative Writing at the University of Maine at Fort Kent, USA. She holds an MFA in creative Writing from the University of Arkansas, Fayetteville (1998), and an MA in depth psychology from Pacifica (2014). She has published creative work and essays in magazines and peer-reviewed journals, including *The Pedestal, From East to West, Between, Chrysalis: The Journal of Transformative Language Arts*, and *Spring Journal*. She also leads Journaling/SoulFlowering community workshops, is a member of WE LEARN's board of directors, and is co-founder of North Woods Jung Society and Old Sylvain House Press. geraldine.becker@maine.edu

Jessica Becker is a freelance copy editor, graphic artist, and writer, and she holds a second-degree black belt. A graduate of the Savannah College of Art and Design (SCAD—2016), she has a special focus on sequential art and storytelling. She is co-owner of the arts dojo Bushi and Brush, Lancaster, PA. jessicacembecker@gmail.com

Joanna Becker is a freelance illustrator and has a first-degree black belt. She is attending the Pennsylvania College of Art and Design (PCA&D—2021) for a degree in illustration and has a special focus on medieval art and a passion for teaching. She is co-owner of the arts dojo Bushi and Brush, Lancaster, PA. joannacreatesart@gmail.com

Joseph E. Becker is Professor of English at the University of Maine at Fort Kent. He teaches world literature, composition, and other literature courses. He has presented and published varied works on Blake and other Romantic period authors. He is co-founder and director of the North Woods Jung Society and Old Sylvain House Press.

Jodie Bowers is an Assistant Professor in the Communication Studies and Mass Media Programs at Ancilla College in Donaldson, Indiana. Her research interests straddle the intersections of computer-mediated communication, interpersonal communication, and how the lack of physical presence of others has affected one's understanding and app-lication of acceptable behaviour.

Jessica Boynton is an adjunct English Professor at University of Maine at Fort Kent (UMFK). She graduated from the University of Southern Maine (2020) with an MFA in Creative Writing, with a focus on pop-ular fiction. She also graduated from UMFK in 2017, with a double major in English and criminal justice.

Mary Bronstein, MA, MS, is a writer/rogue feminist scholar/film-maker. Her scholarly work includes feminist analysis of *The Babysitters Club* (Lexington), *The Lonely Doll* series (MacFarland), original theory about metaphysical relationships between mothers and daughters (Demeter), and analysis of father-daughter incest in alternative comics (NY Review of Books). For eighteen years, Mary worked directly with children in hospitals and educational settings. She is currently writing fulltime for film and television.

Emily Colpitts is a Postdoctoral Fellow at the Centre for Feminist Re-search at York University. Her research interests include sexual vio-lence policies and prevention efforts at Canadian universities and efforts to engage men and address masculinities in antiviolence act-ivism. Emily also volunteers as a frontline service provider at a local antiviolence organization.

Carolyn M. Cunningham is an Associate Professor in the Comm-unication and Leadership Studies Department at Gonzaga University. She teaches classes in social media, digital storytelling, and women and leadership. She is the author of *Girls Games Play: Contexts of Girls and Video Games* published in 2018 by Lexington Books.

Katherine J. Denker is an Associate Professor and is Director of Graduate Studies as well as the basic course at Ball State University. Her work centres on issues of power and voice in both the instruction-al and interpersonal context, with a further focus on couples' cocon-structions of work-life concerns.

Angel T. Dionne is an English Professor at the University of Moncton Edmundston campus in New Brunswick, Canada. She is currently completing a PhD in Creative Writing at the University of Pretoria with both a creative and critical component. Her interests include contemporary literature, Jewish literature, and creative writing as well as the teaching of English as a second language. Her creative work has appeared in various publications, including *Chicken Soup for the Soul, The Missing Slate Magazine,* and *Good Morning Magazine.* angel.dionne@ umoncton.ca

Leigh Gaskin is a doctoral candidate in American studies at Washington State University. Her dissertation is about the social and economic impacts of the rape culture industry and the biopolitical mechanisms used to enforce rape culture in the United States. Beyond academe, she enjoys walking through forests and thinking about how humanity can love one another more fearlessly.

Kirthi Jayakumar is a lawyer, writer, researcher, artist, and gender rights activist based in India. She is the author of *Gender in War and Peace,* among other books, and is also the founder and CEO of The Red Elephant Foundation, a civilian peacebuilding initiative that works on gender equality.

Erin R. Kaplan is a feminist and queer studies scholar interested in the intersection between performance and social justice. She holds an MA from New York University and a PhD in Theatre and Performance Studies from the University of Colorado Boulder. She is currently a lecturer at University of Colorado Boulder and the Community College of Aurora.

Sona Kaur is a doctoral student studying social psychology at the University of California, Santa Cruz. Her research interests include gender and media socialization, objectification, and violence against women. Her current research examines links between exposure to Bollywood media and gender and sexual attitudes among South Asian viewers.

Faith R. Kellermeyer is the Social Media and Digital Marketing Coordinator at Drexel University's College of Computing and Informatics. She earned her master's in communication studies from Ball State University. Her research interests include public art and advocacy, public health, and sexual assault prevention.

Olga Marques received her PhD in Criminology from the University of Ottawa. Her research focused on women who use sexually explicit materials for their own sexual pleasure, and centred on the inter-relationships between social norms, social control and resistance in an area where questions of deviancy, regulation, and censorship continue to surface.

Abigail L. Moser (MA, University of Arkansas, 2006) is a Blackboard staff specialist in University Information and Technology Services at the University of Arkansas. This chapter is a research report based on Moser's 2006 MA thesis in communication, directed by her co-author, Lynne M. Webb. A copy of the interview protocol, including the prompts to begin the conversation, is available from the first author upon request at almoser@uark.edu.

Priyanka Nupur is pursuing a PhD from the Centre for the Study of Law and Governance, Jawaharlal Nehru University. An earlier version of this paper was presented for the course Enculturing Law, during her coursework for M.Phil. Her research interests include gender, developmental politics, the environment, social justice, and the city.

Jen Rinaldi earned a doctoral degree in critical disability studies at York University. Funded by the Women's College Hospital, her work engages with narrative and arts-based methodologies to deconstruct eating disorder recovery and to reimagine recovery in relation to queer community. Rinaldi also works in collaboration with the arts-based collective Recounting Huronia.

Tracy Royce is a feminist writer, poet, and sociology doctoral candidate at the University of California, Santa Barbara. Her work examines violence against women and fat oppression, and has appeared in *The Fat Studies Reader* (NYU Press), *The Fat Pedagogy Reader* (Peter Lang Publishing), and in the forthcoming *Body Stories: In and Out and With and Through Fat* (Demeter Press).

Carole Sheffield is Emerita Professor of Political Science and Women's and Gender Studies at the William Paterson University of New Jersey. She has taught courses on violence against females, feminist theory, and social justice. She received several teaching awards, including being named by the Carnegie Foundation for the Advancement of Teaching as the New Jersey Professor of the Year in 1997. Sheffield authored "Sexual Terrorism," which has been published in several anthologies. An update, "Sexual Terrorism in the 21st Century," will be published in a forthcoming edition of *Gender Violence: Interdisciplinary Perspectives*.

Lynne M. Webb (PhD, University of Oregon, 1980) is a Professor Emeritus in Communication, Florida International University. She has coedited three scholarly readers and authored over eighty essays, including multiple theories, research reports, and pedagogical essays. Her research examines romantic communication, family communication, and social media.

Eileen L. Zurbriggen is a Professor of Psychology at the University of California, Santa Cruz. Her research focuses on behaviors in which power and sex are linked, on psychological linkages between power, objectification, and sex, and on media representations of sex, power, and gender. She coedited the book *The Sexualization of Girls and Girlhood: Causes, Consequences, and Resistance.*

Deepest appreciation to
Demeter's monthly Donors

DEMETER

Daughters
Naomi Mcpherson
Linda Hunter
Muna Saleh
Summer Cunningham
Rebecca Bromwich
Tatjana Takseva
Kerri Kearney
Debbie Byrd
Laurie Kruk
Fionna Green
Tanya Cassidy
Vicki Noble
Bridget Boland

Sisters
Kirsten Goa
Amber Kinser
Nicole Willey
Regina Edwards